Anti-Capitalism: A Beginner's Guide, Simon Tormey, ISBN 1–85168–342–9
Democracy: A Beginner's Guide, David Beetham, ISBN 1–85168–363–1
NATO: A Beginner's Guide, Jennifer Medcalf, ISBN 1–85168–353–4
The Palestine–Israeli Conflict: A Beginner's Guide, Dan Cohn-Sherbok and Dawoud El-Alami, ISBN 1–85168–332–1
Political Philosophy: A Historical Introduction, Michael J. White, ISBN 1–85168–328–3
Global Terrorism: A Beginner's Guide, Leonard Weinberg, ISBN 1–85168–358–5

GLOBAL OUTRAGE

The Impact of World Opinion on Contemporary History

Peter N. Stearns

ONEWORLD

OXFORD

GLOBAL OUTRAGE

Oneworld Publications
(Sales and Editorial)
185 Banbury Road
Oxford OX2 7AR
England
www.oneworld-publications.com

ISBN 1–85168–364–X

Cover design by Mungo Designs
Typeset by Wordstop Technologies (P) Ltd., India
Printed and bound by WS Bookwell, Finland

Cover photographs: Pakistani Shi'ite Muslims Attend a Procession
During the Month of Moharram © digitalvision direct 2004;
Globe © Syed Zargham/Getty Images 2003

For Aidan Stearns,
with a welcome to the world

CONTENTS

ACKNOWLEDGEMENTS

A number of people have contributed to this book. Jake Woody and Brian Gipson provided valuable research assistance. Johanna Bockman, Peter Mandaville, Sumaiya Hamdani, Chris Hill, Luke Brindle, and various members of George Mason University's global affairs program offered useful advice and specific references. I am grateful to the Global Affairs group at Mason more generally for their interest and suggestions. Debbie Williams's work in preparing the manuscript was indispensable. My thanks to Christina Wipf Perry and others at Oneworld Publications and to the anonymous readers whose suggestions and enthusiasm were both helpful.

PREFACE

This is a book about world opinion, a subject familiar to anyone who follows world events but which has not been systematically studied. Timeliness is crucial: we have just seen arguably the most massive expression of world opinion ever recorded, against then-imminent war in Iraq, and we have just seen the same expression fail, at least in the short run. Questions about what world opinion is, where it is heading, and what it should be abound, and the analysis of how the phenomenon emerged and how it has evolved will contribute greatly to the answers.

Timeliness aside, there are two principal reasons for studying world opinion. First, of course, despite recent limitations, it has become a significant force in world affairs, capable of causing change and emerging as a factor in the decisions of states great and small.

And second, more boldly: world opinion has, with minor qualifications, always been right, serving as a constructive human conscience on a growing array of issues. This statement must be proved, of course, and it will be debated, but it reflects more than coincidence. The arousal of moral outrage on the part of people in many (not necessarily all) different countries provides a stamp of validity that has been demonstrated in many specific cases for over two centuries. The problems with world opinion involve consistency and tactical effectiveness, not moral power. Validity does not guarantee the future, of course, but it commands attention, or should command attention, when world opinion is expressed.

We deal, then, with a potent, though not omnipotent, element of the contemporary global environment, and a resoundingly positive one. Both features more than justify a new level of attention.

PART I
Origins and Initial Successes
1780s–1880s

1

INTRODUCTION: WHYS AND WHATS OF WORLD OPINION HISTORY

This is a book very much shaped by recent events, which triggered my desire to trace and use a history of a phenomenon in order to understand it better. We hear about world opinion recurrently – there's even an annual summary of sorts in the reference sections of libraries, from Gallup International polls – but the chance to think about it in any systematic way is less available. This introductory chapter is intended to remind readers of the current importance of the subject, to offer some preliminary definitions and talk about how the book will approach world opinion, and to relate the subject very briefly to some larger issues in social science scholarship.

Like many Americans, I watched in considerable awe at the weekly procession of huge protests against imminent American war on Iraq, as they unfolded in many of the world's great cities in February, March, and early April 2003. Cities in Britain, Spain, and Italy had rarely if ever seen such large demonstrations. Equally interesting were the voices from East Asia, in Japan and particularly South Korea, and also from Mexico, along with the possibly spontaneous rallies in Moscow. Joining in, of course, were significant outbursts in centers within the United States, as well as the more predictable risings in Islamic strongholds, from Indonesia to Egypt.

It was not a matter of rallies alone. Opinion polls showed up to eighty-five percent opposition to American intervention, again fairly widely around the world. Only the United States public stood apart, but even it was hesitant until the war actually began, with a majority inclined toward the legitimacy of war but uncertain, in the face of the rest of humanity, about going it alone.

Americans dissented from international norms for the most part, but they were affected by them. It is also important to note that U.S. military policy had long been constrained by world opinion, and had made huge investments in new guidance technology that would allow aerial bombardments, the military strategy in which the nation excelled, without extensive civilian casualties. Quick victory in the first phase of the ensuing military operation in Iraq helped explain why world opinion was not sustained, as fully as might have been expected, for what many people had expected and feared, in masses of bystander deaths, did not materialize. Anticipation of international reactions in this regard helped counter the vehemence of the pre-war demonstrations and polls once the war actually began.

This was world opinion, unprecedented in the strength of its opposition to a great power, unusually coordinated thanks both to the passion involved and to high-speed technologies headed by the internet. Many governments, as in France and Germany, saw their own policies constrained, partially guided, by the sentiments of the public, while a Spanish regime that backed the war was threatened by punishment at the polls and the British government faced sustained criticism.

But this was also world opinion aborted. The United States government, despite some bows to the United Nations, largely ignored the world (except in the kind of military technology it utilized), went to war, and encountered few immediate adverse consequences.

Some bottles of Coke were ritually spilled in the streets of Europe, lots of nasty editorials were written, but for all intents and purposes nothing happened. Secretary of Defense Donald Rumsfeld mused, "One or two or three or four countries have stood up and opposed it [the war], and that is considered the world by people for some unknown reason to me. It's utter nonsense, that's not the world . . . There are lots of countries in the world." It's a reaction worth noting when one is defining world opinion, and it certainly described official U.S. policy even as it understated the extent of the outburst.[1]

It was not even clear at first that there would be a legacy, despite the fact that the U.S. not only defied the world but also failed to find the fabled weapons of mass destruction on which the war's rationale had been principally based. To be sure, the U.S. President at one point told the world that weapons had been found, despite the evidence to the contrary; but this bald assertion merely highlighted world opinion's impotence.

Yet it increasingly became clear, as the war ended and a difficult occupation period began, that this unusually strong statement of world opinion would continue to have consequences. This story is not over at this writing, of course. But the British government of Tony Blair was beaten up rather badly for its defiance of world opinion and possible efforts to mislead. The United States remained more aloof, but its difficulty in finding partners for the arduous and expensive task of reconstruction in Iraq derived directly from its need to ask the rest of the world to step in despite the United States' previous unilateralism. World opinion could not prevent a war, in other words, but it helped shape a postwar aftermath that proved more difficult than American leaders had expected. For the longer term, it was probable that a bitterness had been planted that would continue to work against the United States, that the next time American power was asserted world opinion would rise up even stronger, not just with a louder voice but with more effective methods, to impede it. The second shoe may not have dropped. Months after the war had ended, the unfavorable-to-favorable balance of opinion toward the United States had tilted considerably, particularly outside the West but even in the major European nations. Was this a meaningful development? An invitation clearly exists to explore the unfolding of world opinion in order to assess American reactions at a difficult impasse.

The subject is inherently elusive. Does an entity "World opinion" really exist? I will argue yes, though world opinion always over-claims and is never as global as the term implies. How, in a world clearly and bitterly divided, does any agreement on world opinion ever emerge? In fact claims to world opinion are often disputed, particularly by the opinion's targets, but the disputes do not necessarily overshadow a substantial moral consensus. Should anyone care about it? Another tough question, open to discussion, but answered to an extent by the simple fact that various societies, including very powerful ones, have recurrently decided to care or have been affected when they tried to override world opinion.

History offers a way to probe world opinion and its obvious limitations. When did "world opinion" start? How can it be defined? What consistent features mark world opinion, and when have major changes occurred? What successes has it had, if any, and when, besides in 2003, has it largely failed? More important still: Is world opinion changing yet again, gaining strength despite its inability as yet to thwart the "world's only superpower"? And what should world opinion accomplish and claim?

Surprisingly, almost no one has yet examined world opinion in any systematic way, despite the fact that we hear about it frequently and that annual international polling compilations have existed since the 1970s.[2] World opinion is, admittedly, difficult to pin down. It tends to emerge around single issues, it is fickle, and it can dissipate rather suddenly. Further, as the Iraq war demonstrates, its success is often quite hard to measure. Yet both its existence and its impact are open to assessment.

It can be argued that, at a time when the forces capable of reshaping human lives around the world have outstripped normal political controls, whether the issue is war or environment or exploitation of labor, world opinion stands as one of the only available correctives to abuse. The existence of world opinion is itself a product of increasingly intense global contacts – in technology, through the worldwide dissemination of news and views, and in culture, through the legitimacy and receptivity involved in passing judgment on distant problems and (sometimes) responding to these judgments in turn. As globalization has intensified in recent decades, world opinion takes on new importance as an international conscience, however flawed and however inconsistently effective. A host of non-governmental organizations (NGOs) have emerged, from Amnesty International to Greenpeace, that rely primarily on world opinion or the threat of world opinion to implement their values. Other, established institutions, like the papacy, have increasingly added efforts to lead and shape world opinion to their more traditional functions. The questions are: How well does world opinion do in constraining some of the less desirable implications of globalization, and how effective might it become in future? We need, as part of this evaluation, to recognize cases in which world opinion may have done more harm than good, or may have won individual victories while leaving fundamental problems unchecked.

For an American audience, along with the general relationship between world opinion and globalization, a second key set of issues revolves basically around the question "So what?" The United States, as the world's only superpower, can afford to ignore world opinion, at least in the short run. It has done so not only in the case of Iraq, but also in areas of domestic policy such as the administration of the death penalty. At times, indeed, world opinion undoubtedly goads many Americans into a sense of defiance (a reaction visible elsewhere as well): if outside interferers want us to do this, then we'll most certainly insist on doing that. Yet, given the end of the Cold War, world opinion is one of the only real constraints on the United States, and its presence will surely increase simply because it's the available outlet. Americans are accustomed to participating in and using world opinion against what they view as excesses elsewhere. We have less experience in pondering what it's like to have the shoe on the other foot, yet, quite apart from Iraq, it's an experience we need to think about. There has never, in world history, been a superpower like the United States; but there has never been a time when a great power has faced such a potentially hostile international audience. The combination is both intriguing and significant, for all parties involved.

We emerge with several central issues: defining world opinion and its impact; looking at the phenomenon in terms of mounting globalization; and considering the implications from the standpoint of American policy and the American public, all the more interesting given a demonstrable national desire to be liked.

Although a historical assessment of world opinion is not the only approach to the subject, it does allow not only the establishment of a clearer record, but also an opportunity to talk about the major forms of the phenomenon, as they have unfolded over time, and the tally of successes and failures. It allows an evaluation of the nature and impact of world opinion that goes beyond the abstractions that often permeate some of the more theoretical excursions in international relations.

A preliminary definition is essential, though the book intends actually to offer a running commentary on what world opinion is, so this is only for starters. World opinion involves the capacity to react to developments (real or imagined) in distant parts of the globe with some sense of impassioned outrage and a belief that there are or should be some common standards for humanity, plus a recognition in many societies, at least in enough cases to make world opinion plausible, that such evidence of outrage may need to be accommodated, at least superficially – that world opinion counts. This barebones definition can be elaborated somewhat, and then further enhanced by a forecast of the kinds of components involved in assessing what world opinion is.

Although world opinion is rarely in fact global, it does enlist support from significant segments of the public in more than one nation, and recently in more than several. The expressions of outrage and concern, about conditions affecting people in other nations and cultures, are designed to press governments or corporations or other entities to change their behavior in line with what are assumed to be just standards for people wherever located. The expression may or not have significant results, but there is an attempt at impact and not just idle venting.

World opinion is a special form of public opinion, and it is important not to make the subject unduly diffuse. World opinion as defined here goes beyond strong but purely national beliefs about foreign affairs. Public opinion in the 1890s urged Britain not to back down to France in the imperialist struggle for Africa, and vice versa; but this was not world opinion, because the focus was strictly on national foreign policies. World opinion also goes beyond polling results, available in more recent decades, in that it involves more active expressions through petitions, demonstrations, and boycotts, though polling may confirm the strong views involved. Again, world opinion and public opinion are not interchangeable. Although world opinion often involves the media, it captures interests from a wider public and cannot be summed up by collecting newspaper editorials; there must be wider resonance. World opinion, in sum, involves a measurable degree of public passion about developments outside parochial boundaries.

Any analysis of world opinion, from basic definitions on up, needs to look at several components. The first is technological. The emergence of world opinion depended on some degree of global reporting that went beyond traditional travelers' accounts, if only in conveying a greater sense of immediacy and timeliness. The steady progression of global news is part of world opinion's march. Some years back the U.S. State Department began referring to the "C.N.N. effect," in terms of predictable outpourings of outrage or support when C.N.N. dramatized some particular development in otherwise remote parts of the world. But world opinion could take shape even earlier, when reports were less immediate, so long as there was regular access to news well beyond one's own national and cultural borders.

The second component, more complex, involves determining who makes world opinion. This brings in the media again, from a slightly different angle. It involves looking at social groups that are particularly influential. World opinion partly reflects the emergence of a global "middle class" capable of receiving the same kind of news and sharing enough values to form transnational reactions. It can also reflect global ties among even more focused segments, like university students. The making of world opinion also requires regional judgments: To what extent is world opinion, still, mainly Western? (It was in its origins, and to some extent remains, disproportionately European.) Have other parts of the world begun to gain some real participation in forming, as well as merely receiving, world opinion? Does Africa count yet at all? Finally, deliberate manipulation of world opinion is a vital issue. Governments try to do this (recent American efforts have been tangible if somewhat pathetic). So do individual groups – like the independence seekers in East Timor, who ultimately roused world opinion quite effectively. The emergence of movements frankly dependent on their capacity to stir world opinion fits into this final category. Discussion of the participants in world opinion thus involves both general contexts, like the regions most or least involved, and attention to particular efforts to galvanize and manipulate.

The making of world opinion depends, more broadly, on beliefs that there are certain standards of behavior that can or should cut across boundaries and that allow groups in one society to pass judgment on events and processes in distant places. Here is the fascinating source of the combination of earnest moralism and smugness that so often characterizes the expression of world opinion. World opinion demands high standards in behaviors as varied as the treatment of women and children or the conduct of war. At the same time, world opinion operates on the assumption that people in one part of the world are, at least temporarily, falling short, requiring correction by the superior values of their global judges. At an extreme, world opinion expresses a "white man's burden" that can easily rouse resistance. Understanding the making of world opinion has to take the underlying assumptions – the sense of certainty and responsibility – into account and to consider the groups, institutions, and manipulators that generate its expression. What kinds of issues call forth the periodic statement of international standards with enough passion to rouse significant numbers of otherwise ordinary people to rally, petition, or otherwise demonstrate their sense of outrage?

Another component involves mechanisms: How is the expression of world opinion manifested and supported? Editorials and demonstrations often play a vital role, backed by pervasive opinion polling. But world opinion can also involve boycotts and other economic action; some of the most interesting cases of world opinion's impact involve reactions to corporate activity, backed by economic sanctions. And world opinion obviously interacts with international political and religious organizations. The emergence of the contemporary Catholic Church as a shaper and promoter of world opinion, beyond its capacity to rouse its own faithful, is an intriguing case in point, along with the more obvious links between world opinion and the United Nations or, earlier and more dismally, the League of Nations.

An obvious specific aspect of world opinion involves relationships not just to mainstream international organizations but to special efforts to organize conferences or associations to deal with specific issues, such as, for example, voting rights for women. There is overlap between associational efforts and world opinion, and some campaigners have opted to express world opinion more through conference pronouncements than through grassroots mobilization. We will keep on evaluating grassroots support in our core definitions of world opinion, but we have to deal with alternative claims and methods as well – a point that also relates to what some scholars have called "world culture," discussed below.

The next component, probably the most interesting of all, involves receptivity. Why should anyone care? To paraphrase Stalin's comment about the Church, world opinion (usually) has no military divisions. It's almost inherently annoying to an offending party, in that it asserts the validity of outside interference, often in a patronizingly preachy fashion. Yet, even apart from the fact that world opinion does sometimes have some teeth, as with commercial boycotts, key groups and nations do turn out to care. There is a desire, at least at some times and in some places, to appear respectable in the eyes of the world. World opinion requires this kind of acknowledgement on the part of various players that the views of distant others count for something – that it is both possible and meaningful to be embarrassed about falling short when global standards are applied. To give some illustrations: Why did Koreans, in 1988, even as nationalist pride was cresting, decide that their place in world opinion required that restaurants serving dog meat be closed during their hosting of the Olympic Games? Why did American southerners, back in the pre-civil-rights 1950s, carefully serve black people with French accents in restaurants (some of them, crafty and sophisticated locals) when they ignored unmistakably American black faces? Why have some institutions and individuals even taken to apologizing for past wrongs – as the Pope did in regretting the Church's treatment of Galileo – as if even history had to be placated in the interests of good standing in world opinion? Here are illustrations of the belief that there are, sometimes, some global standards to be applied: the belief not only undergirds the assertion of world opinion but also inculcates some receptivity in apparently offending parties.

The importance of assessing the reception component when examining world opinion obviously has a flip side: why do some groups, states, and individuals resist the embarrassment factor, as the United States has done recently? Power is a factor, but so are dignity and the extent to which the issue involved seems deeply attached to a cherished identity. The long, agonizing, and still-current debate in the Islamic world about how to react to "world opinion's" hostility to the veiling of women is a fascinating case in point, at some remove from the crudest power politics. Examining the rejection of world opinion includes attention to recurrent efforts to form alternative structures. Before its collapse, the Communist world promoted its own world opinion, defiantly rejecting capitalist sources; *Pravda* provided media fodder for Communist outlets around the globe. More recently, through television and the internet, the Islamic world has generated its own outlets, clearly more compelling, at least for millions of Arab viewers, than the media bases for world opinion more familiar in the West.

Impact is the final topic, and in some ways sums up the whole set. When does world opinion get results? What kinds of topics (for example, human rights or the environment) seem to be most open to world pressure? What parts of the world are most susceptible to global blandishments? How does China, a great power and long proud of its superiority to world standards, compare with a smaller country in the same region or with another great power like India with a different tradition toward the outside world? What support mechanisms work best? What kinds of issues seem to elicit the most consistent global reaction, as opposed to a cause-of-the-month fickleness?

Diagnosis of world opinion thus involves technology, opinion makers and the assumptions they maintain, support mechanisms, receptivity (including resistance), and results. It's a complicated but intriguing brew, which this book will pursue through a combination of specific case studies and a larger pattern of historical evolution. Ultimately, diagnosis must also lead to prognosis: the assessment of where world opinion seems to be heading, and what changes are most and least desirable for the future.

This book is not intensely theoretical, offering instead a set of historical instances and patterns that permit an ongoing but informal analysis of what world opinion is all about. As noted, the absence of even a first stab at a historical record of world opinion is both odd and remiss, though happily there are many accounts of particular instances which this larger survey can build upon. But this book does touch on two kinds of discussion current in the social sciences which should be laid out early on and then resumed in the final assessment.

By some accounts the most compelling theoretical formulation in social sciences during the 1990s involved the idea of globalization (both for and against). Yet also on the table was the rather different "clash of civilizations" model put forth after the Cold War by Samuel Huntington. Globalization advocates, and some opponents, saw an increasingly intense set of global linkages, particularly in the economic and cultural domain, that some viewed as opening a new and unprecedented period in world history. Huntington, while not denying global contacts, saw a future shaped by the reassertion of traditional large cultural identities, and their mutual hostility. Western values versus Islamic values headed the list, but a third camp of neo-Confucianists was also envisaged.[3]

The examination of world opinion relates to both these visions but confirms neither. Obviously, globalization and world opinion are related, though world opinion pre-dates what even the most ambitious proponents claim as the beginnings of globalization. World opinion depends on global contacts and judgments. But aspects of world opinion protest aspects of globalization, so the relationship is nuanced. And world opinion can be modified or thwarted by the values of particular civilizations. To be sure, if clash of civilization turns out to trump globalization, world opinion will probably no longer be an issue. But world opinion in practice continues to play out against different receptivities on different topics, which means that it operates in and sometimes contributes to no small amount of civilizational tension. Attention to the complexities of world opinion will improve the dialogue between the globalization theorists and the clash camp.

Over the past decade, an interesting branch of sociology has explored the nature of what its proponents call "world culture." Here too there is a connection with world opinion, but here too it is complex. The world culture school argues that since the later nineteenth century (it is, happily, convinced of the utility of a historical approach and generates very useful findings in the process) a set of international standards has emerged that explain why almost all societies, despite their apparent differences, pursue so many similar goals. World culture thus holds that mass education systems should exist, that some welfare protections should be offered to protect the unfortunate, that population growth should be limited, that states should seek to expand their economies, that women should have increased access to higher education, that the environment needs protection, that human rights must be defended, and so on. World culture rests on assumptions of universality: "Humans everywhere are seen as having similar needs and desires." World culture also asserts the validity of regional identities, a point that is granted as a realistic tension within the phenomenon. But the primary emphasis rests on "world citizenship," on a set of "common world forces."[4]

This approach overlaps the grander theories of globalization, but it is more focused on beliefs and on the organizational apparatus, particularly international NGOs, that both reflects and sustains them. And the approach obviously relates to the emergence and operation of world opinion. But the world culture school tends to be both too detached and too assertive, which means that its relationship to this study of world opinion must be stated carefully. While the world culture sociologists have amassed a great deal of information, they tend to assume rather than really illustrate the existence of this array of shared beliefs. The basic assumptions have an abstractness that recalls some of the worst features of modernization theory, which the approach resembles without acknowledgement. World culture is just there, operating unseen but powerfully;

we don't have actually to find it. When an NGO states a global principle, it tends to be assumed as widely operative. Similarly, the harmony projected by world culture flies in the face of much of what is actually happening in the world. Agreement on welfare obligations? Why then are so many children at work in South and Southeast Asia? Women in higher education? Yes, to a degree, but doesn't it matter a lot whether they're in the same classes as men or shunted off to separate schools and, often, separate subjects?

This study of world opinion shares with the world culture school a great interest in exploring beliefs that there are common world standards and in trying to find out who, exactly, holds such beliefs and with what effect. The study will add some concrete cases to the world culture arsenal. But we must also be conscious that world opinion has a narrower range than what is commonly defined as world culture. World opinion requires not only beliefs but also wide audience and real passion, and in fact excited world opinion has not pronounced on many of the issues central to world culture. Most world opinion has focused on human rights broadly construed, not on education per se, or science, or the importance of international commercial standards. Furthermore, the exploration of world opinion must constantly acknowledge dissent and counter-reaction, not just some benign triumph of global standards. Because of its more precise focus and its greater tolerance of complexity, the study of world opinion may advance examination of world culture in useful ways, even as it benefits from some (not all) of the world culture claims and findings. The two subjects must not be conflated.

Another body of scholarship, more historical than sociological, has taken shape recently, on the nature, evolution, and geographic distribution of human rights activities. World opinion often organizes around definitions of human rights, and it is to be hoped that a history of the subject will contribute to this literature in turn. The human rights studies do not usually concentrate on opinion, however, so much as philosophical principles embodied in organizational manifestations. Again, there are clear relationships and real contributions to an understanding of world opinion on particular topics, as the ensuing chapters will make clear. But the human rights work has not sought explicitly to explore world opinion as a phenomenon.

World opinion has been gaining momentum and changing significantly, but it is not simply a contemporary phenomenon. Having started this account with Iraq, let us take an example, from the same general part of the world, over a century before, to see world opinion in operation in an earlier time. There's a fair amount we'd recognize as characteristic of world opinion today (including some limitations on results), but also some distinctive flavor that can help us define what's consistent in world opinion and what has changed.

Between 1894 and 1896, at least several hundred Armenians were assassinated in the Ottoman Empire, others tortured, at the hand of various ethnic groups with the apparent connivance of the Ottoman government. As news of these developments reached Western Europe, sometimes amid apparent exaggeration and definite press manipulation by Armenian representatives, expressions of outrage quickly followed.

European public opinion had a long-standing mistrust of the Ottoman regime and was drawn to the Armenians (without a great deal of actual contact or knowledge) as fellow Christians. Armenian advocates in Europe became increasingly adept at fanning the flames.

Feelings ran particularly high in Britain. Popular newspapers devoted many articles to the apparent atrocities. Protestant leaders took up the charge, as did many politicians in the Liberal Party, which saw itself as something of an international conscience. Former Prime Minister Gladstone, at the age of eighty-seven, gave a stirring speech to a substantial gathering in Liverpool. Other rallies developed in London, one around the home of the Lord Mayor. The surge generated repeated questions in Parliament about what actions the British government was planning to take to provide greater assurances for the suffering Armenians. Queen Victoria, though less active publicly, expressed her own deep feelings in a series of private letters. One historian has commented on the "thrill of horror" that ran through the nation.[5] The show of public opinion had some echoes elsewhere, such as in France.

There were some definite results. The Ottoman government, though furious at the accusations, had to agree, under Western pressure, to set up a commission of inquiry, though it tried to divert its task toward an investigation of the activities of "Armenian brigands." A Conservative prime minister in Britain was forced to resign in part because he seemed insufficiently zealous in reacting to the atrocities. A durable historical memory began to be generated. Even in the early twenty-first century, Turkish authorities have continued to dispute Western claims of widespread massacres, and Western and Armenian groups have periodically sought to recall the episode, even proposing formal memorials.

None of this did much for the Armenians at the time. While public outrage spurred even the British Conservative Party toward greater hostility toward "the Turks" than normal, political divisions in Britain limited the potential for action. Public opinion in other relevant countries was less aroused. There was no particular outcry in Russia, either because public opinion was stunted in a society with less media and a smaller urban population, or because the government did not want to associate itself with actions that might increase Western influence in the Middle East, or a bit of both. Opinion in the United States was also more sedate, since Americans – though referred to during the crisis – were not yet full participants in what passed for world opinion at the time. Even the British public might have done more. It was noted that the demonstrations, though frequent and large, were less substantial than those that had rallied on behalf of the Bulgarians two decades before. Even 125 years ago, world opinion had a certain fickleness, depending on how much was known about the injured parties (Bulgarians were at least European, which the Armenians were not) and what else was going on. Britain's moral stature had itself deteriorated in the interval, because of its eager involvement with imperialist expansion; it was not as easy to pretend disinterested commitment to oppressed peoples. In the end, some people worried that the whole episode had provided false hope to the Armenians, with little concrete gain. On his deathbed, Gladstone was reported to have murmured "those poor Armenians."

Yet, for all the hollow bluster, there was real fervor, a belief that civilized people had a responsibility to prevent deadly cruelties halfway around the world, with no particular self-interest beyond a certain sense of Christian solidarity. A Conservative leader, speaking to a Nonconformist audience in 1896, captured the emotions eloquently:

> I hold it morally to be a very high honor to the religious people in this country that they have taken so intense and deep an interest in the fate of the Armenians. They can have nothing naturally to gain by it, politically or otherwise. It is merely the outcome of a genuine feeling of sympathy for those who suffer and of horror at the cruelties under which they suffer.[6]

The best way to get a handle on world opinion, including an analysis of technology, expressions, and receptivities, is to sketch the major historical stages in its formation and evolution, pulling out the component parts at each principal phase. This is how we can most clearly see how each of the pieces of the phenomenon developed. At the same time, by marking major changes, we can determine what contemporary world opinion is all about. What follows, in the principal historical chapters, does not pretend to pick up every major instance of world opinion, even recently, for the list would be too long. Some readers may object to certain omissions, or at other points feel that I have stretched the definition of world opinion (a definition not easy to pin down) in unacceptable ways. There are doubtless further discoveries to be made, further refinements to add beyond this pilot effort. But the delineation of major stages provides coherence while providing a framework within which additional case studies can be fitted, while allowing us to note some consistent features of world opinion – the definitional core – and also to trace change, including prospects for the future.

This is, however, a historical approach with a twist. The focus is not on past episodes for their own sake, but on what they reveal about components of world opinion today. Alongside outlining the principal historical phases in the evolution of world opinion, we shall periodically jump forward; features present earlier on still merit attention when assessing the phenomenon today. The hope is to combine a standard historical exercise with a present-day focus by considering throughout, rather than simply in a final chapter, significance of past developments for present and future.

The pre-modern background to world opinion merits brief attention. The Catholic Church, for example, long maintained a capacity to rally Christian opinion across political boundaries and sometimes turned its power toward more remote parts of the world, as in the Crusades or in missionary endeavor. International Islam had some similar capacities.

The first set of issues the really evoked world opinion was the campaign against slavery and the slave trade in the late eighteenth and early nineteenth century. Here was the point at which the technology, broadly construed, was emerging to provide opportunities for exchanging vivid information about slavery – as in the transatlantic success of *Uncle Tom's Cabin* – and for loosely coordinated international groups, including antislavery conventions. Still more important: here was the point at which humanitarian opinion in Western society was gaining sufficient coherence and confidence to offer compelling judgments about how things should be done and about how other parts of the world were failing to measure up to the best standards of civilization. Here was the point, in other words, at which a confident sense of global responsibility first emerged, and it's an intriguing moment to capture and explain an attitude that continues to operate in the world today. Through the nineteenth century, this combination of confidence and new technology and organizational capacity provided a context for recurrent expressions against apparent atrocities such as those visited on the Armenians, as an admittedly Western-based world opinion flexed its muscles fresh from the successes against slavery. Although not yet labeled as such, a human rights focus continued to organize the most vigorous expressions of world opinion.

The beginnings of global opinion, in Western-sponsored technologies and evolving Western beliefs about the world at large, already raise questions that still apply to the phenomenon today. To what extent is world opinion still a disproportionate expression of Western values? To what extent has world opinion served as a recurrent distraction, encouraging the judging societies to ignore their own shortcomings, including their ongoing abuses of global power, by focusing on the vivid evils that can be conveniently located elsewhere? But also: why was the first large outpouring of global opinion, against slave trading, more successful (if gradually and incompletely) than some expressions of world opinion have been in more recent times?

World opinion began to branch out after the 1860s, partly perhaps because the leading slavery issues seemed to be resolved, partly in association with the growing reach of Western imperialism. It is in these decades that world opinion periodically asserted itself in the foreign policy field, the Ottoman Empire being a frequent and revealing target. It is also in this period that a host of global organizations began to form, designed both to influence and to benefit from world opinion. International women's groups, for example, began to shape a characteristic approach to world opinion that has turned out to offer a distinctive balance of strengths and weaknesses.

Developments in the first half of the twentieth century, shading off from the late-nineteenth-century expansion, present several of the key diagnostic issues in dealing with world opinion: new questions arose both about world opinion's geographic base and about resistance to it; the need to find new supporting mechanisms became urgent. But on the positive side a new set of societies became open to the use of international embarrassment as a motivation for internal reform, and at least in principle the targets of world opinion began to broaden, to include a wider range of social issues.

Although Westerners still assigned themselves a disproportionate right to judge the rest of the world, other societies were finding a voice as well. How would world opinion interact with the growth of Asian and African nationalist movements and, soon, with the contraction of imperialism? (In a sense, we're still grappling with this issue today.) How could world opinion express itself with the decline of Western power to enforce its judgments? It was fine to use the forces of imperialism to back up world opinion's condemnation of slavery; but what would happen when the imperialist powers lost their relative military edge, when world opinion had to depend on its own momentum for much chance of success? During the first half of the twentieth century a variety of experiments reacted to this new context, often with limited effectiveness. World opinion clearly counted for little, even when sanctioned by new institutions such as the League of Nations, against the brutalities of some of the great powers. Whole regimes such as Hitler's deliberately defied world opinion, while through the Communist International and media like *Pravda* the Soviet Union began to establish an alternative basis for world opinion, international in principle but non-Western and non-capitalist in structure. Failures of world opinion up to and including World War II would provide new impetus for efforts after the war.

Beneath the surface, even before 1945, there were some interesting new developments. The targets of world opinion became more complex, in part because of changing standards in Western society, in part because of the activities of agencies associated with the League or other organizations. International standards for the treatment of workers, norms for children, and other social issues began to gain ground, with periodic expressions of world opinion not far behind. Even as imperialism receded, efforts to gain respectability in global eyes could involve sweeping attacks on cherished traditions, such as the veiling or foot binding of women, in order to meet global standards. New regimes, such as Ataturk's in Turkey, were designed to utilize and recognize world opinion as a goad for change.

It was after 1945, however, and especially after the worst of the Cold War in the 1950s, that world opinion began to blossom fully in the third and to date most impressive phase of the phenomenon. Several strands must be interwoven here. Technologies developed further, providing opportunities for virtually instantaneous recording of events almost anywhere. The emergence of international news channels both reflected and encouraged world opinion, though the same development could prompt resistance to sources regarded as biased toward the West. The United Nations became more active than the League had been in seeking to organize and to guide world opinion, around issues such as the treatment of women. Institutions like the Catholic Church, branching out in their judgments about global ethics to reach an audience beyond the faithful, became significant players in world opinion as well. The emergence of organizations like Amnesty International, almost entirely dependent on the power of world opinion to influence repressive regimes, was noteworthy. Finally, the range of issues subject to world opinion continued to expand, to include the death penalty and environmental concerns. The misbehavior of global corporations began to gain attention as well: a key example was the role of Nestlé in providing to parents in Africa infant foods whose use often threatened the health of their children, until blocked by global protest.

Amid this efflorescence, crucial issues involved the role of public opinion outside the West not only reacting to but also participating in global expression. One of the most intriguing aspects of the protest against American moves on Iraq was the coordinated involvement of significant publics in East Asia and, of course, the Islamic world along with Europe, Russia, and Latin America. But global involvement also included new resistance to world opinion, in the form of less tolerant national expression (e.g. the growing resistance of Indian Hinduism to outside views) and in the effort, particularly in the Arab world, to create alternative global media.

It is concerning the past three decades that crucial judgments must be formed about the limitations and impact of world opinion. What kinds of issues are most amenable to global pressures, and what kinds provoke the greatest resistance? The impact of world opinion on the leading powers, not only the United States but also countries like China, constitutes an intriguing topic; we might expect a mixture of defiance and susceptibility. New efforts to manipulate world opinion suggest the public's vulnerabilities on certain issues. Even more troubling is their fickleness in responding passionately to some incidents while virtually ignoring comparable events elsewhere. A vital question involves the tension between highly publicizable individual atrocities – the Hispanic sentenced to death in Texas, the Nigerian facing death by stoning for adultery – and pressure on more systematic policy formulations. Always, there's the question of enforceability. Is the power of international embarrassment fading? Are there methods, such as trade sanctions or boycotts, that demonstrably support world opinion short of the use of force? How does world opinion relate to the other, more familiar aspects of globalization?

The year 2003 brought more than the clash between world opinion and the United States. An American trade union imported some women textile workers from Lesotho to New York and the United Nations, to rally world opinion against labor abuses practiced by multinationals in that impoverished African country; the effect was unclear. The government of Indonesia began to resume efforts to form partnerships between global environmental groups and local and international companies, after a previous environmentalist failure in using potential global product boycotts to reduce the clearing of Indonesian rain forests; it was not clear how sensitive the government was to world opinion on this subject, or whether world opinion could really be mobilized. There was no question about world opinion's passion in defense of Amina Lawal, a Nigerian

Muslim woman accused of adultery and sentenced to death by stoning; but it was long uncertain whether Nigeria's Islamic or national courts would pay any attention or whether outside intervention might simply generate defiance. The world opinion plate seemed to be filling steadily, but the capacity to digest might not be expanding accordingly. There were lots of questions for the future.

On the other hand, world opinion has also progressed in some measurable ways. It has become more broadly based, which means that righteous indignation is no longer a Western monopoly. It has forced policy changes and it has saved individual lives. It has affected the operations of some multinational companies – with the ironic result that multinationals, exposed to world opinion, sometimes behave better than more isolated local operations. The range of topics on which world opinion may be brought to bear has widened. Its impact remains inconsistent. Its relationship with the United States is certainly problematic. More systematic examination of world opinion may well suggest possibilities for improvements in articulation and in policy response. But the phenomenon is here to stay, and its role will surely expand in future.

One final comment by way of introduction. Human rights studies in the 1990s tended to be fairly optimistic about the role of international standards and advocacies in improving the human condition. Current discourse has turned sour, wondering whether massive efforts make any difference.[7] The present study will probably rate an optimistic label: I do think that history shows not only what world opinion is and why, but also a list of favorable impacts. But there have been huge gaps and failures as well, and whole periods in which world opinion wilted in the face of massive problems. I hope that this book contributes to understanding world opinion and also toward making it more useful; I do not join some current pessimists in fearing that its force is about to weaken in face of new international tensions. But complexity is undeniable, and I'd like to avoid the simplistic labeling of "optimist" or "pessimist."

2

HOW WORLD OPINION GOT STARTED

Exploring the first sustained outburst of world opinion advances our definition of the subject, by illustrating and explaining the changes that were needed to generate the initial attempts to pronounce on distant matters in the name of humanity. The same exploration also highlights crucial differences between formative world opinion and its contemporary counterpart. Some preliminary comments on even earlier manifestations of key components of world opinion, coupled with explanations of why they did not really constitute world opinion, both improve the definition and help prepare the case for why real world opinion emerged when it did.

Historians love to fuss about origins, for reasons that are fundamentally sound. This chapter seeks to avoid the sometimes excruciating detail and pickiness the love can generate ("When did it really begin? Let me count the ways") while elucidating when and why previous historical elements coalesced into the phenomenon we know today.

Three elements in earlier world history provide the backdrop. Some seemingly natural, if not entirely admirable, social prejudices around identifying "otherness" showed up early on, and elements of them persist in world opinion today, though they also initially generated barriers to the wide application that world opinion implies. Receptivity to external standards, also apparently natural though less predictable, contributes a recurrent factor as well; that is, there are signs of response to outside opinion in various premodern situations. More specifically historical are the implications of somewhat more recent commitments to ideas of natural law or missionary religion.

First, human societies quickly developed a capacity to distinguish otherness and to delight in their own superiority. Classical China and classical Greece both readily identified "barbarians," by which they meant most peoples whom they encountered other than themselves. Traveler accounts, like that by the Greek historian Herodotus, though sometimes a bit more open-minded, similarly focused on what was different and, often, bizarre about the distant lands visited. Modern world opinion continues this ancient tradition to a degree, in insisting on identifying certain practices as different from one's own standards and probably inferior if not downright weird. Even more specifically, world opinion will sometimes make reference to civilized standards and behaviors that hark back directly to the older distinctions – though it has become unfashionable to call other people "barbarians." But the tradition, unlike modern world opinion, almost always stopped with the identification: what was other was other, and there was nothing to do about it except celebrate one's own enlightenment and its contrast with the deplorable deficiencies of the non-we. World opinion, in contrast, depends on an ability to argue that in crucial areas the other can and should be changed in light of shared human values.

In point of fact, even ancient societies sometimes worked to bring certain groups in line with accepted standards, as part of the integration necessary to make territorial expansion work. The northern Chinese strove diligently to meld various southern ethnic groups into a common pattern of belief and behavior, by sending northern immigrants, pressing for a single official language and elite educational system, and so on. The Romans ultimately expanded opportunities for citizenship to a minority of elite individuals around the Mediterranean, including people like St. Paul who were very proud of this status. And they believed that a common legal system could set standards for the diverse peoples of the empire, while even developing broader ideas of natural law that, in principle, could embrace the whole of humanity. Early religions like Judaism, although focusing on individual groups, could project a sense of shared ethics for humanity more generally. These developments were important, in moving beyond the narrowest condemnation of otherness, but they did not lead to any efforts to work for rights or remedies beyond political or cultural boundaries. Knowledge of the world as a whole was far too sketchy to permit anything like a global view; the Romans, although they traded for Chinese silks, barely knew that China existed, and vice versa.

The advent of major missionary religions, with a desire and capacity to move beyond established cultural boundaries, was potentially of great significance in moving closer to world opinion. When the Indian emperor Ashoka sent Buddhist missionaries to spread the truth as they saw it to other parts of the Indian Ocean basin, the assumption was that there was a common humanity capable and deserving of spiritual enlightenment. Buddhism, Christianity, and Islam all assumed a single humanity open to conversion, possessing souls that merited the opportunity for salvation, even though the people involved were distant and, in many other respects, quite different from those from whom missionary activities emanated. Both Christians and Muslims hesitated about this universality, early Christians often assuming that only Jews were ripe for truth, early Muslims often believing that their religion was for Arabs alone. But the universalizing implications soon triumphed. In the process of proselytization an unprecedentedly wide base for certain kinds of opinion arose. By the end of the eleventh century, there was a Christian public opinion (in Western and Central Europe, not all of Christendom), open to papal appeals to crusade for the conquest of the Holy Land from Islam, across the welter of political boundaries and separate vernacular languages that characterized the medieval period. The Crusades depended on a belief in the spiritually appalling conditions of the Holy Land, which created an urgent sense of obligation to an otherwise unknown and distant locale – evocative of what world opinion could produce later on. Islamic opinion was a bit more diffuse, because there was no centralizing agency like the papacy, but the spread of beliefs and of practices like the pilgrimage to Mecca united Muslims from West Africa to Indonesia[1]. Muslim travelers like the thirteenth-century Ibn Battuta could pointedly note ways in which certain Muslim groups did not entirely live up to appropriate standards – Battuta was highly critical of the public openness of women in sub-Saharan Africa, for example – but they readily modified this sense of otherness by recognizing a common devotion to Islamic belief and practice. Islam could also create a sense of embarrassment among non-Muslims which might compel them to convert in order to measure up to civilized standards – another foreshadowing of world opinion. Chinese Muslims visiting Indonesia in the fifteenth century commented on how local non-Muslims were "very ugly and had strange faces," besides being infidels and possibly possessed by the devil; this in contrast not only to the Chinese (Muslim or not) but also to Muslims from the Middle East. This kind of derogation, expressed even implicitly, could certainly annoy but could also influence local behavior, as world opinion would later do. With the expansion of Islam, Buddhism, and Christianity, identities became less narrowly subdivided than they had been previously.

Particularly for Islam, expansion and growing trade greatly increased knowledge about the wider world, another precondition for world opinion later on. Muslim scholars did occasionally comment on conditions in societies beyond direct Islamic control, for example in Africa, noting (like the Arab travelers) issues such as conditions of women. This capacity of judging the appropriateness of other societies may be seen as approaching a basis for world opinion, though the component of moral responsibility was not yet fully articulated; it certainly underlies more recent efforts to develop Islamic counterparts to Western-based world opinion.

These developments were truly important. We have seen already the significance of Christian elements in modern world opinion, for example against the presumed atrocities against the Armenians, and Islam will enter our consideration later on as well. But the world religions, by themselves, could not generate world opinion in the modern sense, quite apart from considerable ongoing ignorance of developments in more distant parts of Afroeurasia and complete ignorance of the world as a whole. Christianity and Islam recognized a common humanity that might be converted, but they sharply divided humanity between those who had converted and those who had not; there was no sharing of rights across religious lines. Christian crusading interest in the Holy Land was not really directed to the people there, save insofar as they might be converted; it was the place, not the common humanity, that generated the passionate sense of obligation. Atrocities committed in regions devoted to other religions were either of no interest, since they did not affect that part of humanity worthy of consideration, or were positively to be expected as part of God's punishment for unbelief. They might even be welcomed, and crusading Christians generated their own cruelties in confronting Muslims in Jerusalem. The world religions helped set a base for a wider understanding of common humanity, but they did not create this understanding and in many ways actively impeded it – in many ways, indeed, continue to impede it to this day.

A third facet of the human experience before modern times deserves note. Just as many societies readily identified others, and found them wanting, so many societies, confronted with apparent superiority, proved willing to try to change in order to measure up to higher standards. Japan, first copying Chinese culture and institutions, went through a seventh-century phase of trying to be Chinese in virtually every way possible, before it became clear that this was impossible and in some respects undesirable. Many non-Arabs, awed by Arab conquest and culture as well as the attractions of Islam, quickly worked to become as Arab as they could; in places like North Africa they succeeded. Germanic groups on the fringes of the Roman Empire and the Russians in contact with the splendor of Byzantium are other cases in which knowledge of a superior culture, combined with the sneers or suggestions from representatives of that culture, produced an active desire to improve the level of civilization by active imitation. This human impulse, to acknowledge inferiority amid new levels of contact but to seek to adjust to the apparently higher standards, is a vital component of receptivity to world opinion, when this opinion is seen as the contemporary statement of superior values.

The impulse began to apply to Western standards well before the formation of Western-based world opinion, once Europe began to flex its military and commercial muscles from the sixteenth century onward. Russia, beginning with Peter the Great, began to define aspects of its progress by its ability to mimic Western fashion and cultural life. It became embarrassing, for the Russian upper class, not to dress and coiff in the Western manner, not to define painting and literature by Western standards, not to have a Western-style scientific education. Even more intimate aspects of life had to change. Peter the Great decreed that the old custom by which a daughter's father handed a whip to her new husband, as part of a marriage ceremony, was uncivilized and must stop, and stop it did. None of this was the effect of world opinion directed at Russia, because world opinion did not yet exist. But it showed a sensitivity to Western standards that were now manifest through Western merchants and diplomats present in Russia, plus the fruits of widespread elite Russian travel in France and elsewhere. This sensitivity to Western standards, though simply the latest stage in a common process of reacting to contact, would play a vital role in the emergence of and reaction to world opinion, in Russia and elsewhere. To be sure, even the most ardent Russian Westernizers, in this pre-modern world, did not seek to bring every aspect of their society into alignment; even as Westernization proceeded, the conditions of Russian serfs continued to worsen, in contrast to social patterns emerging in other parts of Europe. And the Westernization that did occur brought urgent protest from more traditional sectors, such as much of the Russian Orthodox clergy, who found imitation dangerous and demeaning. These features – the incomplete application of "civilized" standards and the reaction against them in the name of traditional values and relationships – would also be part of the age of world opinion, when it finally dawned.

Well before the emergence of world opinion, then, many societies were accustomed to a pattern of self-definition and self-congratulation when confronted with evidence of otherness; a significant expansion of a sense of humanity had occurred with the world religions, but not an ability to transcend religious divisions themselves; and a frequent willingness to adjust showed an awareness of inferiority, once revealed by contacts with a more successful or confident society, that would continue to play a role after world opinion began to operate. But though all of this provided elements that would feed the formation and implementation of world opinion, the modern product was, for better or worse, still out of reach.

Two developments had to be added in to convert traditional attitudes into world opinion, including transforming an ongoing statement of otherness into a plea for common standards of humanity. Both developments initially emerged strongly in the formation of world opinion against slavery and the slave trade. First, there needed to be wider knowledge, less limited by myths and fancies, about distant parts of the world. This knowledge also had to be more promptly delivered, creating an atmosphere of urgency as well as direct connection. Second, most crucially, there needed to be a new sense of shared humanity, across even religious boundaries, that could generate an expectation of common minimal rights and a torrent of outrage when these rights were being violated. The articulation of world opinion against slavery was, to be sure, less than global; it began in the West and only gradually gained any support from people in other parts of the world. We will return to this limitation. On the other hand, the impressive campaign against slavery testifies to a new kind of passion and a universalist humanitarianism that continue to feed world opinion to this day, directed in this first instance against an institution virtually as old as human society. The story is familiar. We will review it only to establish what it illustrates about the new capacity for global outrage.

World opinion also depended, of course, on the emergence of public opinion – a combination of new media to disseminate strong views (and early newspapers were decidedly opinionated) and a sense among segments of the public, particularly in the cities, that their views should be both expressed and heeded. Although there had been hints of public opinion earlier – in Christian communities or in the cities of Islam – a clearly modern version of the phenomenon emerged in the eighteenth century in Western Europe. World opinion, branching off toward global targets, followed quite quickly, and it was slavery that served as lightning rod for this extension.[2]

Hostility to slavery was not new, but it had never been systematic. Individuals had spoken against slavery, and many owners had freed slaves (usually, conveniently, after the owner's death). Systems of slavery had declined in key societies, like China, though rarely disappeared entirely. Major religions, like Christianity and Islam, raised new problems for slavery, particularly when co-religionists were among the enslaved. But the religions had managed to accommodate slavery even so. (Islam disavowed the enslavement of Muslims but was more neutral concerning non-Muslims, an obvious difference from later world opinion.) Practitioners were most comfortable when slaves came from other places, through trade or war, but some internal slavery proved acceptable as well, for example in Christian Russia. The Jesuit order had some success in resisting the enslavement of South American Indians, whom it was trying to convert, but it did not intervene against the African slave trade. In sum: the systematic protest against the whole institution of slavery, and the international trade that sustained it, that began to take shape in the later eighteenth century was a truly novel phenomenon, directed against a time-tested practice in human affairs.

The central innovation that made this campaign possible, and would fuel world public opinion from that point forward, was what historian Thomas Haskell has called a "new sensibility." This sensibility extended the assumption of moral responsibility, on the part of the people central to the formation and furtherance of world opinion, so that the conditions of distant peoples – like slaves – became as relevant to the application of ethical norms as conditions of near-neighbors. The norms were not necessarily new – the golden rule and other elements of Christianity loomed large – but their application was unprecedented. Here were the cultural determinants of the soaring campaign against slavery, from the 1780s onward, motivating some leaders to mount the campaign but, almost as significant, also motivating a growing number of people to listen and respond. The evils of slavery became immediate, and the moral condemnation central to this first outpouring of world opinion required implementation.[3] Here was a force that could impel proponents to seek changes even against their obvious material interest, as the formation of world opinion against slavery impatiently brushed aside economic arguments in favor of moral justice.

The new sensibility had two sources, oddly paired. The first source involved new Protestant groups, Quakers and Methodists particularly, who emphasized the universality of their moral code and who provided much of the initial leadership of the antislavery movement. Baptists also became heavily involved, on both sides of the Atlantic. These new forms of Christianity, concerned with a proper moral order in this world, would continue to play a role in global opinion well into the twentieth century – as the movement for Armenian rights in the 1890s illustrated. The second source, more obviously novel, was the secular movement of the Enlightenment, whose advocates emphasized the fundamental equality of all human beings and of their natural rights. The Enlightenment directly spurred reevaluation of conditions in Europe and North America, helping to set the stage for the wave of revolutions that crisscrossed the Atlantic, but it also generated the larger world opinion as well. Combined with the religious fervor of the Christian antislavery proponents, who sometimes directly shared elements of Enlightenment belief as well, the new assumptions about common humanity were central to the insistence that people in one area had the right and obligation to seek fundamental changes on behalf of people thousands of miles away.

Almost as important as the emergence of the new humanitarian universalism was the array of tactics that emerged, periodically from the 1780s through the 1830s and beyond, to rouse public opinion and to use it as a force for change. Almost all the mechanisms of world opinion still present today appeared during this fervent half-century. Specific technologies differed, of course, but they count for less than might be imagined given the entrepreneurial zeal of the antislavery advocates in what was not only the first but among the most successful explosions of world opinion over the past two centuries.

Organizations proliferated. Central coordination came from groups like the British Abolition Society, founded in 1787. A succession of such associations like the Society for the Amelioration and Gradual Abolition of Slavery (1822) were established on the principle that slavery was "repugnant to the principles of justice and humanity."[4] But each such national society generated a host of local branches, where the real mobilization occurred. Within a year, for example, the Amelioration society had 250 regional affiliates. These groups sponsored meetings, lectures, and other activities designed both to widen public opinion and to translate it into action. Specialty groups formed, for example for young people. A vital innovation, much discussed, involved the inclusion of women, both in general meetings and in special ladies' organizations, which spread widely. The associational movement, from its British roots, also had international ramifications. Ireland offered a direct connection, and antislavery advocates frequently took organizational and propaganda trips to the island. Denmark responded as early as 1792, curtailing its slave trade. The French Revolution introduced its own measures on slavery in the colonies, few of which endured. French organizations were coordinating with British groups, and citing British example, by the 1830s. Also in the 1830s came the formation of Canadian organizations, with close ties to their British counterparts. German groups were loosely linked in by the 1840s. United States interaction with the British movement occurred at a number of levels. Denominational churches, not only the Quakers and Methodists but also Presbyterians, heard from their British co-religionists in ways that helped fire up their own antislavery efforts.

In the United States, as in Britain, the opportunity to use established organizations, as well as setting up new ones, was crucial to the elaboration of public opinion. American leaders in fact asked for British backing, because, as two of them put it, "the literature of Great Britain exercises so vast an influence over the public opinion of America."[5] Daniel O'Connell, the Irish leader, directed explicit appeals to Irish Americans.

Building out from the proliferation of organizations was the formation of international congresses on the subject, from the 1830s onward. Several conventions were held in London, with active backing from a number of nations. An 1839 invitation was issued in a number of languages to "friends of the slave of every nation and of every clime." As the American poet Whittier put it, "Yes, let them gather! Summon forth the pledged philanthropy of Earth. From every land, whose hills have heard the bugle blast of Freedom waking." Here was a classic opportunity both to gather and to intensify world public opinion, and the tactic has been repeated many times since.[6]

Historians have noted the impressive efficiency of the antislavery movement's effort to organize meetings and local associations. By the 1830s many businessmen, such as James Cropper, were directly applying business techniques to the whole apparatus of generating this aspect of public opinion.

Tireless pamphleteering was a vital part of the strategy, often building on both central and local organizations. Books, pamphlets, and an occasional regular journal, like the 1830s *Slavery in America* periodical in Britain, drove home two themes. First were the basic moral principles reflecting the transformation of sensibility toward global responsibility. But second was a vigorous effort to seize on highly personal, dramatic (often tragic) accounts, so that slavery and its evils acquired human faces. *Slavery in America*, for example, highlighted experiences in slave auctions, discipline, and family dissolution. Branding and public punishments drew great emphasis, and accounts of family disruption were designed particularly to rouse women's concern. Events like the seizure of the slave ship *Amistad* or the capture of John Brown greatly furthered antislavery propaganda, because they were ideal for stirring outrage. French poet Victor Hugo wrote of John Brown's conviction, to a British paper, "the whole civilized world was witnessing with horror a travesty of justice" – not in Turkey, where such things were expected, but in America.[7] British papers expressed the hope that, if Brown were executed, individual citizens and public meetings would drive home their disgust to "American travelers whenever they set foot on the shores of England."[8] Theatrical versions of *Uncle Tom's Cabin*, as well as the book itself plus the author's international lecture tour, spread like wildfire, again because they so vividly personified the human suffering of slavery, in contrast to the standards of civilization.

Personal tragedies could easily translate into the larger principles. "Let us remember that they are God's creatures, created by the same power, sustained by the same goodness . . . as ourselves; that they have a capacity for suffering and enjoyment like our own . . . Think of these things, and let your zeal be enkindled and your pity excited, that your exertions may henceforth be commensurate with the miseries of these unhappy beings, and your own responsibility."[9]

Petitions were vital, both to press domestic governments to take action against slavery and the slave trade and to urge the same of foreign regimes. Protestant ministers in Lancashire gathered thirteen hundred signatures to protest to the government of South Carolina against the possible execution of John Brown. Within individual countries, Britain unquestionably at the head, petition drives to attack foreign evils were impressive beyond any precedent – the biggest outpourings of opinion that had ever occurred. Petitions in the several thousands were routine. In 1788 ten thousand people in Manchester, a city then of fifty thousand in total, signed; by 1833 twenty percent of all British adults were joining in. In early 1833 alone, over five thousand petitions reached Parliament. Though the idea of public opinion made sense particularly to the middle class, large numbers of artisans and others were joining in. As one newspaper put it, "*Vox populi, Vox dei* – that slavery shall be no more."[10] Petition movements in Sweden, Denmark, and The Netherlands added to the clamor, though with smaller numbers involved. The idea was to insist to one's own government that action must be taken to eliminate slavery (efforts here were supplemented by urging voters to apply antislavery litmus tests to candidates in elections) and to press foreign regimes, and individual slaveholders, to the same end.

Boycotts were proposed, particularly as the campaign moved past the slave trade, which the British abolished in 1807, to foreign slavery more generally. A number of campaigns sought to persuade people to boycott West Indian sugar. One antislavery business leader organized sugar imports from Indonesia to provide a morally approved alternative. This particular dimension was sketched, more than widely implemented, but it foreshadowed yet another common tactic of world opinion in the twentieth century.

The impact was undeniable, even amid significant historical debates about the role of humanitarian sentiment versus new kinds of economic calculations including the availability of other forms of labor. Measures by the British government, from the initial abolition of the slave trade to later emancipation in the British colonies, directly reflected the bombardment of public opinion.

Public pressure, both domestic and international, played a role in slave trade decisions from Denmark to France to the United States. Internal decisions about slavery or serfdom were more complex; it would be wrong to exaggerate the role of world opinion, for example, in the emancipation debates in the United States. Furthermore, as is often the case with world opinion, invocation of the moral views of foreigners could actually enhance local stubbornness, and the southern sense that abolitionism was "foreign" facilitated arguments to hold the line. But a sense that the values of civilized society demanded some redress of forced labor did affect the American debate. It played a role – again along with other factors, including a sense of economic and military decline relative to Western Europe plus concern about peasant uprisings – in discussions about the emancipation of serfs in Russia, leading up to the reform decree of 1861. Partly because of awareness of world opinion, in a context in which embarrassment about appearing backward was already established, virtually no one in Russia disputed the moral grounds for unseating serfdom by the later 1850s. There was direct impact in the United States as well. One of the several reasons for President Lincoln's 1863 Emancipation Proclamation had to do with international opinion – a desire to elicit British and French backing for the Union cause, once a partial commitment to freeing the slaves was built into war plans. Reference to the values of being civilized sustained abolition movements in Brazil, prior to slave emancipation in 1888. A classic and time-tested institution had been rethought, thanks to the creation, imaginative tactics, and sheer insistence of world opinion and its self-appointed leaders.

This first instance of world opinion had some special features, not surprisingly. The movements I have sketched were hardly global. This was a Western phenomenon, rooted in changes in Western culture, with Britain predominant. It is the global outreach, far more than any international base, that qualifies the whole phenomenon as seminal in the history of world opinion – though the affiliations and tactics that crossed borders within the Western world, and slightly beyond, remain relevant. It is also true that mass manifestations of antislavery were transient and fickle, cresting at a few passionate points but then falling back. Sustained agitation came from a few elements of the middle and upper classes. But this is a characteristic of world opinion generally, important in assessing it but hardly a distinctive limitation of antislavery.

Though deeply traditional, slavery, and particularly the slave trade, was a relatively clear target for world opinion, in contrast to more amorphous efforts later on. The slave trade was highly visible, and though occasional ships could slip past international prohibitions the high-volume operation that had characterized the Atlantic commerce during the eighteenth century could not. When rules changed, results would follow. The same held true to a degree for domestic slavery and serfdom. The systems depended on laws and state support; if these were withdrawn in face of pressure from world opinion, real change would occur. Other forms of coercion might, and did, persist and expand, but formal slavery could be largely ended. All of this may help explain why world opinion first focused here. The fact that campaigns brought visible results helped sustain the phenomenon.

It is also worth noting that, during the half-century high point of world opinion against slavery, there were really no other causes that global opinion leaders decided to rally around. Candidates abounded; for example, the growing opium trade. But nothing sparked interest the way slavery did, until after the 1860s. In this sense, the first episode of world opinion was a distinctive moment. Later periods, including the present, always saw an array of causes vying for attention on the stage of world opinion, and the sheer volume inevitably has threatened to dilute results. The single-minded focus on slavery permitted limitations on the new moral sensibility before the 1860s – outrage against opium was reduced by beliefs that the Chinese were degenerate anyway – plus some ongoing constraints on the availability of world news that might dramatize other kinds of evils. But the same single-minded focus undoubtedly helped produce results, again in contrast to some subsequent efforts that displayed the same kind of zeal but demonstrated less staying power.

Several characteristics emerge from this first explosion of world opinion which remain applicable today despite significant change. First, given the frequent defiance of world opinion, it's worth remembering that the phenomenon began with a success. Combined with other factors, including massive global population increase that helped drive down the costs of "free," or wage, labor, the expression of deep moral conviction, supplemented by clever tactics ranging from demonstrations to petitions to heart-rending drama, could promote basic change. World opinion could sway governments to become more active forces against slavery; it could influence the powerful tsar of Russia to reconsider serfdom (along, again, with other factors involved); it could trump the counter-pressures of slaveholders and estate owners. To be sure, the process took time. Victory was less complete than the formal legal abolition of slavery and serfdom suggested, in that various forms of coercion, including the recruitment of powerless children, the use of company stores and the resultant binding debts, and the revival of indentured labor, persisted and persist to this day. But there was real change, and world opinion played a role – which was one reason that the weapon seemed worth using later on for a wider array of causes.

Second, world opinion, from this first instance onward, has been particularly concerned with human rights causes. Beliefs in a common humanity, which constituted the most fundamental innovation in the antislavery campaign, work best when directed against blatant denials of freedom or rights of survival. References to physical suffering – the harsh punishments of slaves – figure prominently in defining the civilized standards that most readily rouse world opinion, even within a larger human rights context. A host of potential targets for world opinion, but ones less definable in terms of basic human rights and physical degradation, have not attracted effective expression; or their advocates have turned to other mechanisms. Only the significant adoption of environmental issues, in the past thirty years, has seen a core addition to the human rights impulses that most clearly activate global outrage.

Third – and this obviously follows from the human rights thrust but requires separate comment – world opinion was broadly speaking a liberal rather than conservative force at the outset, and it has remained so. A few antislavers were conservative in other respects, and they were ultimately able to persuade many conservative politicians to join their cause, but the movement used world opinion to promote major change in the status quo. Because world opinion is normally directed toward change, or against the doings of established powers, its non-conservative quality may be self-evident. But it's worth noting that conservative forces, though sometimes interested in mobilizing world opinion, have some characteristic difficulties. Because they defend existing positions, their credentials in the human rights field may seem less than pure. The conservative embrace of nationalism which began in the later nineteenth century, while providing a vital vote-getting tool at home, also limits conservative capacity in the world opinion field. Conservatives still tend to push the nation state as their source of strength in the international field (sometimes quite successfully); although this is obviously true in the United States, it also applies to other situations such as China, where conservative Communists have their own set of dances with world opinion. Here is another aspect of the subject to which we will have to return.

Fourth, world opinion was born West European, with the United States providing a bit of a complement. It resulted from the addition of humanitarian sentiment to Western Christianity and from the related outlook of the Enlightenment, and it built on a European sense of power and superiority.

These characteristics have been modified, with the addition of other centers of global authority, but they have not been obliterated. The global standards that undergird world opinion remain disproportionately Western. World opinion has outlasted Western imperialism and has surpassed some of its limitations, but elements of its original incarnation persist. To a surprising degree, European, not more generally Western, leadership persists as well. With a few exceptions, the United States has not pioneered in world opinion formulation, even though it has surpassed European leadership in other respects. A greater parochialism – Americans remain much less likely than Europeans to belong to international non-governmental organizations, for their penchant for joining things applies more clearly to national or regional units – plays a role here. So does a distinctive American moralism that often differs from the moralism of world opinion, a point to which we will return. More recently still, the status of the United States as the only superpower more predictably has turned it from proponent to target; but Europe's disproportionate role in world opinion was established long before.

Fifth, the antislavery campaign also formed a first instance of the considerable hypocrisy that often nestles in the baggage of world opinion. The humanitarian fervor that anchored world opinion against slavery is incontestable. But it had many blinders. The shapers of world opinion decided that slavery merited their attention – which from a contemporary vantage point seems valid enough – but also that current conditions of factory labor largely did not. Some historians have suggested that much of the fervor of antislavery in Britain was designed to distract from the huge evils of factory conditions. Although this is too harsh a view, there's probably some truth in it. World opinion picks and chooses, as it doubtless must to be successful, but in the process it can gloss over problems that are almost as severe as those it singles out. In the slavery case, there was more still. Fervent antislavery did not extend to much concern about what happened when slavery was abolished. Immense poverty and lack of land did not rouse the kind of campaign that slavery itself had generated, partly because the issues were more diffuse, partly because different kinds of property rights came into play, but partly because many antislavery advocates were tainted with a racism that precluded much attention to the real people involved as opposed to the abstract principles and symbolic dramas. Here are some other characteristics that will re-emerge in later instances of world opinion, where principle may overshadow human beings and where follow-through finds world opinion fading away when the complexity of real-world situations becomes clearer. Furthermore, world opinion against slavery got caught up in nineteenth-century imperialism. Both sincere concern and colonial self-interest prompted imperialist ventures, particularly in Africa, to continue the battle against slavery and, in the process, to establish new bastions of European control. This crude relationship between world opinion and empire has largely disappeared, but a broader link with recurrent assertions of economic and political power has not disappeared from the world opinion stage.

Finally, the antislavery campaign was rooted in beliefs in the power and validity of opinion, and though this is obvious it does warrant comment. Well before major extensions of suffrage, people in many Western countries, again Britain at the head, were coming to believe that they had the right to express themselves and that some results would or should follow this expression. This reflected new opportunities for information and expression, like circulating newspapers, but also a new sense of entitlement. The same belief sustains world opinion today and has spread beyond the Western world (though not uniformly or universally). Wedded to the also novel sense of moral obligation, the belief in the validity of strong public expressions completed the establishment of the cultural prerequisites for world opinion.

The campaign against slavery provided both precedents and illustrations for world opinion in subsequent decades. The force of moral zeal, religious or religious-like in fervor but applied to the defense of basic human rights, remained at the core of the phenomenon. This was the cultural sea change that allowed world opinion to emerge in the first place, in advance of some of the technological apparatus that would come to be associated with modern media and opinion formation. But there were also lessons in the use of parliamentary advocacy, tactics of mobilization, and dramatization of information. As European world dominance continued to advance, opportunities for world opinion expanded as well. It was hardly surprising that a number of features of the first and triumphant outpouring continued to inform its successors.

The campaign against slavery itself continued to reverberate, with increasing global impact and participation. By the 1870s new reports on slavery within Africa, from the pens of people like David Livingstone, provided vivid reminders of the brutalities involved. Organizations proliferated in Europe and the Americas, including Brazil, in imitation of British progenitors like the British and Foreign Anti-Slavery Society. As one observer noted, this continued to illustrate the first transnational moral movement that was not specifically religious. Brazilians, for example, expressed themselves eager to "imitate every

European progress, and possess each new material, moral, intellectual, or social improvement of civilization."[11] Public opinion campaigns were mounted against the East African slave trade, leading for example to an 1873 treaty that ended the traffic from the territories of the Sultan of Zanzibar. (This move also supported British imperialist interests in the region.) New organizations and opinion campaigns in the 1890s and 1900s were directed against Belgium's harsh labor regime in the Congo, where vivid stories helped bring an end to King Leopold's tyranny. Edmund Morel, a British shipping employee, led a campaign of outrage against the treatment of Congolese workers, bringing the horrors to public attention in Europe and North America. His work was a bridge between antislavery and more modern human rights work.[12] Another achievement for the ongoing British Anti-Slavery Society was an attack on the methods of a European company in Peru which used debt peonage to create a labor force for its rubber production. The Society also worked against a Chinese practice of selling young girls from poor families into domestic service for extended periods during their youth. Efforts continued after World War I, when the major Allied powers invited the Society to draft those parts of the League of Nations Convenant which dealt with "backward territories." The League subsequently conducted several inquiries on various forms of exploited labor, with particular attention to debt bondage, forced marriages for women, and the purchase of children for work. A variety of conventions were signed by a number of states around the world. Decisions such as a 1923 decree by the King of Nepal or the 1963 move by Saudi Arabia, both abolishing slavery, continued to show the practical impact of this focus of world opinion and the organizations it fostered. By the decades after World War II a host of NGOs were at work on forced labor issues, as the initial thrust against slavery expanded into concerns about child labor, prostitution, and the like. In 1990 the Anti-Slavery Society changed its name to Anti-Slavery International, while continuing to rouse global outrage against practices such as child prostitution in Asian tourism. A 1998 Global March against Child Labor, and an attendant campaign against conditions of domestic service for girls in the Philippines, showed the continuity that had led from initial expressions of moral outrage, two centuries before, to the ongoing mobilization of a world public on behalf of human rights in work. The linkage was clear, in tactics and moral sentiment alike, even as world opinion broadened within the field of labor and beyond and even as its range of participation gradually expanded as well.

PART II
Expansion, Innovation, and Constraints, 1860s–1930s

3

WORLD OPINION EXPANDS ITS RANGE

With the strength, culture, and many of the methods of world opinion firmly established by the 1860s, it was hardly surprising that its mobilization began to be applied to a growing array of international topics and problems. This section deals with a second phase in the emergence of world opinion, in which the expansion of issues addressed was matched by a growing diversity of approaches, from the 1860s through the troubled years of the 1930s. This was not a period of unalloyed triumph, and the 1930s indeed saw world opinion either fail or hesitate as part of the looming international chaos that led to World War II. Failure, but also some less heralded successes, set the stage for the fuller blossoming of world opinion after 1945. At the same time, decisions about how to organize international pressure – and whether world opinion was in fact the best vehicle, and how world opinion could best be mobilized or professed – varied during this period as well, with consequences that have endured to the present day. The later nineteenth century, in particular, was a fertile breeding ground for new kinds of global movements, and various expressions of world opinion were a key part of this process.

This chapter and the two that follow deal with the eighty-year span between the substantial triumph of antislavery and the disaster of World War II. The twin themes are innovation and limitation. A steady advance of world opinion did not occur, for several reasons. Some of the issues that now came under its purview were simply more intractable than slavery had been – when great power interests were involved or when more intimate aspects of life, like gender relations, came into play. The growing impulse to invoke world opinion not only against major military powers but in more personal interactions such as control over children invited frequent failure, which in turn raised questions about the whole phenomenon and could discourage its use. Some states, as well, became more clever about concealing abuses, precisely because world opinion was now a potential force; this had some bearing on the horrendous doings of Nazi Germany. Growing conflicts among the great powers themselves, cresting in the 1930s, also hampered public opinion; it was harder to pretend consensus and the results of too much earnest insistence became scarier. During the 1920s and 1930s, some of the moral zeal that normally fed world opinion now went into pacifism, which again diluted the effort against specific abuses.

In this context, the development of alternative methods of pressure also challenged world opinion. The emergence of international agencies, global negotiations among great powers, and international non-governmental organizations all provided the leaders of some causes – like women's rights – some tempting channels for pressure without turning directly to world opinion. A revealing, and important, incident: the signing of the Geneva Convention. In 1859 a Swiss-Italian banker, Henry Dumont, became appalled at the lack of medical attention to soldiers during the wars of Italian unification. He wrote a book urging international standards and caught the attention both of the press and of celebrities like Victor Hugo and Florence Nightingale. An international committee was established, which later became the International Red Cross; global action, not provisions by individual states, was clearly essential. But Dumont and his distinguished colleagues worked this issue from the top down, with no particular effort to enlist public passions. Although there was some publicity, elite support was primary. Dumont managed, for example, to gain the ear of Napoleon III in France, who then altered national legislation to permit the application of international standards. In 1864 the Geneva Convention was signed, and an array of governments beyond Western Europe gradually adhered: Japan observed the Convention in its 1890s war with China, for example, even though China had not yet signed. Here was an important gain for international standards, but world public opinion in any literal sense was peripheral at best. A number of global advocates would follow this precedent, which became still more attractive when formal international organizations, like the League of Nations, emerged.

But the opportunities for world opinion widened as well. News of distant doings became more available. The expansion of antislavery agitation to Africa, noted in the previous chapter, followed from growing publicity in the Western press. Japan and Korea were opened to international scrutiny. The sprawling British Empire generated news mechanisms that shared information widely to the English-speaking world, with an eagerness to identify challenges to "civilized" standards. Shock and outrage, or ridicule, not infrequently followed.

International news services, like Reuters, gained increasing leverage. The related expansion of Western power also created a new sense of embarrassment in some quarters about falling short of the standards of the world's dominant civilization. Even casual assertions of Western opinion about global issues could have deep impact, although they could also generate resistance in the name of cherished identities and against European imperialism.

The establishment of the Nobel Prizes, in 1901, indicated the growing confidence in identifying global standards in a variety of fields. The Western base remained clear: not until 1936 did a Peace Prize go to someone other than a European or North American (the winner was Argentine), and not until 1960 did the prize clearly escape Western bounds (the award went to Chief Luthuli in South Africa). But the prizes, particularly for peace, did advance the idea of world opinion. Many Peace Prize winners, particularly from the 1960s onward, had done much to rouse world opinion in favor of conflict resolution or in attacks on human rights abuses, and prize-winner status in turn would help some world leaders inspire global opinion on the same subjects.

This chapter explores the new openness to Western pressures, which often passed as global opinion, but also some of the reactions that complicated the late-nineteenth century suggestions of a looming "world culture." Then we turn, in chapter 4, to the mobilization of global forces through mechanisms that touched, but did not centrally invoke, world opinion. Chapter 5 deals with world opinion per se, particularly as it expanded into a wider array of human rights abuses and then failed against the onslaught of national rivalries in the 1930s.

Opportunities to gain vivid knowledge of remote conditions, and exposure of regions to impressions of Western opinion both expanded rapidly during the nineteenth century, particularly from mid-century onward. Journalists began to score points for sensationalist reporting about unknown areas and shocking native practices – the famous trips of Stanley in Africa were one example. Western publics were entertained by patronizing satires, like the Gilbert and Sullivan spoof of Japanese rituals and punishments, in the *Mikado*, which drew outraged protest from the Japanese government but proceeded nevertheless – with impact on Japan as well as on London audiences. Protestants began to support missionary activity, along with Catholics. Protestants were less tolerant of local vagaries than Catholics had been, and more vocal about conveying their standards of behavior both to the "natives" and to publics back home. Business travel increased. Clusters of European merchants in cities like Buenos Aires helped publicize European norms, inspiring new interests – like soccer – but also a new effort to shape up.

The new sense of moral obligation, which had fed the antislavery drive, increasingly blossomed into wider humanitarian efforts in the later nineteenth century. While not a function of world opinion directly, charitable outpourings in response to disasters in remote parts of the world – both natural and human made – tapped and extended the moral sentiment fundamental to world opinion. In this sense the development of the Red Cross, with its assumption that people should be helped in disasters around the globe and that limits should be imposed on the suffering of innocent populations in war, both illustrated and expanded essential features of world opinion.

On a slightly different front, the expansion of imperialism created some situations in which wider European standards could be imposed directly. British control in India grew from purely economic exploitation to a wider effort to create a durable, and up to a point responsible, political administration. This larger goal entailed some circumspection – there was no reason to interfere unduly with traditional practices, lest undesirable resistance be roused. But there were circumstances in which European standards simply begged for application, in which local customs were so at variance with what seemed right that correction proved inescapable. Partly, to be sure, for economic reasons, the British thus refused to enforce the caste system on Indian railway lines (though the British class system was just fine). The growing British presence, including the addition of some British women as wives or daughters of the imperial bureaucrats, soon generated conflicts between their values and those implicit in established Indian practice. Supreme British confidence in their own superiority helped persuade some Indian leaders that certain traditions must be rethought. A British East Indian company official as early as the late eighteenth century had noted scornfully, "Nothing can exceed the habitual contempt which the Hindus entertain for their women." Missionaries, trying to raise money back home, often pointed to the deplorable treatment of Indian women as a reason to support conversions to Christianity. Even businessmen were shocked by some of what they saw around them in India. Particular targets were female infanticide and the striking, though in fact limited, practice of sati – where widows threw themselves on their husband's funeral pyre because in principle they had nothing else to live for. The British banned sati outright in 1829, though it continued to occur into the 1860s. More to our point was the fact that many Indian reformers joined in the campaign, developing a critique through their contact with British values. Rammohun Roy wrote a pamphlet against sati in

1818, arguing that the practice denied women "the excellent merits to which they are entitled by nature," and he ultimately thanked the British for their law, arguing that it restored original Hindu values against the distortions Hindus themselves had introduced and thankfully eliminated "the heinous sin of cruelty to females."[1]

Pressures on India's gender arrangements continued, as British feminists launched a variety of campaigns later in the nineteenth century around such issues as the treatment of prostitutes in the colony. One leader, Josephine Butler, particularly noted Britain's role as both government and Christian nation, in ways that invoked the moral basis of outside opinion: "We have an additional responsibility in respect to India."[2]

This was not, to be sure, a world opinion campaign, though some people in Britain were undoubtedly roused and some domestic outrage was expressed as part of the general blessing of empire. It did, however, illustrate the extent to which growing Western presence roused a new level of sensitivity that created some local acceptance for imperial reforms and that could prepare other areas of receptivity to outside (largely Western) standards. Similar stories would repeat in other imperial areas – for example Polynesia, where missionary outrage against apparent sexual license and scanty costumes quickly led to local opinion that also insisted on change as a measure of advancing civilization and global respectability. Here American as well as British and some French perceptions were involved in stimulating local reform reactions.

Along with imperialism, perhaps ironically, a series of internationalist aspirations erupted in the late nineteenth century, which added to the context in which world opinion could expand and various domestic publics become more receptive to it. Esperanto was created, in hopes that a genuine international language could catch fire and expedite global understanding (language was a patchwork of purely Western tongues and ultimately had little impact; but as an optimistic symbol its significance for a period of expanding internationalism was quite real). Emanating initially from the Islamic world, the new Bahai faith sought to emphasize the spiritual union of all humankind, and again it had some, if modest, resonance.

Three centers outside the West proper proved particularly receptive to measurement by outside, Western standards, and through this to what seemed to be the global standards of civilized society. Russia experienced a heightened sensitivity to values from the outside as it fell farther behind the West militarily and economically yet built on prior patterns of Westernization. By the 1840s many Russian intellectuals and political leaders routinely referred to selected Western standards as models for Russia to emulate. In 1843 Professor Timofei

Granovskii offered a series of lectures on Western medieval history, at Moscow University, designed to show key aspects of the Western experience that Russia had missed, to its disadvantage – including a tradition of religious independence from the state. At the end of one lecture, as the professor turned to his audience, as one observer noted, "to remind them what an immeasurable debt of gratitude we owe to Europe, from which we have received the benefits of civilization and a humane way of life, which she had earned by blood, toil and bitter experience, his words were lost in a surge of applause from every corner of the auditorium." A host of efforts to achieve political reform, but also changes in cultural life, including attacks on the backwardness of the peasantry, were motivated by this responsiveness to an abstract West as the beacon of civilization. Major developments, such as the 1861 emancipation of the serfs, were spurred by the sense of backwardness when measured by relevant world – that is, Western – standards. During the ensuing reform period, the government itself often spoke in the language of the Westerners. A major reform in law courts and punishment was thus guided, in the words of Tsar Alexander II, by "those fundamental principles, the undoubted merit of which is at present recognized by the science and experience of Europe."[3]

To be sure, even Russia's Westernizers frequently criticized the West for its own lapses, and they deeply resented patronizing attitudes toward Russia. It was often tempting to tout special Russian values, such as the imagined solidarity of the peasant village, as preferable to Western individualism and disarray. Here, as in many other cases, openness to world standards also bred reaction. This was even truer of an openly anti-Western camp, fueled by Slavic conservative nationalists, who felt that Russia's only problems derived from its efforts to imitate. These Slavophiles argued that Russia had its own merits, from village cooperation to innate spirituality and orderliness, that should not be sacrificed to any outside standards. Here was a nationalist-based alternative to any idea of Western-derived world opinion, and as a model it would have great power in many parts of the world, in addition to Russia itself. In no sense, then, was Russian leadership swept away by embarrassment at gaps between the nation and what seemed to be the prevailing global norms of civilization. But there was continued sensitivity, and this, along with the direct reach of Western imperialism, contributed to a sense that such global standards existed.

A sense of falling short of global values was even more pervasive in the more heavily European parts of Latin America during the final decades of the nineteenth century. The norms involved were variously phrased – sometimes Western Europe was cited (more rarely the United States), sometimes "civilization," sometimes "modernity" or "modern society." But they involved the same kind of appeal to higher, and globally applicable, standards of law and behavior, the same mixture of apology and reform zeal, that had developed among Russia's "Westerners."

The late nineteenth century saw an outburst of Western imitation in countries like Argentina, Uruguay, and Brazil. Whole city centers were designed in the image of modern Paris. Western standards in education and science were widely emulated, though economic constraints prevented full convergence. By the 1860s, European sports had gained ground, headed by soccer, as local teams, initially drawn from the upper classes, emerged from pick-up clubs organized by European businessmen and diplomats. In this context, many Latin American liberals also began invoking European criteria in a wide array of public policy and personal conduct areas, using a fear of falling short of global civilization norms as an explicit argument for change. By 1900 a host of campaigns aimed at attacking hygiene conditions in the urban slums or regulating popular leisure outlets were justified in terms of the demands of modern civilization and the opprobrium attached to laggards. Global standards provided cover, if not real motivation, for a host of middle class groups eager to force the lower classes into greater respectability.

Prostitution came in for specific comment, and here world opinion was definitely in play. European communities living in cities such as Buenos Aires developed great concern about the levels of prostitution and the presumed forced import of women from abroad, as part of the larger, late-nineteenth-century white slavery scare. (Historians have established that there was a problem, though not as great as world opinion claimed.) Vivid articles and books also appeared in Europe, and the subject came up frequently at international conferences on the white slave trade. At first, Europeans not only noted the problem but also condemned the lack of local disapproval – as one Briton put it, "the absence of any [local] public opinion on the moral question."[4] These strictures hit home, and by 1904 a number of Latin American governments were grappling with regulating both prostitution and the immigration of unattached females. Leading reformers, like Alfredo Palacios, who sponsored regulatory legislation to provide women protection from pimps, specifically noted how embarrassed, even shamed they were by the European belief that Buenos Aires was "the worst of all the centers of the immoral commerce in women." Associations, including local chapters of international groups, proliferated. European accusations of Latin American immorality persisted into the 1920s ("the hotbed of the abominable trade is Argentina"[5]), sustaining the domestic anxiety to measure up to global standards. Embarrassment surfaced again in 1924, when a League of Nations commission made a special, highly publicized visit to Argentina. Again, reformers responded with new policies designed to bring the nation up to global standards. Only after World War II was the international taint fully overcome, as a result (in Argentina) of two major laws and a significant public relations effort.

What was happening in Latin America, at least in its more European-leaning regions, and to a degree elsewhere was the formation of a new middle class based partly on receptivity to Western culture and to Western-based signals about world opinion. This middle class took root with some difficulty, against a traditional social and cultural structure that had emphasized landholding juxtaposed with an impoverished lower class. Adhesion to global standards helped provide identity, against the upper class, and clear canons of respectability against everyone else. Brian Owensby has described the formative process in Brazil, from 1888 onward. White-collar professionals and employees were urged to be *culto*, to steep themselves in Western music, theater, and reading materials, with emphasis on the classic literature of Greece and the Renaissance. As one association put it, "COLLEAGUE! If you aspire to a higher position, think first about the cultural level of your spirit. Sign up today for the self-improvement class sponsored by the Bank Functionaries Union . . . Results are sure to follow."[6] More than erudition was involved, for familiarity with clothing fashions and Western-type sports joined in as well. The package included a commitment to Western-derived habits and manners that embraced a sensitivity to global standards and a willingness not only to accept them but to begin to join in the chorus of world opinion. The Latin American expansion of associations aimed at international efforts on behalf of women, discussed in the next chapter, was part of this new movement toward middle class identity defined in part in global terms.

Japan constitutes a final case of pronounced new receptiveness to global standards, in many respects the most interesting of all. Here was a country that, save for a brief period, had never been exposed to Western ideas and techniques, except for the gradually growing trickle of contact through Dutch merchants and their Japanese translators in the controlled port of Nagasaki. Here was a country that, prior to the response to new Western power, had severely limited international contacts of any sort, from around 1600 until the West forced open entry in 1853. Yet here was a country that, with extraordinary rapidity, deliberately sought global knowledge from 1868 onward, eager to modify or jettison existing practices that did not pass the international litmus test. The imperial

Charter Oath (1868) that sent Japanese emissaries to study foreign achievements specifically stated that "knowledge shall be sought throughout the world," and though this world was in fact Western the leaders meant what they said. Western commentators made clear their sense that Japan was a strange place, in need of some serious reordering. Although the intense hostility directed toward things Islamic was missing, spoofs like the *Mikado* (directed against presumed despotism and unreasonable punishments, in the best global opinion / human rights fashion) revealed the usual sense of superiority and could easily put Japanese leaders on the defensive.

Japan's eagerness for Western-style reforms during the Meiji era of the later nineteenth century is well known. Military systems, public health, and mass education saw widespread imitation from 1868 onward. Technology and science were extensively imported, and enthusiasms for Western consumer products spread widely as well, from the adoption of humble devices such as the toothbrush to the importation of the department store format. To be sure, zeal could prove excessive. By the 1880s the government was pulling back on educational imitation, maintaining Western standards in science and engineering training but insisting on national distinctiveness in the social sciences and related political training, with emphasis on group loyalties over Western individualism. So (as in Russia) an openness to Western-style world opinion was not unbounded. Still, a sensitivity to potential Western criticism in some key areas developed quickly.

Prostitution, once more, was a case in point. Japanese officials retreated quickly from traditional toleration, seeking systems that would avoid too much openness and, by the same token, adverse outside commentary. Individual incidents were carefully handled to avoid eliciting comments from Western visitors: a ruckus in 1900, for example, generated a ruling that an individual prostitute had the right to cease her trade without any authorization from her brothel owner – an affront to traditional employer rights, clearly designed to mesh with apparent world opinion in a touchy area. Even earlier, missionaries and other visitors had provoked criticisms of previous patterns of official toleration and regulation, the government being anxious to demonstrate its civilized status. Concubinage also came in for new official disapproval and for downgrading in law, at cost to traditional arrangements. Local branches of Western organizations, such as the Women's Christian Temperance Movement and the Salvation Army, played a role in conveying the new standards directly, urging the protection of prostitutes as individuals and greater equality between men and women. Similar vulnerabilities emerged over the issue of homosexuality, another area of wide traditional tolerance in Japan. Numerous reformers headed the charge, seeing custom in terms of barbarism, the West in terms of enlightenment and civilization. Western-language papers in Japan periodically expressed concern about homosexuality, for example among students, and urged fuller imitation of legal prohibitions that were gaining ground in the West. Even lesbian acts, never singled out previously in Japanese commentary, came in for new disapproval under the spur of Western attitudes and potential embarrassment. The point is obvious: even in relatively intimate areas, the prospect of outside criticism combined with genuine reformist zeal to produce a new sensitivity, in some cases reversing traditional practices and policies. A growing list of regulations in areas such as public nudity or urination, though more obvious, added to the trend. Except in categories seen as vital to national identity, like group loyalty, it was important to keep below the world opinion radar screen.

While Russia, Latin America, and Japan became particular centers for interaction with Western standards during the later nineteenth century, there were other important transitions. Sensitivity to global standards, again as defined by Western ideals and institutions, also developed in the Middle East. A number of reform efforts sought to respond to Western norms of law and constitutional practice and to Western-style education. Articulate Westernizing reformers wrote on a variety of subjects from the early nineteenth century onward. Along with increasing travel to the West, by students and businessmen, and a growing Western presence in various parts of the Middle East (including outright imperialist conquest, particularly in North Africa), their work provided growing awareness of the gaps between regional habits and the values of what now constituted global leadership. The frequency and condescending hostility of the Western press toward Islam created a genuine challenge to the region, provoking both a desire to establish greater harmony with the wider world and a bitter reassertion of the superiority of regional traditions.

A growing debate over the treatment of women, and specifically the practice of veiling, revealed the new pressures involved. Western commentators, and even popularizers, including pornographers, had long criticized what they saw as degrading Islamic practices concerning women. Lord Cromer, British imperial administrator in Egypt, listed the treatment of women as the "first and foremost" sign of the failure of Islam as a social system. (This was the same Lord Cromer who headed an organization opposed to women's suffrage back home.) British scholars chimed in correspondingly: as one put it, "The degradation of women in the East is a canker that begins its destructive work early in childhood, and has eaten into the whole system of Islam." Missionaries and journalists made similar representations. Social seclusion and presumed sexual excess were the twin, if not logically compatible, targets of this kind of commentary. To criticism was joined insistence on change. Cromer again: it was essential that Egyptians "be persuaded or forced into imbibing the true spirit of western civilization," and veiling and seclusion were a "fatal obstacle" to the Egyptian's "attainment of that elevation of thought and character which should accompany the introduction of Western civilization." The noise was loud enough, and sufficiently focused, that no Islamic reformer by the late nineteenth century could avoid some awareness of this challenge to claims of civilization.

New and partly Western-inspired proposals for women's education and for reforms in the laws on polygamy and divorce had surfaced widely among intellectuals by the 1870s. In 1899 an extreme Westernizer, Qassim Amin, an Egyptian, published a book entitled *The Liberation of Women* that put veiling, for or against, first and foremost on the agenda in discussions about the future of Islamic society. Amin had accepted the views of Cromer and his ilk: veiling was incompatible with the standards of global, i.e. Western, civilization, and it had to go. Islamic society must become Western, lest it remain defenseless against the West's seizure of its resources. Western standards must quickly predominate, and, because of the centrality of motherhood, changes for women were a vital first step. "It is impossible to breed successful men if they do not have mothers capable of raising them to be successful. This is the noble duty that advanced civilization has given to woman in our age and which she fulfills in advanced societies." The goal is interesting, but also the phrasing: the reference to "advanced civilization," evocative of world standards and possibly world opinion, is more palatable than direct reference to the West, even though the equivalence is clear. Amin added a host of criticisms of contemporary Islam, including the backwardness of its intellectual life, and a revealing number of insults to Egyptian women that suggested a profound misogyny (perhaps also shared with Cromer?). But the focus on the veil, as symbol but also as substantive limitation to full access to education or public life, came through strongly, as "a huge barrier between woman and her elevation, and consequently a barrier between the nation and its advance." Europeans would never countenance veiling, and they knew best – after all, as Amin noted, they had discovered steam and electricity and so "could not fail to know the means of safeguarding woman."[7]

Amin's treatise stirred a huge uproar, provoking more than thirty books and articles in immediate response. Most of the initial reaction was critical, with defenders of traditional Islam at the forefront. But the issue could not be kept down and remains vivid over a century later. If world standards are essentially Western, and if the West condemns veiling, can veiling be sustained? Later reformers picked up the charge. Kemal Ataturk, introducing a variety of laws establishing women's legal rights in Turkey – including the vote – in the 1920s and 1930s, seized on the veil as a sign of backwardness. "In some places I have seen women who put a piece of cloth or a towel or something like that over their heads to hide their faces, and who turn their backs or huddle themselves on the ground when a man passes by. What are the meaning and sense of this behavior? Gentlemen, can the mothers and daughters of a civilized nation adopt this strange manner, this barbarous posture? It is a spectacle that makes the nation an object of ridicule. It must be remedied at once."[8] Similarly the reform-minded Shah of Iran, in 1920, banned the veil as a "symbol of backwardness." Efforts of this sort did not take full hold, and they provoked often riotous resistance. Many Muslims, women as well as men, seized on the veil as a vital emblem of regional and personal identity, rejecting the imposition of global standards (or, more subtly, in the case of some Islamic feminists, viewing the argument as irrelevant to a real discussion of women's rights and conditions). The outcome of this particular extension of Western world standards was less decisive and more embattled than in the case of Chinese foot binding, partly because (despite Western stridency) the practice was less clearly dreadful (or not dreadful at all), partly because Islam mounted a more concerted reaction against Western-inspired globalism.

But the fact that the debate was launched was intriguing. Imposition of outside standards, fueled by apparent moral outrage, spurred a sense of vulnerability in areas like gender that were both deeply traditional and highly personal. That the result was a prolonged, often bitter argument is hardly surprising. As in other cases in the later nineteenth century, world opinion did not sweep over other opinions without serious reaction. The local, usually self-appointed, wielders of world opinion had their own social class and individual agendas that frequently involved the expression of other kinds of hostilities – toward the masses, toward women – through the newer global language, and this too guaranteed dispute. But the ability to assume that there were global standards of civilization, that might apply as readily to how women dressed as to how parliaments should operate or labor should be treated, signaled a major expansion of the context in which world opinion could be formulated and applied.

Interaction with Westerners had more decisive results in China, where women were concerned, if only because the symbolic practice here, foot binding, was harder to defend against Western values than the seclusive but hardly painful practice of veiling. Foot binding, with its restrictive results and painful procedures, had been occasionally criticized in China itself, for example during the earlier nineteenth century, and this provided some basis for adjustment to new global standards. But it was also revealing that purely domestic critique (even from the Manchu leadership) had accomplished nothing. For it was the growing presence of Westerners, as missionaries, businesspeople (including, ironically, opium traders), and diplomats that really provided the basis for reconsideration – again, out of a sense of embarrassment and attendant revaluation. Protestant missionaries were particularly vigorous in arousing a new kind of public opinion within China, organizing local and then national societies from 1874 onward. Young Men's Christian Association (YMCA) and Young Women's Christian Association (YWCA) movements worked hard against foot binding and also encouraged new kinds of exercise among women for which foot binding was entirely unsuitable. A variety of private schools for girls were founded by Westerners, which also worked against the practice. Chinese reformers responded quickly, forming among other things a series of "natural foot societies" and issuing stories about the suffering and indignity the custom imposed. A Confucianist, Ko Huichang, in 1920 summed up the currents of change and the vital role of foreign standards: "I have always had my unquiet thoughts about foot binding and felt pity for the many sufferers. Yet I could not venture to say it publicly. Now there are happily certain benevolent gentlemen and virtuous daughters of ability, wise daughters from foreign lands who had initiated a truly noble enterprise. They have addressed our women in animated exhortations and founded a society for the prohibition of foot binding." Nationalism entered in, reformers being ashamed that all the initial impetus came from foreigners, and Christians at that: "We should establish OUR schools for our girls."[9] A larger national purpose emerged as well, again in a context of growing sensitivity to global influences: "The bound feet of women will transmit weakness to the children . . . Today look at Europeans and Americans, so strong and vigorous because their mothers do not bind their feet and, therefore, have strong offspring. Now that we must compete with other nations, to produce weak offspring is perilous."[10] Concrete results came gradually, but by the early twentieth century the imperial government was seeking to outlaw the practice.

The Chinese and Middle Eastern examples show that the embarrassment factor was hardly a constant. Western disdain could yield impassioned defense of traditional practices, or, more commonly, provoke new debate, as in the case of veiling. It is not always easy to explain why one society championed reform more wholeheartedly than another, particularly in cases in which inclusion in the Western orbit was equally novel. China, more secular in the first place, faced with more abundant outrage against what seemed (to Westerners) a savage practice – outrage complete with internal organizational efforts and not merely rhetorical blasts – picked up on world opinion, in this regard at least, with fewer reservations than did the Middle East. Embarrassment was more complete, and turned more fully into a widespread internal reform effort that, within a few decades, abolished a practice that had existed for centuries. But it was the extent of susceptibility to Western critique that varied; almost no society, by 1900, could avoid some reaction where the assertion of standards of civilization was clear-cut.

One final example drives home the growing range of world opinion, as well as its geographical reach. By the late nineteenth century, world opinion was recurrently roused against lynchings in the United States. Widely publicized lynchings of African Americans drew primary attention, and connected readily to the kinds of moral outrage that the antislavery campaigns had built up earlier. But lynchings of Mexican Americans also provoked outrage from publics and governments in Europe and Latin America. Japanese public opinion entered the fray too, an early instance of the inclusion of this globalizing nation in a world voice. Newspapers commented on lynching, anti-black riots, and American racism from the 1880s onward, with headlines such as "White Brutality: Lynching against a Black" or "An Atrocious Lynching." Commentary continued into the 1920s, spurred in part by resentment of racist measures against Japanese immigrants and a broader concern about Western belittling of Japan. Many Japanese saw lynching as contrary to American ideals: a 1922 article in the *Yomiuri*, for example, noted that "the United States, which loves to win the world's best, has the world record in lynching as well." Japanese delegates at the Versailles Peace Conference introduced a racial equality proposal, which went nowhere (in contrast to United Nations commitments some decades later). But public attention persisted: in a comment on vicious attacks on blacks in Chicago, a correspondent noted, "we can hardly imagine such brutality has occurred in the big city of a civilized country." Here was an issue of potentially wide resonance, capable of expanding the base for world opinion in very specific ways.[11]

United States anti-lynching advocates both stirred and utilized international petitions and media reactions. Ida Wells launched a global (read: European) campaign against lynching in tours of England and Scotland during the 1890s, gaining support from some key British clergy who joined in persuading an initially skeptical public that these events really did occur. The link with earlier antislavery moral indignation was direct and effective. Mary Church Terrell, attending a women's conference in Berlin in 1904, used the occasion to rouse sentiments on behalf of her African American brothers and sisters, clearly invoking world opinion in her letters back home: "The people across the sea cannot understand why educated, cultivated ladies and gentlemen of color are handicapped or socially ostracized at all. Even the most intelligent foreigner finds it difficult to believe that colored men, women and children are still being lynched in the United States."[12] Another African American, William Monroe Trotter, even snuck into the Versailles Peace Conference in an abortive effort to get racial justice included in the peace settlement, and anti-lynching parades back home often invoked a global context, comparing for instance India's moves against the caste system to the hardening de facto caste lines in the United States. Even the white press used international comparisons, in 1914 juxtaposing Germany's presumed atrocities in Belgium with what happened to blacks in places like East St. Louis: in both cases, "we could hardly believe it possible that civilized beings could be guilty of such conduct . . . We confess that we are ashamed."[13]

Foreign press coverage, editorials, and outpourings of letters to American leaders played a definite role in stirring American opinion against lynchings and, gradually, in influencing federal policy. World opinion, combined with specific representations by the Mexican government, induced the federal government to begin paying monetary damages to the families of lynched Mexicans, from about 1900 onward. American embassies were frequently deluged with letters and telegrams after news of lynchings, or on behalf of victims of apparently rigged trials in the south; European papers often sent correspondents to the south to provide eye-witness accounts of the aftermaths of lynchings, and such events had precisely the dramatic human detail so important in stirring global reactions. World opinion gained additional bite in the United States as news of Nazi racial atrocities, in the 1930s and 1940s, belatedly solidified global standards. In 1946, African American groups appealed for United Nations backing against home-grown genocide, again with some effect in enhancing American embarrassment at ongoing evidence of discrimination and violence.

World opinion both shaped and complemented a growing domestic concern about what was often termed, with a global eye cocked, a "national shame" or "national disgrace." The whole series of episodes was a fascinating illustration of the sometimes unexpected relationship the United States has maintained with world opinion, alternating as moralistic participant and moral target. Even more important, the interactions showed the growing availability of world opinion as a weapon against a variety of abuses, and the growing awareness, on the part of victim groups, of this same resource as a means of triggering productive compunction in ways that purely domestic protest could not always achieve.

World opinion tried on occasion to stretch further still. In 1911 reformers from several nations convened a First Universal Races Congress, in London. It was designed to "discuss, in the light of science and the modern conscience, the general relations subsisting between the peoples of the West and those of the East, between so-called white and so-called coloured peoples, with a view to encouraging between them a fuller understanding, the most friendly feelings, and a heartier cooperation." The meeting resulted in various statements of opinion and some general optimism about the prospects for world peace. But there was no chance at this point of any coherent world opinion on racial or imperialist issues, for divisions were too great, shared assumptions too scanty. And the peace momentum, shattered three years later, proved too feeble for a real global opinion movement either, though there were some renewed efforts, naïve from a contemporary perspective, in the 1920s. Still, the 1911 initiative shows the optimism that could coalesce around attempts to mobilize opinion to make the world a better place.

The growing global presence of the West by the later nineteenth century and the willingness of Western pundits to opine with great confidence about the inferiority of most non-Western practices wherever they might be found constitute a familiar chapter in world history. The whole concept of the "white man's burden" assumed that the West held the keys to civilized values and behaviors and that the rest of the world fell short. The only question was whether other parts of the world needed permanent guidance by Western masters, or whether they could be prodded, gradually, into greater harmony with civilized standards. Western success and assurance almost inevitably provoked new sensitivities, from Asia to Africa to the Americas. It was hard, for those aware of Western norms and attitudes, not to feel some embarrassment at newly perceived gaps. To be sure, the issues were framed in terms of Western civilization and responses to it, not world opinion as such. But the context was shifting in ways that were conducive both to the more explicit formulation of world opinion and to wider application and awareness of it. Westerners could easily slide into an equation of their outlook with inescapable global values – indeed, their preachments might be more acceptable if framed this way. The more enthusiastic Westernizers in other parts of the world tended similarly to equate the West with the most advanced standards of civilization, and their willingness to urge reform, in order to measure up to external criteria, also pushed in the direction of global evaluation. The logical next step would only occur later, when reformers in the same non-Western parts of the world became comfortable in their own preachments about global standards, even to the West itself – as in Gandhi's famous response, when asked what he thought about Western civilization, that it would be a good idea. In the meantime, the expansion of the range of Western-derived world opinion – including the groups that were open to it, in various parts of the world – established a context for subjecting additional topics to its purview and for experimenting with different methods for its mobilization.

4

WORLD OPINION THROUGH ORGANIZATIONS: AN ALTERNATIVE FOR SOCIAL ISSUES

Almost inevitably, world opinion campaigns fanned out from slavery to other social concerns, including those of women and labor. In the process, given difficulties in rallying world opinion in the most literal sense, mobilizers explored new organizational options.

The later nineteenth century saw a proliferation of international contacts, mostly under Western egis and some, in fact, entirely Western despite global claims. It became increasingly easy to imagine and to form international non-governmental organizations and to stage international conferences. Some of this potential had been sketched earlier by the antislavery movement. Antislavery associations, however, had been supplementary to the more direct solicitation of world opinion through rallies and petition drives. Now, the leaders of worthy causes might concentrate on the associational channel almost exclusively, implying the backing of world opinion without actually rousing it. Use of international organizations was enhanced after World War I by the formation of the League of Nations and its subsidiary units, notably the International Labor Office: well-orchestrated campaigns by associations could now prompt international action, or at least international inquiries, without much direct recourse to public opinion.

The result was an important addition to the arsenal of global movements and a significant additional complexity in world opinion itself. Why some movements preferred the associational route, rather than turning more directly to world opinion, is not easy to explain, but the habit could become deeply ingrained. This chapter traces the rise of international feminist agitation, which skirted the edges of world opinion and, in the main, continues to do so today; and the emergence of international labor agitation, characterized by a mixture of international organizational effort and periodic (but declining) solicitations of direct worker outrage. The aim is to address two important targets of world opinion, which have persisted to the present from their nineteenth-century origins, but also to embrace the new set of tactical options, which have also persisted and that present an alternative route to world opinion.

The topic of the chapter is not just the associational approach to world opinion. It also involves the expansion of world opinion to additional, but controversial, social agendas. Both feminism and organized labor identified abuses at home as well as abroad. Both were involved in bitter dispute, again both at home and abroad, that inevitably affected appeals to world opinion. Even though some of the same outrage that had fueled the campaign against slavery clearly extended to abuses of women and workers, it proved difficult – indeed, it remains difficult today – to develop comparable unanimity over the issues involved. Women's and labor concerns expanded the social agenda of world opinion, but with incomplete success. International standards emerged, but without the passionate sense of moral responsibility that other campaigns, such as antislavery, had generated, save on the part of more limited groups. The associational approach may have been chosen because world opinion itself was hard to rouse or was divided outright; but the approach also concealed some limitations, implying a force that did not exist. This chapter traces world opinion and emerging social issues up to World War II, but the story, and the confusion, persisted beyond the war, and we will return to the more recent consequences.

World opinion has always depended heavily on the activities of non-governmental organizations – though the term was not yet invented, this is precisely what the antislavery societies had been. Non-governmental organizations have been widely studied of late, and this book relies extensively on these studies. But NGOs and world opinion are not the same thing. This chapter explores the first phases of what remains an ambiguous relationship. Non-governmental organizations may generate world opinion: discussion of the campaign against white slavery, below, is a clear case in point within the larger deployment of international feminism. But NGOs may also decide not to rally wide public outrage, but rather to claim a public mantle without the voice to match – and they may or may not get away with this tactic (or even be entirely clear about the distinction themselves). We will see this in international feminism as well. Because social issues like women's and labor rights were more contested than slavery had been, world opinion flickered in and out of the associational efforts – particularly before the later twentieth century, but to some extent still. Hence the two topics of this chapter: the somewhat sporadic expansion of world opinion into the social domain; and the development of international organizations that sought strengths besides world opinion, while sometimes courting it and some-times successfully rousing it. This early relationship, with all its complexities, will help explain the emergence of newer NGOs, since the 1950s, that under-stand more fully what their relationship to world opinion is and should be.

Organized feminism and its first hints of international cooperation were both encouraged by the evolution of the antislavery movement, by the middle of the nineteenth century. Women's involvement in antislavery, particularly in Britain and the United States, raised obvious questions about rights issues that applied to them directly and not just to slaves. Women's growing organizational experi-ence and participation in international meetings, but also their exclusion or downgrading by male antislavery leaders, spurred the cause as well, from the 1840s onward. It was therefore understandable that a transnational context emerged along with the national feminist campaigns, with recurrent collabora-tion or at least contact across the Atlantic. This meant that it was also inevitable that international women's rights agitation picked up the largely Western con-text in which antislavery campaigns had emerged.

At the same time, concerns about women's rights were different from those about slavery, in that advocates were inevitably talking about their own situa-tions, and not just those of others; for a long time there were no clear examples of suitable conditions, to contrast with inadequacy – nothing as dramatic as the free labor in Western Europe or the northern United States, against which slav-ery could be seen to fall short. This greater complexity diluted the force of inter-national efforts, even though these emerged quite early.

Pinning down the very first transnational meetings about women is not easy, but they followed initial national gatherings within two decades at most – a tribute to the belief that global standards were involved and there was merit in assembling strengths beyond conventional borders. Marie Gregg, of Sweden, organized an International Association of Women in 1868, and a women's rights conference occurred in Paris in the 1870s with American and British as well as continental delegates. The year 1875 saw the first international crusade for women's rights, aimed at abolishing state regulation (and therefore implicit condoning) of prostitution – British leaders were central to this effort. In the best world opinion fashion, advocates worked to mobilize European public opinion to "produce the necessary revolutions in the minds of people, the peo-ple of the whole civilized world."[1] Attention soon broadened to suffrage and working conditions, the latter often in some relationship to ongoing antislavery activities that, as we have seen, now focused on unfree contexts that frequently involved women workers. Temperance interests could also chime in, for purity crusades could transcend boundaries and appeal to the special needs and virtues of women. An American-based organization headed by women visited Asia as well as Europe, under the banner of the "World Women's Christian Temperance Union." The international socialist movement also generated discussions of women's issues, though the first explicit conference under these auspices did not occur until 1907.

Some hesitations were interesting. Pressed, in the 1880s, by American leaders like Elizabeth Cady Stanton to form a transatlantic suffrage campaign, the British feminist Millicent Fawcett refused, claiming that it was "quite impossible that European and American women should have anything in common, the conditions of their lives and the purposes of their respective societies being so different."[2] Again, distinctions from the antislavery campaign showed through. The women concerned with suffrage or labor conditions were directly battling inequities in their own societies, not simply addressing evils elsewhere. It was hard not to feel the weight of national differences, because so many problems related directly to the policy and legislation of particular governments; and it was hard also not to concentrate primary energy on the more immediate issues, the issues at home – one reason that significant public opinion, as opposed to organizational spin-offs, did not form around women's rights issues globally.

But the associational impulse remained strong, based on a sense of solidarity and of ultimately common values. More durable organizations, like the International Alliance of Women (initially, the International Women's Suffrage Alliance), the International Council of Women (I.C.W.), and the Women's International League for Peace and Freedom, formed from 1888 onward, differing in specific focus and degree of politicization but sharing a desire to mobilize women in various parts of the world. The International Council of Women, organizing regional and national women's clubs and shunning controversial issues, claimed a membership of four to five million by 1907 and twenty-five million by 1925. The I.C.W. aimed explicitly at women of "all races, nations, creeds and classes." Elizabeth Cady Stanton, the American feminist leader, referred to the "universal sense of injustice, that forms a common bond of union" among "the women of all nationalities." By 1915 global conferences could claim to provide a voice for "women of the world" in the name of the "great ideals of civilization and progress."

The international gatherings were small, mainly drawing from Western Protestant groups, despite modest representation of Catholics and Jews. (Until after World War I, most mainstream international meetings began with prayers from a Protestant New Testament.) Financial barriers discouraged attendance by, for example, most interested women from Central and Eastern Europe. There were language issues as well, for though women's global leaders urged their followers to learn at least one other language, it was difficult in practice not to insist on English. A Dutch leader thus wrote a Hungarian feminist, Rosika Schwimmer, in German, offering to translate her pamphlet into English, "because the poor monolingual Americans must know what is going on with you." Even in the early 1920s a Chinese feminist living in Germany refused an invitation to participate in an international gathering "merely to speak for a few minutes in a language probably all of the congress participants could not understand;" this would interrupt her work and constituted an "unreasonable demand that I cannot reconcile with my self-respect." It was still hard to avoid the appearance, indeed the reality, of tokenism beyond the Western framework.[3]

The range of areas represented had expanded beyond the antislavery effort, even before 1914, and the fervor could run quite high. Meetings against global trade in prostitutes, for example, drew delegates from Austria, Belgium, France, Denmark, The Netherlands, Norway, Russia, Sweden, Switzerland, Britain, and the United States. Some Hungarians were also involved, and, by correspondence at least, leaders from Australia and Canada.

One specific effort took off in a big way, in this case combining the organizational thrust with direct solicitations of editorials and resolutions that suggested a wider appeal to public opinion. "White slavery" – as the term suggested – could capture much of the same fervor that had been applied to slavery in general, sometimes heightened by a sense that it was one's own daughters whom one was seeking to protect. The campaign against seizure and transportation of women for prostitution has been termed one of the largest global movements of the nineteenth century, carried on mainly by representatives of women's groups but backed by vigorous mobilizations of national public opinion. Initial pressure emanated particularly from Britain, with campaigns led by Josephine Butler in the 1870s and 1880s, but the United States and other nations were heavily engaged. Although government legislation figured prominently, real (if largely Western) world opinion was involved too. As regional excitement – sometimes near-hysteria – about stories of the capture of young girls mounted, a global effort took shape somewhat apart from the mainstream women's organizations. An International Federation of Friends of Young Women was founded in 1877 by thirty-two women from seven countries. International Jewish organizations played a prominent role in the movement, both to protect immigrant women and to counter charges of Jewish involvement in procurement. (This was the first clear case of a traditional religious constituency adhering to world opinion, beyond the Protestant base.) A series of national congresses in the 1890s yielded a World's Purity Federation in 1900 and an ensuing Paris conference in 1902.

The campaign won an international agreement against white slavery, in 1904, to be monitored by a new International Bureau; French officials took a prominent role in this effort. Echoes of the antislavery movement resounded strongly, public opinion being anchored in the middle classes of Western nations and there being a clearly identifiable evil against which moral fervor could be roused. As many historians have noted, the real phenomenon was compounded, and exaggerated, by scare stories and by a desire to believe that foreign villains were responsible for much of the prostitution that so troubled turn-of-the-century consciences. Novels and early movies portrayed the snatching of innocent young women, and often their transportation abroad, in the most lurid tones, and reached a wide audience. ("Our daughters are being trapped and violated and held prisoners and sold for fabulous sums.")[4] The white slavery movement continued after World War I, appealing for support from the League of Nations.

Even this fervent effort, though intentionally reminiscent of world opinion in many ways, had distinctive features. The women involved were either one's own – the daughters about to be abducted – or immigrants into one's country, sincerely pitied but also feared as sources of immorality and disease. Compassionate interest in a real other was largely lacking; though the lot of prostitutes roused sympathy, a considerable motivation was protecting one's own kind, even one's own family. A strong dose of xenophobia marked many comments. Butler disparaged the low level of civilization of Indian women. American commentators proudly claimed that Anglo-Saxons would almost never be found among the white slavers, whose ranks were filled with an unsavory assortment Mediterraneans, Jews, and Chinese. (Some comments also included the French, which testified to sexual reputation but seemed particularly unfair given the French organizational lead in international measures.) The white slavery effort, in other words, does not dispel the impression that mobilizing genuine world opinion on behalf of distant women was oddly difficult compared with the readier outrage that had fueled the campaigns against slavery.

Yet there were results, as we saw in the previous chapter. The potential to induce embarrassment by singling out a country in the name of global standards was quite high, as officials from Argentina to China could attest. But the success of the white slavery agitation remained exceptional, on an international level, up to World War II and even beyond.

For the more common pattern applying to women's issues, particularly legal and voting rights but also working conditions, was different, involving organizational meetings and conferences rather than strong appeals to public emotion. If the movement against white slavery was a genuine, if somewhat self-interested manifestation of world opinion, the same did not hold for the wider range of feminist concerns. A steady trickle of international non-governmental organizations, run by women and devoted to women's issues, maintained the tendency to rely on associational efforts more than public opinion. Twenty-two organizations were formed between 1875 and 1914, followed by another thirty-eight between the world wars. Most were small, but convinced of their service as vanguards of international justice and as representatives of a real, if not always clearly expressed, global opinion.

This approach, essentially consisting of pressure group activities targeting various governments and international bodies, spiced with periodic conferences, continued after World War I. The existence of the League of Nations provided an obvious target for associational tactics, and women's groups achieved considerable success in getting issues on to a study agenda. Splits within the women's movement during and after World War I, with a strong pacifist current, affected organizational activities but also complicated any efforts to appeal to a wider public opinion: without much question, women's organizations were more pacifist than most publics were, at least outside Great Britain.

The war and its aftermath did provide new opportunities and arguments, however. Discussions of a common motherhood (often invoked as a woman's response to militarism) added to the earlier invocation of global rights. Thus one pacifist group referred to the "growing despair" felt by "mothers everywhere" at the prospect that their children might be sent again to war. Rosika Schwimmer added, "Even women who are not physically mothers, feel all as the mothers of the human race."[5] Violence more generally evoked the need to defend women's rights, and military rape became a powerful theme in potentially uniting women across cultures. These arguments added to the earlier rhetoric about the universality of women's goals. This crucial belief, fundamental to world opinion, continued to apply to campaigns for suffrage. Carrie Chapman Catt saw Chinese suffragists sharing "the same vision which is arousing the women of all the Nations of the Earth," for "the wrongs of women are common to all races and nations." Mary Sheepshanks more simply noted "the bond of their common sisterhood."[6] To be sure, as women did win the vote in some countries, new gaps developed between them and women elsewhere, as the successful groups wanted to move on to other issues. Yet international meetings routinely noted that women with suffrage felt "that their work is not done . . . as long as the women of any country remain disfranchised." Attention turned particularly to Asia – the "East" – as "probably needing our help more than any others."[7]

And this spilled over into increasingly successful efforts to enlist some participation from women outside the West. By the 1920s Chinese feminists were writing pamphlets for international women's groups. Siao-Mei Djang referred in one to "the problems which are universal to womenhood." A group of Indian women declared their willingness to attend a conference so long as their representation would be distinct from the British. Delegates from Egypt and the Middle East began to pepper some conferences, though Europeans feared that they (like the Indians) were excessively nationalistic. Thus an Arab delegate in 1935, at an international conference in Istanbul, warned the women from the great powers that "no amount of effort on your part will ever achieve your high aim while imperialism reigns in any corner of the world." European pacifism was also an issue, for, as another Middle Eastern representative noted, Eastern women wanted peace just as much as did their sisters in the West, but "they want it based on justice and respect for the rights of the people." Within Europe, Scandinavian and French women gained increasing voice, though German delegates found at best a mixed reception because of widespread beliefs among other Europeans that Germany was particularly at fault for World War I: internationalism could be overridden by new animosities within Europe, a key problem with world opinion during the interwar decades. Decisive gains occurred in enlisting Latin American participation in the global women's movement, a number of branches emerging from Cuba to Argentina. Finally, Australian and also white South African participation increased.[8]

The various international women's organizations maintained a lively interest in making sure that global principles would prevail. Although national flags were allowed at some interwar conferences, there was also work on explicitly global medals for suffrage activities or achievements. One group created a "world section" so that women who were without country or hostile to their sisters' national organization would have a clear home. As a British delegate noted, seeking to belong to one group without joining her national section, "there is always a danger . . . of the national side being developed at the expense of the international." To be sure, bitter arguments surged in the 1930s about whether conference voting should be strictly by national sections; some leaders despaired about the "world spirit" in this context. Nevertheless, the organizational approach of the global women's movement could claim real success in moving beyond a strictly Western base. An Estonian delegate to a meeting in Washington, in 1925, put it this way, with some hyperbole: "The world's map is, so to speak, now peopled for me . . . There are friendly faces in all corners of the World, hands which are ready to help, kind voices calling from everywhere, from Iceland to South Africa." Editor Karleen Baker agreed, in noting, "it is these friendships made between members in different countries that can be counted as one of the most fruitful results of any international gathering."[9]

The resultant capacity to claim wide support for women's rights could, in turn, conceal relatively modest numbers, and this is where world opinion, in at least one of its manifestations, comes in directly. Thus an urgent petition to the League of Nations, in 1935, for a resolution on international women's rights could claim support from thirty-six countries, which was doubtless correct; but aside from this petition the League received only a few more than two hundred telegrams and letters in support of the same cause. Association and organizational clout, not high-volume passion, largely served to represent women's issues on the global stage.

Specific campaigns also developed that involved more explicit efforts to rouse opinion, though never with the vigor that the white slavery campaign had managed. In 1919, for example, Clare Haslewood and her husband Hugh went to Hong Kong, where Hugh had an appointment in the British colonial administration. They soon discovered the practice of *mui tsai*, in which young girls were sent to other households to do domestic chores, usually in return for money paid to the family of origin. To observers like the Haslewoods, this was "slavery," pure and simple, though many scholars have since disputed use of that term. The Haslewoods moved quickly to rouse international sentiment with outraged speeches, press conferences, and pamphlets, particularly in Britain and the United States, but with backing also from Chinese reform groups, despite vigorous opposition from British officials. The cause turned into a massive argument about imperial responsibilities, relationships to the new republic in China, and whose definition of *mui tsai* best described the practice. The movement continued into the late 1940s, when it was overshadowed by the rise of Chinese Communism.[10]

By World War II, there were international standards on women's issues, but considerably less real world opinion. Associational efforts infused bodies like the League of Nations, and soon the United Nations, with sincere and pious sentiments about women's rights. But the real passions devoted to women's causes were more purely national, or were simply lacking. On the global level, relatively little effort went into dramatizing abuses or mobilizing expressions of mass outrage, the movement against white slavery and a few other campaigns being the exceptions that proved the rule. Negotiation and representation, though referring to presumably civilized standards, set the criteria. This approach paid off in international acknowledgement, but it could mask wide disagreements among actual publics and it could seriously limit implementation. All of this – the successful strides but also the limitations – would become clearer in the second half of the twentieth century, when sweeping proclamations advanced more rapidly than ever before, but impacts remained both varied and questionable.

The leaders of organized labor, emerging toward greater maturity from the 1860s onward, quickly realized the potential of developing an international voice. Under Marxism, something like a labor world opinion gained theoretical backing, for Marx and his followers were correctly convinced that capitalism was a transnational force and that workers must unite across national lines to oppose it. Hence the formation of International Workingmen's Associations under largely Marxist auspices. The claim was global class solidarity, but as with feminism the approach turned out to rely more heavily on organized international conferences than on consistent bursts of widespread public opinion on anything like a global scale.

There were several constraints. First, though some workers thrilled to the idea of international solidarity, most were preoccupied with local or at most national issues and campaigns. It was hard to muster much extra energy for larger causes. Here, the similarity to the feminist situation was most pronounced. Second, again rather like in feminism, labor organizers encountered huge gaps between industrialized and largely agrarian societies. It was fine to trumpet international labor issues, but, given the divisions in economic patterns around the world, it was hard to generate much that went beyond a Western industrial outcry. Even among industrial countries, variations in specific conditions – exact wage levels, or the nature of trade union law – tended to focus attention domestically, rather than encouraging the development of more than very general international standards. Third, labor issues did not resonate with large segments of middle-class opinion, or they roused explicit resistance. Yet forming a plausible and consistent world opinion without middle-class backing was, and probably remains, quite difficult. And, fourth, even for workers and their leaders, divisions among types of labor organizations (labor parties versus trade unions, for example) and among labor ideologies (particularly, Marxist versus reformist) severely hampered a coherent voice sometimes even within individual countries, much less more widely. For all these reasons it was frequently much easier to organize conferences and conference proclamations than to agree on campaigns that would actually succeed in rousing widespread expressions of opinion on issues in other countries.

Many workers harbored a deep sense of injustice; for some this could be activated by reports of problems in otherwise unfamiliar societies. But some of the most internationally committed workers or labor leaders often focused on generalized goals, relating to the larger economic system rather than the kinds of personalized, emotionally evocative problems that more easily roused world opinion. The passion was there, in other words, but it sometimes seemed rather abstract and did not always translate into a wider global outcry.

The First International (International Workingmen's Association, 1864–74) was truly international through the participation of hosts of refugee labor leaders in Britain, but it had a limited popular audience and it consumed much of its time on specifically ideological disputes among Marxists and anarchists, trade unionists and socialists. The Second International, formed in 1889, played a greater role as an associational representative on labor standards (though it, too, remained resolutely Western in composition). Differences among national labor movements turned many of the International's periodic meetings into negotiating sessions on tactics or, again, ideologies. After 1900, concerns about the prospect of war generated much attention. A 1913 meeting saw ringing statements, like this one by a Belgian socialist: "The proletariat, which from today henceforth must be recognized as the herald of world peace, demands peace in the Balkans . . . (and) the abandonment of alliances and diplomatic intrigues which carry with them the seed of every war . . . For France and Germany the hour of reconciliation has struck. There is to be no more war between Germany and France."[11] As with global feminism later, the anti-war movement, though both appropriate and sincere, limited popular support for labor internationalism and distracted from the establishment of more specific transnational labor standards. All this suggested world opinion of a sort, but diffuse and, except among the truly committed leaders, excessively abstract. In the labor case, the approach collapsed entirely with the onset of World War I.

Some important developments did occur before 1914, particularly in the final decades of the nineteenth century. Workers in one country could be galvanized by information about gains in another. International cross-referencing, at least within the industrial West, was particularly meaningful over issues of hours of work. French workers, for instance, campaigned vigorously for what they called the *semaine anglaise*, or "English week" – a half-day off on Saturday afternoon to go with Sunday for leisure and family activities. This was not world opinion in a strict sense, but rather expropriation of one national movement for another. But there did begin to emerge some perception, across national lines, that limitation of excessive hours of work had a degree of sanction in global morality. Labor leaders were also quick to organize sympathetic demonstrations in one country to protest a particularly shameful attack on workers' rights in another. Excessive police or military action could draw international attention and induce a real, if often fleeting, sense of solidarity. Major drawn-out strikes often elicited monetary support both from unions and labor parties and from individual workers in other countries. Here, among the working classes, was a real world opinion (if mainly within the industrial nations), sensitive to abuses of police power that had nothing directly to do with one's own life. Even in this category, however, it was far more common for an annual socialist or trade union congress meeting, or the labor press, to issue blasts against oppression in other nations than for much of a spontaneous rally to develop.

It was true that internationalist sentiment among workers and their leaders helped develop an unusually powerful global symbol of organized labor, the celebrations on May Day. In the campaign for international recognition of May Day as a day off designed to celebrate workers and their cause, a real sense of solidarity across boundaries was both reflected and encouraged. (It was revealing, of course, that United States leaders successfully countered this impulse for American workers by providing an alternative September Labor Day date; as ever, United States commitment to global public opinion was highly qualified.) Long before it was legalized (mainly after World War I), thousands of workers in industrial countries took May Day off, to parade on behalf of class and organizational unity nationally and internationally alike. Speakers at May Day celebrations could list recent cases of oppression in other societies, though they most commonly centered on the latest national issue in a widespread strike or legislative conflict. During the 1890s May Days tended to focus on the eight-hour day, supporting an emerging international standard in the Western world.

Another approach to international labor issues, based on a combination of labor leaders (particularly of the reformist stripe) and reform-minded economists and other social scientists, began to generate a different kind of conference activity. A first International Congress on Labor Legislation was held in 1897, under the leadership of Professor Ernest Mahaim, and a second followed in Paris, in 1900, on the initiative of other academics and government officials. The second congress adopted the statutes for an International Association for the Legal Protection of Workers and created an International Labor Office, with its headquarters in Switzerland. Subsequent conferences promoted international agreement prohibiting the use of white phosphorus in making matches and limiting night work for women, and several governments signed up. Here was the associational approach pure and simple: there was an assumption of global standards of labor treatment in the case of extreme problems of safety or vulnerable categories of workers, but there was no effort to generate expressions of opinion on the subject, because compliance depended on organizational pressure on established governments. There were further moves to set a maximum working day of ten hours for women and children, but these were interrupted by World War I.

During the war the idea of international labor standards advanced with meetings of government representatives, trade unionists (like the American Samuel Gompers), and academics. This momentum generated the creation of the International Labor Organization (I.L.O.), in 1919, with an explicit mandate to work toward international standard setting in the name of social justice and humane conditions. Government representatives dominated the I.L.O., but there were also labor and employer participants.

The I.L.O. quickly became both a vehicle of, and a substitute for, global opinion on labor issues. The post-1918 splintering of organized labor between the now Communist-dominated Third International and a variety of socialist and reformist movements further reduced the possibility of seeing a clear international voice emerge from workers' organizations. The Moscow-run International helped maintain a strong international focus in the Communist movement, with frequent demonstrations on behalf of causes in other countries; but except occasionally, particularly in Popular Front coalitions in the 1930s that targeted the rise of fascism, there was no wider sense, outside the Communist orbit, that the result constituted a global expression of workers in general. Even the Popular Front movements proved brief and fragile. Reliance on the I.L.O. to articulate global standards, and through this global abuses, and to work for implementation became unavoidable. The results were often striking, but they depended on the power of association, not world opinion.

Two features of the I.L.O., though eminently defendable, tended to move it far from any reliance on opinion, worker or otherwise. First, reflecting its partially academic origins but also the severe economic problems of the interwar period, the I.L.O. frequently undertook complex research tasks on issues such as the economic cycle or exchange rates. These were designed to improve conditions for labor, but they were far too complex and protracted to rouse much popular interest. They often led to massive compilations of data about violations in particular countries, but not usually a great deal of passion. The reliance was on expertise, not groundswells of popular opinion.

Second, as critics often noted, the I.L.O. often became enmeshed in legalism, debating the force in law of the standards – called "Conventions" – the organization adopted and what to do about recalcitrant governments. Issues of fundamental importance were often involved, but the capacity to rouse a sense of global injustice was muted by the terminology and procedures employed. When the I.L.O. turned to topics like a suitable minimum wage or basic standards for social insurance, the complexity of the research base and the careful articulation of legal issues moved any sense of global standards far from the reach of world opinion.

It was not surprising that one of the earliest and clearest foci of the I.L.O. was directed against ongoing instances of forced labor, and a number of Conventions were drafted from the mid-1920s onward. This built on the anti-slavery campaign but led to discussions of other issues such as prison labor and various kinds of compulsory work for children – discussions that began in the interwar decades but continued after World War II. A second target, developing in the 1920s but receiving clearer articulation from the 1940s onward, involved freedom of worker association, including protection from political arrest or economic sanction. Related Conventions dealt with collective bargaining and the right to strike. The I.L.O. also worked, from 1919 onward, for recognition as a matter of "special and urgent importance" "that men and women should receive equal remuneration for work of equal value,"[12] though here too more elaborate discussion occurred after World War II. We will see that still other topics, including racial discrimination in the workplace, were later added to the list. In these areas and beyond, a sense of international standards emerged, forged in a genuine commitment to social justice, but without significant intermediary from a wider public opinion. While national unions and labor parties sometimes pronounced on I.L.O. issues, no one organized large petition campaigns or rallies about bargaining rights or minimum wages in some distant land.

In labor, then, as in women's questions, a partial disjuncture developed between widely shared emotions and the articulation of global standards. Passion tended to be reserved for domestic injustices or, on the part of a small but devoted leadership, for more abstract ideological issues across national boundaries. Slavery, always a foreign problem to its main opponents, however proximate the moral responsibility involved, had not presented this dilemma. It had not been necessary to choose, even implicitly, between domestic and global outrage. The reliance on associations to do the work of formulating and trying to implement global standards on specific issues produced important results, many of them more visible after 1945 than before, as more and more governments submitted relevant portions of their legal codes to the scrutiny of international bodies. As the I.L.O. began its work, national divisions and soon the overwhelming impact of the depression held back much more happening than initial definitional work and related research programs. For labor and feminism alike, we will be able to assess the success of the associational approach more fully when we turn to social issues in world opinion in more recent decades (chapter 8).

Still, the habit of reliance on international associations and conferences, rather than strategies to elicit outburst of public sentiment, was clearly established in labor issues before 1945. It reflected division – in this case, among worker organizations and beliefs as well as wider social conflicts between employers and workers. Despite genuine internationalism, it was tempting to view distant workers – like distant women – as retrograde, or as competitors, rather than as targets for support through world opinion. National differences encouraged the associational approach, in the absence of a marked sense of moral responsibility: it proved easier to use international organizations to issue standards than to have workers in one country shout about the backwardness of conditions in another.

The emergence of the I.L.O. suggests the validity of the associational approach – and here feminist efforts lagged behind, for there was no international women's group with this much official sanction. Here was an agency that could not only delineate international criteria in complex matters but also try to negotiate for them some force in law. Even without this institutional focus, advocates of global standards, from missionaries and the press through outright feminists, had their own successes to record before World War II, as in galvanizing reformers who worked against specific practices like foot binding and (less conclusively) veiling.

But the associational approach had at least two deficiencies that followed from its distance from world opinion. First, it lacked drama and the power of international attention that a more passionate denunciation of abuse might bring. Lack of a vote for women, routine husbandly domination, and excessive work hours for adult males were, and remain, legitimate issues in human rights terms, but they may be inherently difficult to dramatize save in immediate, local or at most national contexts – though it may also be that internationalist leaders turned too readily to associational support without attempting to rally wider voices through dramatic appeals. The second weakness of reliance on conferences and expert surveys was that success in claiming international standards often masked huge differences of opinion, even among workers or women themselves, that made associational pronouncements and even negotiated legal arrangements hollow in fact, because little effort was made to persuade the parties actually involved in abuse that the standards involved deserved attention.

The growing capacity to define social rights, for workers and for women, was a powerful extension of the idea of international standards, an amplification of claims of a global morality. The lack of emergence of a corresponding world opinion was at the least an interesting anomaly, at most a telling weakness. The question will be, when we return to social issues, whether the support base has been significantly amplified in the decades since World War II.

5

HUMAN RIGHTS ABUSES AND FOREIGN POLICY: NEW CLAIMS AND NEW SETBACKS

The final extension of world opinion, from the late nineteenth century onward, involved attention to real and imagined human rights issues in many countries (though particularly in and around the Middle East), and a growing response to foreign policy concerns. This brought world opinion in contact with some of the leading world powers, either to press for remediation of domestic injustice or to press for activism with regard to injustice elsewhere.

In a sense, this extension followed logically from the antislavery campaign: the same passionate sense of global obligation was involved, and the same need to embarrass offenders into compliance. The use of media, assemblies, and petitions often resembled antislavery, and there were dramatic, personalized accounts to foster outrage. But the extension did have distinctive features. First, it applied to abuses that were less well defined than slavery was – that depended more on the veracity of media reports and on definitions of what constituted injustice. We know today that even slavery is not always easy to pinpoint, as it continues to surface in contemporary societies despite its illegality. But in the heyday of slavery the institution was ensconced in law; one might argue about how real were the hardships that it entailed, but no one denied the existence of slavery itself. Accounts of unjust imprisonments, torture, or even massacre involved definitions that were less clear-cut, more dependent on observers and on passions of the moment. One symptom: the antislavery movement was concerned about slavery everywhere, though in practice its attention first turned to the Americas. The more diffuse concern about human rights has proved to be more fickle, seizing with magnificent fervor on some horrors while leaving others, no less awful, essentially unattended because the victims simply did not seem as appealing or because information was not handled in a provocative fashion.

The extension of the rights abuse concern also bumped world opinion against the interests of great powers, including governments of countries from which such opinion emanated, such as Great Britain. Antislavery also had involved great power policy, which sometimes retarded action, but its main targets were slave owners, not governments. In the later nineteenth century world opinion often targeted the Ottoman Empire, and therefore also British or French or Russian interests in the region, which complicated its application and frequently thwarted its impact. In the two decades between the world wars, world opinion, called upon to confront a welter of conflicts, blatantly failed, proving no match for the kinds of abuses it now confronted. This sad passage in world history is familiar enough, involving, for example, the collapse of the League of Nations, but it requires brief review for its role in chastening, but ultimately re-stimulating, the efforts to direct world opinion toward a broader array of causes and a more formidable set of protagonists.

Within the period from the 1870s to the 1940s, what seemed a logical focus for the passions and methods of world opinion soured steadily amid the tensions of World War I and its aftermath. Had the world opinion story ended in 1941, there would be little to report beyond lament. Happily the story had a sequel, partly because of catastrophic failures, yet weaknesses in the application of world opinion to war and diplomacy persist.

Suggestions of what would develop into world opinion on foreign policy issues emerged during the Greek war of independence (from the Ottoman Empire) in the 1820s. Among upper class and government circles, sympathy for the Greeks was widespread. The French artist Delacroix painted a poignant memorial after a Greek defeat in 1826, and various individuals from Britain, France, and Russia expressed active sympathy, some (including Lord Byron) even joining the fighting forces or hoping to do so. The Ottoman Empire had fallen far in European opinion by this point, the twin target of both (old) Christian and (new) Enlightenment critique as a largely Muslim, backward, oppressive regime. The Greeks, who evoked classical splendor, were fighting for freedom and national identity, and these images resonated widely in the West. Large-scale public involvement had yet to materialize, and most Western support was quasi-official, but there was more than a hint of causes to come, based on a mixture of prejudice, older religious values, and some new human rights rhetoric. The key component, also present in outright imperialism, was the belief that higher values justified interference in what otherwise would seem the domestic concerns of an established government.

Further growth of Western power and larger public involvement generated more widespread manifestations of opinion after the 1850s. Heavy focus on the Middle East and Mediterranean continued. Independent Greece came under the fire of Western (particularly British) public opinion, for corruption and for toleration of brigandage. Assassinations of British citizens by outlaw gangs drew emotional press coverage, though, since this involved Western interests directly, it does not qualify as world opinion in the fullest sense.

Attacks on Bulgarians in the Ottoman Empire in the 1870s attracted the first really clear manifestation of world opinion in the foreign policy field. A Bulgarian nationalist rising was put down with great force and brutality by Ottoman troops in 1876. (The territory had been part of the empire for centuries.) Ottoman policy was supported by Britain, eager to maintain the Ottoman Empire as a means of protecting free entry to the Black Sea and preventing Russian encroachments that might threaten British interests even in India. According to some accounts as many as thirty thousand people were killed and many villages were burned to the ground. (Current historical wisdom suggests there were about four thousand deaths.)

When news of the massacres reached Western Europe, reaction, on the liberal or progressive side, was widespread. The great Italian leader Garibaldi sent a letter to a Bulgarian nationalist organization expressing his support, and several protest meetings took place in Italy – where the sentiment of national liberation was still fresh. Victor Hugo spoke on Bulgaria's behalf in France – another reminder of the importance of doughty public figures in galvanizing wider sentiments. The French press covered Bulgarian suffering extensively. Slavic intellectuals in parts of the Habsburg monarchy wrote poems against both the Ottomans and the British. Romanian poets, artists, and fledgling socialists added to the general protest. In Russia both conservatives, eager to defend Slavic nationalism and to befriend their Bulgarian little brothers, and worker and peasant organizations collected money on behalf of the Bulgarians. Leading intellectuals, including Tolstoy, Turgenev, and Dostoevsky (again, a mixed group politically), publicized their support. Tolstoy sent his hero Vronsky as a volunteer to fight the Turks, in *Anna Karenina*, and Turgenev wrote a whole novel around a Bulgarian hero; Turgenev also issued a bitter denunciation of Queen Victoria and the British for their inaction. Russian artists contributed moving paintings of Bulgarian suffering, including one by Makosky called *Bulgarian Martyrs*.

The British people chimed in as well, spurred by their government's stubborn policy. Newspaper accounts detailed tortures, which Prime Minister Disraeli dismissed as "to a large extent inventions" and unlikely because the Ottomans usually adopted "more expeditious methods." But ongoing news accounts stimulated mass protests, particularly when British officials themselves reported extensive slaughter. (A *Daily News* account talked of rivers blocked by dead bodies, churchyards covered with human parts, and babies killed and mutilated. Specific references, even in advance of available photography, drove home the claims: "a woman was sitting moaning over three small skulls with hairs clinging to them, which she had in her lap.") Public horror spread. Trade union weeklies repeated and exaggerated the accounts, joining attacks on Disraeli's nonchalance. The Mayor of Manchester convened a protest meeting. Journalists were at pains to describe the Bulgarians as civilized and European (against widespread ignorance in the West), one claiming that literacy rates were as high as those in Europe. Liberal and Nonconformist groups met widely, again recalling the support base and some of the public methods of the antislavery campaign. The growing mass press, spearheaded by the *Daily News*, kept up a drumbeat of accounts of the atrocities: "Pregnant women were ripped open and the unborn babies carried triumphantly on the point of bayonet and sabre, while little children were made to bear the dripping heads of their victims" – according to an American diplomat.

William Gladstone, who had dropped out of politics two years before after a Liberal Party election defeat, used the issue – with all apparent sincerity – as a means of making a comeback. His pamphlet on the atrocities, *The Bulgarian Horrors and the Question of the East*, denounced the Ottoman government in the strongest terms, while supporting immediate Bulgarian independence: "Let the Turks now carry away their abuses in the only possible manner, namely by carrying off themselves." And he directly appealed, in best world opinion fashion, "to the civilization which has been affronted and shamed, to the laws of God, or, if you like, of Allah; to the moral sense of mankind at large. There is not a criminal in a European gaol, there is not a cannibal in the South Sea Islands, whose indignation would not arise and overboil at the recital of that which has been done." Gladstone also addressed huge public meetings, though in slightly cooler language, and his pamphlet sold 200,000 copies in a matter of months. Some rhetoric continued unrestrained: a writer for *Public Opinion*, some months into the crisis, wrote that "Turkey" had committed a "deep and lasting crime against humanity" and "as a nation having ruling power she should die . . . should be utterly wiped out from the face of the earth." Tens of thousands of people participated in ongoing marches and rallies; thousands of petitions were sent to Parliament to change government policy.[1] A letter to Lord Lytton captured the essence of this kind of outrage: "I have never had such strong feeling to exist on any questions as on these."[2]

All this had real, if limited, effect. The British government was forced to yield and to press the Ottoman regime for concessions. The minister cited "a universal feeling of indignation in all classes of English society" as the reason that Britain could no longer defend the Ottoman Empire against Russian attack. And the Ottomans did promise reforms, including a new constitution. But when Russia did in fact go to war, British and other Western opinion divided, because a victory for the tsarist regime could hardly be seen as a progressive gain, even if Bulgaria benefited. In this situation, continued manipulations by the Ottoman and British governments served to limit concessions. The whole episode did yield an independent Bulgaria – and, while recognizing the impact of the great power conflicts involved and the efforts of the Bulgarians themselves, this can be rated one of the real triumphs of nineteenth-century world opinion. But the pure world opinion moment lasted only a short time, before complexities and divisions dulled the sense of moral purpose.

Yet for that moment, mainly for the final eight months of 1876 after the atrocity stories broke in April, the components of this episode of world opinion – in many ways the first that fully entered the arena of great-power diplomacy – are worth analysis. The growing role of the media, eager to sell papers to an outrage-hungry audience, is one point, and with it came considerable exaggeration. (At least in this instance. The distortion factor is less prominent in current world opinion formulations, though it must still be considered. It is also worth noting that many of the atrocities of the twentieth century have required no inflation.) Exaggeration aside, the swelling of outrage across national boundaries and across many standard social and political divides makes this a true outburst of world opinion; these criteria deserve application to more recent episodes to help distinguish full and less full manifestations.

The same crescendo of outrage meant that this version of world opinion served a host of interests beyond those of the Bulgarians, including those concerned with the Liberal Party in England, eager to see Disraeli's regime attacked, and Russian diplomatic interests, eager to have another reason to bludgeon the Ottoman Empire. The power of world opinion as moral cause combined with various self-interests as well as individual aggrandizement.

On the purer side, the ability to lament Bulgarians as fellow humans (who also happened to be Europeans and Christians) was an obvious factor, though it was interesting that some organizers felt they had to beef up the Bulgarians' image to make sure they qualified not just as humanity but as civilized humanity. The widespread capacity for hating the Ottomans not just because of their real or imagined cruelties to the Bulgarians, but for wider deviations from civilization, was a crucial element, which again deserves comparison with more recent outpourings. During the crisis the Ottomans were labeled not only brutal and oppressive, but depraved and barbaric. As one writer put it in *The Nonconformist*, a key Protestant periodical, "Testimony that cannot be impeached declares that Constantinople is Sodom-cum-Gomorrah," while an Anglican Canon of St. Paul's Cathedral claimed that Turks and Islam represented "arrested development." Many intellectuals and publicists saw the chance to condemn Islam ("the Mohammedan religion is probably inconsistent with good government and human progress") while praising Christianity as the only true religion of humanity. Feeding from this, for many leaders, was an inescapable moral fervor: journalist and meeting-organizer William Stead noted, "I felt the clear call of God's voice: 'Arouse the nation or be damned.'"[3]

This instance of moral outrage, in the context of the nineteenth century, compares a bit uncertainly with the fervor so clearly present in the antislavery movement. The links both to Christianity (particularly English Protestantism) and to Enlightenment beliefs (including in this case liberal nationalism) remain clear. Deep sincerity existed in both cases. So did the capacity to exaggerate suffering and wrongdoing, in however good a cause. So did the mixture of moralism with personal and partisan advantage – world opinion does emanate from human beings. But the moral outrage in the Bulgarian case was suffused not just with compassion for victims, but with extensive cultural prejudice against Muslims and Turks, and this complexity was less obtrusive in the antislavery crusade, where the focus on common humanity was less qualified. Ultimately, despite the real and poignant images of suffering that launched world opinion in the first place, the Bulgarians risked getting lost in the shuffle of a larger and more partisan crusade. As a speaker put it in one rally, "These Turks must no longer pollute with their filthy and bloody feet this Christian Europe of ours."[4] An interesting question: How pure can world opinion be in the complexities of world diplomacy, when so many ethnic and religious hatreds can equally be involved?

Finally, world opinion was both stimulated and ultimately constrained by the fact it could be directed not just against an outsider power, but against the world's great power, Britain, seen as defending petty self-interest against a clear ethical imperative. Opinion outside Britain could vent larger frustrations about British imperial and world-policy success, while within the nation the embarrassment about a government that preferred diplomatic convenience over human rights fanned the flames for months. Yet, despite some impact, it was hard to sway the British leadership, which bent but did not break in its support for the ongoing integrity of the Ottoman regime. World opinion had real impact in the Bulgarian crisis, but its voice was muted when great power diplomatic complexities intervened; ultimately there was much compromise. None of this is surprising, of course, and the episode remains a model for measuring success, if limited success, in more recent cases.

The Bulgarian episode was followed by other world opinion crises involving the Ottoman Empire, particularly around agitation by and massacres of Armenians in the 1890s (when opinion was especially aroused) and again after 1900. The situation was conditioned by the Bulgarian episode in several respects. Growing independence in the Balkans, including Bulgaria, stiffened Ottoman resolve to keep Asian minorities in check, including the Armenians. (The British had downplayed Armenian interests in their zeal to settle the Bulgarian issue.) For their part, Armenian nationalists and their Western friends thought they had learned that news of atrocities, often exaggerated and dramatized, could induce successful great power intervention. Without question, deliberate provocation, including some terrorist acts, marked the build-up to the most publicized Ottoman repression. By the 1880s and 1890s, it was steadily easier to get real or imagined news from the most distant reaches of the Middle East. Western missionaries, self-interested in their desire to aid Armenian Christians, and Armenian leaders both on the spot and in the West provided conduits for stories of tragedy.

We traced the new expression of shocked world opinion in chapter 1, noting the mixture of moral zeal and Christian or liberal partisanship. The Armenian crisis was not as striking a case of world opinion as the Bulgarian episode had provided. There was less continental interest, though French newspapers took up the cause to a degree, and the growing ability of Americans to articulate their moral concern did not yet compensate. The British were not as easy to rouse, given less knowledge of the Armenians (and their non-European status) and given a certain skittishness after the somewhat complex and limited results of the 1870s fervor. Too much agitation, for example, might authorize yet another Russian tsarist incursion, which was not likely to represent moral gain. There was enough outcry, however, to stimulate the British government to express its concern, and the Ottomans (who pointed out that the British repressed Indian nationalism in ways not entirely dissimilar to the measures taken against the Armenian minority) promised inquiries. Little happened before the wider disruptions of World War I, and the outcry illustrates more the limitations of world opinion amid diplomatic complexity than its recurrent capacity to protest injustice.[5]

World War I, and even more its aftermath, tested the constraints of diplomatic world opinion severely. The force surfaced recurrently, but the context for successful results deteriorated. The war provided backhanded testimony to the existence of broader world opinion, even though primary attention was devoted to nationalist, not internationalist, arousal. Stories of atrocities – particularly the widespread claims of German mutilations of Belgian children, as the German troops quickly moved through to northern France – were designed to show the justice of the Allied cause not only to British or French citizenries, now mobilized for total war, but to potential supporters beyond – especially on the other side of the Atlantic. Propaganda-conscious governments increasingly recognized the potential for a broader world opinion, and sought to rouse it to their side by fabricated or exaggerated stories of human rights abuses and outright barbarism. The contrast with manipulations at the outset of the Franco-Prussian War, forty years earlier, was interesting: at the earlier time Prussian Chancellor Bismarck arranged matters to inflame the opinion of his emperor, not a wider public. From 1914 onward, however, international conflict was routinely graced by efforts to justify actions and rouse support from a wider global audience.

It is impossible to talk about actual world opinion during World War I, because the whole point was the division of the European-civilized world, the basis of the world opinion available at that time, though various belligerents tried to stage-manage certain claims, like German atrocities against Belgian children, in the process of seeking wider backing. Nationalist passion drowned disinterested moral responsibility. To some degree blatant, propagandistic manipulation of public susceptibilities to stories of atrocities and to depictions of enemy barbarism cast doubts on the credibility of world opinion in the future, in the diplomatic–military arena. In these ways, the war set back the development of world opinion, even as the propaganda activities confirmed its existence and potential importance. The purest successors to earlier world opinion efforts probably came from the pacifists, but they found no extensive voice during the war itself.

The war's immediate sequel showed another limitation: under stress, world opinion remained fiercely Western. Efforts by various groups to win world opinion backing for nationalist causes in Africa or Asia were turned aside. The new African National Congress, organizations representing Indochina, and notable leaders like Marcus Garvey appealed to world opinion as they sought audience at the treaty discussions in Versailles, but they made no headway. The most successful non-Western movements, like Ataturk's creation of an independent Turkey, used force, not world opinion. Even the Bolshevik revolution, though eager to foster and exploit international Communist sentiment, had no significant interaction with world opinion as its forged a new regime. American isolationism was another blow to world opinion, a clear statement that, despite Wilsonian moralism, it was better to withdraw than to press for protection of rights across borders.

The new League of Nations provided a forum for discussion of world opinion, and in special interest areas, like women and children, it undoubtedly reflected and furthered the action of this force. But in the diplomatic arena, world opinion fell short, as national disputes soon outweighed any ability to mobilize a larger public sentiment in the interest of resolving disputes or maintaining the peace. The whole Versailles peace process was a monument to nationalist divisions (as well as outdated European claims to dominance) and foreshadowed further setbacks to world opinion in the arena of international relations.

The diplomatic record of the interwar decades traces a sorry performance for world opinion, ineffective at best, nearly mute at worst. The problems combined an inordinate number of crises, particularly during the 1930s, with a set of insurmountable divisions in the putative centers of world opinion. The rift between Western and Central Europe was one problem. Although Germany and Italy had not been centers of generation of world opinion, and although there was a brief sense of healing in the later 1920s which generated almost desperate hopes for international peace, the shattering of European unity both weakened world opinion and reduced European confidence in the ability to generate it. It is also true that as powerful European countries themselves generated the most obvious atrocities, amid ideologies (fascist or Communist) that largely inured them to outside critique, the effectiveness of world opinion was inevitably challenged.

World opinion was also constrained by the increasingly open division between Western Europe and Asian and African nationalism. Enough Western idealism persisted for Gandhi to believe that nonviolent protest could evoke British support (there was little reliance on international backing more generally), so the picture should not be overdrawn. In the main, however, what passed for political realism trumped moral world opinion when it came to dealing with nationalist protest in the colonies, and this in turn limited the credibility, and the moral certainty, of world opinion in other diplomatic venues.

Social disputes within Europe, and the new division between capitalism and Communism, took their toll as well. Many people who might normally have been active in world opinion movements, as least as sporadic supporters, were preoccupied with domestic issues, especially after the onset of the depression. Furthermore, it was hard to formulate world opinion from a European base when most issues immediately provoked division between conservatives and socialists, the liberal centre steadily eroding. Moral outrage tended to go out the window when each case had to be examined in terms of its implications for advancing the cause of the Soviet Union (anathema to conservatives) or for advancing fascism (anathema to the left). The shared moral sense that could periodically unite middle-class liberals and elements of the working class, for example during the Bulgarian atrocities, had largely disappeared.

Finally, the growing tide of pacifism, in a number of European countries, headed by Britain, tended to divide world opinion from yet another angle. Pacifism picked up much of the moral sentiment on which world opinion had been based. But its tenets emphasized avoidance of war over defense of human rights, and in this way it split potential world opinion – for example, in resistance to fascist advances and atrocities – right down the middle. During the crucial mid-1930s, mobilizations for peace in Great Britain consumed much of the organizational and emotional energy that might otherwise have fed a more active world opinion on specific foreign policy issues. Large numbers of people – over eleven million participated in the British "Peace Ballot" of 1934–35, half a million distributing forms door to door – organized on behalf of efforts to limit armaments and curtail dangerous diplomatic and military entanglements of the sort believed to have led to World War I. Huge majorities of those voting professed support for the League of Nations, disarmament agreements, and so on, and this was public opinion of one sort. The vote did include approval for military measures against aggression, though the mandate was vague. Although British pacificism had echoes elsewhere, including among some American supporters of isolationism, it did not manage to become a global movement, a full expression of world opinion. So, without dismissing the sincerity of the effort, it is legitimate to see it as distracting from the issues that might have called forth strong global reactions during the period. British pacifism also enhanced tensions with France about how to handle many of the threats of the 1930s, another division that limited the capacity for international outrage.

The hesitations of world opinion in the interwar years constitute a clear failure, not only because of other preoccupations and nationalist divisions, but because of disputes among people who tried to think about international issues in moral terms. Not only did world opinion fail to have successful impact, but it was not always clearly articulated in the first place. What moral outrage there was, amid clash and apathy, did not find coherent focus, despite an abundance of earnest advocates.

These various factors – diplomatic and social divisions, the moral dilemmas posed by anti-colonial movements, with pacifism as added diversion – led to the two dominant patterns of world opinion in the increasingly ominous diplomatic climate of the interwar decades: ineffectiveness and neglect.

Ineffectiveness was obvious, in part because hopes were placed on the League of Nations which could not be realized, in part because almost any expression of outrage was quickly counterbalanced by other agendas: the contrast to the focused attention given to earlier presumed atrocities in the Ottoman Empire was striking. Italy's invasion of Ethiopia in 1935, blatantly imperialist, indeed provoked public outpourings in both Western Europe and North America. The Italian government tried to rouse opinion to its side using fabricated stories of Ethiopian barbarism (treatment of prisoners, lack of education, and the like), with little success save among biased groups like many Italian Americans. Here, at least, a wider public had learned some skepticism after the misleading accounts of German behavior in World War I. Much sentiment, particularly on the political left, favored the Ethiopians, and the dignified behavior of the Emperor Hailie Selassie bolstered this support. Newspapers and petitions saw in the Ethiopian cause a vital test for the League but also a campaign for the oppressed in a depression-ridden world. British opinion ran high enough that the government claimed its force in representations to the Italians: a minister, explaining Britain's insistence on economic sanctions through the League, insisted that "any other course would be impossible to explain to the country."[6] But passions did not run deep. There were few dramatic examples of atrocities, and journalists covering the war had a hard time finding much that was interesting as Italian forces swept through the country. Ethiopian complaints about the use of gas were accurate but generated oddly little outcry, perhaps because even the moralistic segments of the public (aside from the pacifists) had given up on taming technology during war. Conservatives quickly dissented from public protest, seeking to bolster the Italian regime as a force for order; so in the United States did Catholic leadership. The French also largely resisted putting pressure on Italy, another blow to Western-based world opinion. And the whole public opinion campaign, culminating in League sanctions, actually served to make the war popular in Italy, another instance in which world opinion and half-hearted enforcement proved counterproductive. Nothing much, in the end, happened, as Italian conquest quickly took hold.

While the force of world opinion against the Italian invasion was inadequate, the mobilization did have a more enduring consequence: enlisting the voices of leaders in Africa and the African diaspora on human rights issues affecting this global community. Building on efforts earlier in the century to identify a pan-African constituency, various individuals and groups in Europe, the Caribbean, and the United States, as well as in Africa itself, expressed strong protest against the Italian action in Ethiopia. Groups like the Council on Africa, an African American lobbying organization, originated in this movement. The existence of an international African movement was an important addition to world opinion. It mobilized both on African issues and on concerns affecting African descendants, like the later civil rights movement in the United States. There was some spillover into concerns about human rights in other colonial or post colonial situations. The African and diaspora contribution to the later formation of world opinion on South African apartheid was particularly important, with direct links to the outrage generated against the Italian campaigns in the mid-1930s.[7]

The Spanish Civil War, opening a year later, roused more genuine global consternation, serving as the clearest test of world opinion in the diplomatic field in the interwar period. Here, more than in Ethiopia, was a cause with which liberals and leftists in many societies could ally, defending a secular republic against a semi-fascist military movement. It was easy to identify with the Spanish masses, and there were stories galore of atrocities committed by Franco's forces to fuel a personal sense of outrage. Undeniable passion brought volunteers from many nations to serve on the side of the republican armies. The leftist press, such as the British *Book News*, systematically provided information and organized periodic rallies, often filling London's Trafalgar Square. Picasso's great painting *Guernica*, protesting Italian–German bombing of Spanish civilians, occasioned large outpourings of support. French as well as British public opinion clamored for more effective intervention on the republic's behalf. Speeches, sermons, pamphlets, letters to the editor, and mass demonstrations – all the apparatus of world opinion appeared in many European countries, the Soviet Union, and North America. Yet little action occurred. Established governments, such as Léon Blum's Popular Front in France, largely spurned public opinion, being worried about counterthrusts from conservatives who sympathized with Franco and profoundly distrusting some of the Spanish Republic's supporters, particularly the Soviet Union and international Communism. In the United States, though large majorities opposed Franco (seventy-eight percent by 1938, according to the fledging Gallup Poll), the same large majorities did not really want the government to get involved at the expense of neutrality. Substantial minorities, such as British and American Catholics, were deeply convinced that it was the Spanish republicans who performed the real atrocities, butchering priests, sponsoring moral depravity, paving the way for a Bolshevist uprising. Global reactions there were, in the sense of deep moral convictions, across many borders, directed at protesting an unfair war and its many abuses of individuals. But aside from spurring individual action, they fell absolutely flat in the interwar context and never really resurfaced in the waning years before World War II broke out.

As striking as the failures of public expression were the substantial silences against even greater evidence of atrocities. In the immediate aftermath of World War I, violence between Turks and Greeks, as part of the Turkish independence struggle, went almost unnoticed in terms of outside public reaction, despite great human suffering. The wounds of the world war were too recent, perhaps, to permit much concern about an area that had previously been a focal point for outrage. Japan's attacks on China, leading to great brutality against civilian populations, certainly occasioned news and attendant dismay, but not the full apparatus of world opinion. Stalin's killings were more concealed and disputed, and their extent still occasions debate among historians; here, too, there was little external outcry. The emerging attacks on Jews in Hitler's Germany, notoriously, generated little global reaction – disapproval, certainly, in the press and in political resolutions, but not the sweeping demonstrations that moral outrage normally commanded. To be sure, the worst horrors of the Holocaust did not occur until Germany was at war, information being severely limited in the outside world. But it was clear, even before 1939, that information was not the only problem: lots of people who in other circumstances might have shaped a global reaction simply did not care enough to mount a significant effort. Fatigue and fear overcame moral revulsion.

In lack of outcry, even more than in ineffectiveness, the divisions and exhaustion of the interwar years proved no match for the bloody series of military repressions in various parts of the world. Global opinion can operate amid some dispute, but it requires a sense of majority concurrence in key societies, and this was normally lacking during the 1920s and 1930s; it also demands some hope that redress is possible, and this too was often missing amid the larger (and justifiable) fears of renewed world war.

World opinion, in sum, had ventured on to the diplomatic stage as early as the late nineteenth century. It lacked consistency, however, and established means of impact, and it was easily overwhelmed or stillborn. Though the next chapter will argue that some of these limitations were modified after World War II, they serve as more than historical reminders. Some similar limitations can reappear when divisions are too great or the range of crises too intimidating.

There was deep irony in the impotence of world opinion during the interwar years, for interest in public opinion was growing rapidly, at least in the Western world and to a degree in the Soviet Union. With the advent of the Gallup Poll, methods of plumbing opinion in the democracies improved and information on what the public seemed to think, on a whole variety of issues, became ever more abundant. But interest and capacity themselves revealed some of the limitations on world opinion during these difficult years. First, key soundings showed the divisions that allowed statesmen to disregard public expressions at many key points – for example, near 50:50 splits in Britain over whether Germany or the Soviet Union was the biggest danger. Second, the organizers of public opinion studies assumed a national, rather than international, base, so that anyone interested in world opinion would have to tally one separate expression after another, which rarely yielded resounding findings particularly in the divided interwar context. (This remains a problem in formulations today, as we will see in chapter 12.) Third – another issue still today – polling could show majorities and minorities, but it did not directly show passion, which remained a crucial issue where world opinion was concerned. To this extent, polling data, which could mix the trivial and the significant (Are you opposed to the Spanish Civil War? Do you think the Duchess of Windsor should be allowed back in Britain?), the lukewarm and the morally outraged, may have diluted world opinion's potential during a crucial period.

The overriding problem, beyond polling, beyond even the specific divisions that inhibited clear-cut outrage in an outrageous two decades, was that the sweep and viciousness of the foreign policy and human rights issues of the interwar years simply overwhelmed the capacity of world opinion to respond. The privilege of being able to set aside a couple of years to focus, say, on Bulgarian atrocities had been swept away by the array of new hostilities. Here, too, there were lessons for the future, and for the world today.

The ineffectiveness of world opinion in the diplomatic arena was ironic in one sense. Diplomatic historians have noted that public involvement in, and awareness of, international policy issues generally increased during the interwar years, in Europe and elsewhere. World War I and Wilsonianism had discredited much of the secrecy that characterized earlier diplomacy (save in special cases of public involvement like the Bulgarian atrocities). A number of elections – in France, for example, in 1924 – hinged on foreign policy issues, which were seen clearly to affect the lives of ordinary people through war or tariffs. Yet awareness and concern generated the partisan divisions and national focus that inhibited the formation of world opinion in the same arena. For many, outrage over the abuses caused by military adventurism either could not be defined easily, because of the disagreements about priorities, or seemed something of a luxury given pressing domestic issues and a fragile peace. Only after World War II did greater public involvement in diplomatic matters contribute to more meaningful statements of opinion on this terrain.

It is important to remember that amid the failures of world opinion in the diplomatic sphere, after a promising if whimsical late-nineteenth-century start, world opinion did continue to have impact in other areas, mopping up pockets of slavery in the 1920s and extending new concerns about conditions for women and labor, often in conjunction with special operations of the League of Nations. A basis remained for further development, despite the disappointing results in the most ambitious arena. How much additional force world opinion could gain in this arena is a legitimate criterion for measuring its more recent history.

PART III
New Tactics, New Targets, 1950s to the Present

6

WORLD OPINION GAINS GROUND, 1950s TO THE PRESENT

World opinion gained new heft in the second half of the twentieth century, particularly from the 1970s onward but with one signal success in the 1950s. Limitations and failures continued; there was no magic breakthrough, particularly in the diplomatic area and where great powers were concerned. But the constraints of the interwar years did not continue to define the field, as world opinion entered a new period of definition and development. In recent decades world opinion has taken on issues, particularly concerning the environment, where it has enjoyed significant influence. Social concerns have taken on new dimensions, though for both women and labor the record of global opinion campaigns, and their associational alternatives, remains checkered. Clearer triumphs for a revivified world opinion include the addition of targets, particularly among international corporations, where it has won some key campaigns. World opinion has benefited from new methods and organizations, especially the groups that have formed explicitly to shape and channel world opinion's force. After the doldrums of the interwar decades, world opinion has contributed to successful change, the attack on South African apartheid heading the list. This chapter discusses some of the preconditions for the ongoing transformation of world opinion in the contemporary era.

Global forces generally retrogressed during the middle decades of the twentieth century, after some dazzling advances around 1900 which generated the growing optimism about the force and range of world opinion. The withdrawal of the Soviet states from the international system from the 1920s onward, the bellicose challenges of Japan and Nazi Germany, even the hesitancies of the isolationist United States all challenged any pattern of growing international contacts. It was small wonder that world opinion suffered from this more general retreat. But from the 1950s onward, and particularly as the Cold War eased in the 1970s, globalization returned with a vengeance. This provided a larger context for the resurgence of world opinion. It also generated a number of new issues for which world opinion offered an essential antidote.

The background for accelerating global commentary is still being examined, and we will learn more as globalization gains increasing historical attention. A recent paper argues that a new set of realistic essays and novels in the 1920s and 1930s, from Orwell on Spain to Tam Lang's *I Pulled a Rickshaw* (on conditions in colonial Vietnam), along with widely circulated photographs, provided new awareness of human rights and labor abuses in various parts of the world. This consciousness, along with the catastrophe of World War II set up the explosion of rights statements, from the United Nations Declaration of Human Rights (1948) to pan-American and European equivalents soon after. The exploration of roots is a work in progress, but changes during and after the war contributed a definite impetus.[1]

Improving technology and expanded international contacts played a key role in the revival of world opinion after World War II. Despite formidable political barriers, it became progressively more possible to obtain global news quickly and with graphic detail. Television, especially after the establishment of international links through satellites, could feed images of misery or abuse to viewers around the world with unprecedented clarity and speed. There was a downside, to be sure: the wealth of opportunities for global lament could multiply almost endlessly, diluting the sustained focus essential for effective manifestations of world opinion. The same bounty of quickly communicable disaster stories offered a premium to the media gurus who would make choices among priorities, almost deliberately encouraging or downplaying opportunities for the formation of global outcry. Regional differences emerged on occasion, based on different media choices. During the 2003 Iraq war, for example, United States and European representations of the conflict diverged sharply, Europeans being given much more information about Iraqi casualties; this variation reflected opinion gaps but even more encouraged them.

New media could raise other questions of accuracy. Great concern about the punishment of a Nigerian woman apparently condemned to death for adultery generated massive petitioning by email in the early twenty-first century. But one Spanish organization created an internet message that exaggerated the certainty of the sentence, and the resultant outcry actually stiffened the resistance of Nigerian authorities until local groups convinced international human rights organizations to back off a bit and to clarify the situation. Error could be disseminated more widely and quickly than ever before.

On the whole, however, changes in technology facilitated the expansion of world opinion. Not only news and imagery but the sheer opportunity for high speed communication, especially with the internet from 1990 onward, encouraged groups bent on mobilizing global views. Time-tested methods of world opinion, such as petitions and letters of protest, amplified with the new speed of transmission and the possibility of recruiting an international cast of participants with well-stocked list-serves. Improved news facilities not only brought more immediate and dramatic evidence of possible abuses, but also encouraged would-be organizers of world opinion to seek methods that would themselves make the news and stimulate wider expressions of outrage. Groups like Greenpeace became expert in creating news events that could be widely and vigorously transmitted.

Technology influenced other developments that primed world opinion. The expansion of global tourism, pretty steadily from the 1950s onward but then accelerating with the decline of Communism, brought new opportunities to form opinions about international conditions and, even more (for most tourists were deliberately oblivious), to extend the possibilities of embarrassment in host countries eager to avoid seeming backward or uncivilized. Many leaders wanted to avoid tourist gibes about things ranging from police behavior to "disgusting" foods. Migration streams were less clearly linked to world opinion, but the movement back and forth of peoples from Third World to first world could enhance some sense of shared standards.

Steady improvements and extensions in polling allowed more accurate representations of opinion in many key countries. Polling expanded from the West to other industrial and partially industrial areas, including much of Asia and Latin America. Polling data in one region, on a topic such as nuclear armament or an imminent war, could influence other areas, thus contributing to world opinion. In turn, polls could encourage interest in participating in expressions about international issues. When polls suggested sweeping majorities, for example in the spring 2003 opposition to war in Iraq, they could encourage other, more passionate manifestations of global opinion, through demonstrations and other means.

A more active component in reviving and extending world opinion, particularly in the period immediately after World War II, was the inescapable contemplation of world opinion's failure between the wars. Growing beliefs that Western publics had been too passive amid the spread of fascism and Nazism and rising awareness of the culpable silence of knowledgeable outsiders amid the evidence of the mounting Holocaust against Europe's Jews helped fuel a sense that world opinion must become more active and vigilant in future. Europe, increasingly reducing internal nationalist barriers, became a more hospitable site for world opinion in part because of this sense of a need, if not to atone for, at least to prevent a repetition of warfare and brutality. The United States accepted new openness to international currents in part for the same reasons. Harry Truman, supporting approval of the new United Nations, caught the theme precisely: the new organization, designed to air international opinion in the interest of resolving conflicts peacefully, "comes from the reality of experience in a world where our generation has failed twice to keep the peace."[2] The American public, backing participation in the U.N. by eighty percent, clearly declared its willingness to host international discussion and to participate more actively in world opinion. To be sure, observers at the time worried that American support was artificially high in the immediate aftermath of war and amid high-powered internationalist press campaigns, and later developments suggest that it was inflated. Nevertheless, the idea of fostering world opinion as a hedge against repeating past mistakes and abuses stimulated new activity. There was some effort to learn from history, and greater attention to a more vigorous world opinion was one of the beneficiaries (along with European unity efforts and other relevant developments).

One specific reaction to the horrors of World War II explicitly extended the assumptions on which world opinion had been based. The Nuremberg trials of Nazi war criminals assumed a basis in international law for defining at least the extremes of abusive conduct. These and later trials, like the current effort against Serbian war criminals, did not necessarily rouse world opinion directly. They assumed, however, that there was global sanction for definite standards of international conduct in war. Postwar efforts and organizations, such as Amnesty International, soon built further on the basic idea of international standards and attendant monitoring of political behaviors, which the wartime collapse and subsequent legal redress seemed both to require and to justify.[3]

The war's aftermath also encouraged new Japanese participation in world opinion, particularly as the nation gained greater global economic clout. The new Japanese constitution prohibited extensive military activity, and this, plus the brutal experience of the war, convinced many Japanese that they had a special mission to seek peace in the world. Frequent Japanese involvement in world opinion followed from this commitment.

The Cold War both encouraged and constrained world opinion. The Soviet Union tried mightily to develop an alternative statement of world opinion to that emanating from the West, something that testified to world opinion's per-ceived power; but the resulting global publicity rivalry seriously limited any agreement about what constituted targets for outrage. The rivalry, with its widely publicized competing versions of truth, soured many people's hopes of world opinion; it was difficult to know whom to trust, what standards were not simply being manipulated by skilled propagandists. From the late 1940s to the late 1950s and to an extent beyond, there were two world opinions on crucial social, economic, and diplomatic issues. The rift had begun earlier, but now it became truly global, seriously complicating any definitions of a global view.

The complexities of the relationship between world opinion and the Cold War were vividly brought home to African American leaders in the 1950s. Several leaders had eagerly seized on the presumed lessons of the Holocaust and on the new United Nations Charter and the organization's human rights policy, hoping to bring U.N. pressure to bear on ongoing American racial injustice. The policy hit home to a degree, in a country eager among other things to present a liberal face to the world in the competition with Communism. Anti-Communism, however, tended to label any dissent from consensus as subversive, particularly during the McCarthy years, and African American efforts to draw on global scrutiny eventually brought their movement into disrepute. At the same time, because of the new competition for global image and the new awareness of international standards, individual African Americans who posed as foreigners could often receive exemption from southern segregation.[4]

On balance, however, at least after the most confrontational decade, the Cold War stimulated world opinion more than it discouraged it, for two rea-sons. First, precisely because it was mostly cold, the Cold War focused attention on allegiances, encouraging both sides to try to persuade peoples around the world of the validity of their cause. Although world opinion rarely resulted directly – division was more common – notions of mobilization and expression developed more fully as both sides competed for global bragging rights. Institutions like the Voice of America or Radio Free Europe, on the United States side, or the efforts of the Soviet news agency Izvestia were designed to shape world opinion as widely as possible. Again, they divided the field and thereby inhibited united expressions of moral opprobrium. But they unques-tionably encouraged the importance of opinion itself. An active cultural com-petition saw both sides promote their visual art, film, music, and theater – again on the assumption that winning the favor of a global audience mattered.[5] Except during specific crises, the Cold War turned into a combination of arms race and competition for popular favor throughout the world.

More directly, Cold War conflicts and dangers encouraged other groups, in the West and particularly in the neutral nations, to seek a more encompassing expression of opinion that could override polarization. The emergence of world opinion leaders from India, while stemming in part from their personal vision and anti-colonial credentials, owed much to a need to seek global statements not tainted by the Cold War and carrying the potential to override it on certain issues. Parts of Scandinavia also enjoyed a special role in world opinion leadership during the depths of the Cold War. Many regions of the world were roused by the Cold War fear of nuclear conflict, which made the disarmament movement a far more significant stimulus to global outcry than the interwar peace efforts had achieved.[6]

There were a few occasions in the Cold War when something like world opinion cut through the standard divisions to condemn one side or the other for a particularly blatant misuse of power. The Soviet repression of the 1956 Hungarian rising drew widespread editorials and public protests, though primarily in Western Europe and the United States; even some Western Communists publicly reconsidered their allegiances. American involvement in Vietnam was even more widely condemned as the conflict dragged on – some American leaders believed that world opinion held the United States to a higher standard than was applied to Communist aggressions. Protests against the Vietnam War figured heavily in student agitation of 1968, not only in the United States but through much of Western Europe. There were occasions, in other words, where global outrage transcended the Cold War rifts, encouraged by the propaganda efforts of one protagonist or the other.

Decolonization, the other great force of the postwar decades, also contributed new elements to world opinion. Here too, there was some complexity. The successful coronation of many national independence movements could create a mood resistant to pressure from outside opinion, and this often occurred. Indonesia long rebuffed global concern about repression in East Timor, in part out of a sense of national pride and responsibility. Many African countries, though willing to sign international agreements about women's rights, later had nationalist second thoughts and retreated to judicial opinions that vaunted traditional male superiority (for example, in property rights). The decline of imperialism also contributed to new currents in Western liberalism, which became more hesitant about imposing single standards on regional diversity; this new-found hesitation might limit world opinion particularly on social and cultural matters.

On the whole, however, decolonization extended the range and impact of world opinion. The greater number of independent countries increased the potential for wider participation in world opinion outside the West, though a strong European focus remained. Decolonization also reduced some of the moral constraints on Europeans and (perhaps to a lesser extent) Americans, making them freer to attack abuses because their own governments were less obviously enmeshed in global systems of oppression. Growing acceptance of decolonization highlighted vestiges of imperialism that deserved global comment, and again the apartheid regime in South Africa proved to be the most important focus here.

For a time, "Third World" leaders attempted to forge a world opinion directed against colonization, as in the formative Banding conference of 1975. Crowds in one former colony could be mobilized against imperialism's hold elsewhere. As independence gained ground, this mood receded, and Western leadership of most global outrage resumed. But the anti-colonial voice continued to contribute to broader world opinion concerning not only apartheid but also the Palestinian–Israeli conflict.[7]

As conflicts over specific decolonization movements declined – with settlements in cases like Algeria and Angola – some of the ideals of the whole current, with its commitment to the legitimacy of national independence, began to enter world opinion, with many Westerners joining with sentiments from the former colonies. On occasion, this kind of agreement could even break through Cold War divisions, as when both the Soviet Union and the United States opposed British–French attacks on Egypt when the latter seized the Suez Canal in 1956. This new facet of world opinion would also inform the groundswell of reaction to the United States' invasion of Iraq in 2003.

The decolonization effort had one consequence related to the expansion of the geographical basis of world opinion. Individual leaders from Asia and Africa gained unprecedented stature through their statesmanlike behavior during the struggle period, which gave them authority in more global pronouncements after the struggle was over. Indian figures like Nehru had a moral authority and penetrating intelligence of their own, but they also benefited from the saintly aura of Gandhi. Later, Nelson Mandela in South Africa gained legitimacy as a world opinion leader through his dignified endurance in fighting for racial justice during apartheid. These exceptional non-Western guides appealed to a global sense of morality, while helping to intensify and shape this moral sense; they proved capable of joining wider audiences, from Asia, Africa, and Latin America, to the more conventional core of world opinion in the West. How durable these moral mantles are is open to question: India has lost most of its opinion-guiding role since the passing of the independence generation. There is no clear successor to Nelson Mandela. Nevertheless, for a few crucial decades the ability to justify leadership from outside the West, while playing on Western guilts about imperialism, added crucial components to world opinion.

The uneven but undeniable spread of more democratic political systems, with at least some freedom of the press, also promoted world opinion. Democracy in Japan, along with growing prosperity and a sense of shared global economic power, gradually encouraged Japanese participation in expressions of world opinion, and later on the same held true for South Korea as well. Germany and Italy, as democracies and increasing economic powerhouses, gradually regained the capacity to participate in world opinion. Israelis sometimes joined in the articulation of world opinion, when not consumed by local tensions. Spain became a player in world opinion with the replacement of the Franco regime. The wider extension of democracy from the late 1970s onward, in Latin America, Eastern Europe, and elsewhere, created conditions for a freer press and greater opportunities for the expression of public views, as opposed to government-staged expressions on more regional or national issues. On the basis of this greater political openness, added to decolonization, world opinion could become more global.

New efforts to lead world opinion from the Roman Catholic papacy reflected some of the changes in the broader context of international affairs, including a desire to avoid the mistakes of the 1930s, and constituted a significant boost to world opinion. The pope continued to emphasize his leadership of the Catholic community and continued to support some causes independent of world opinion. But, from the 1960s onward, there was an increasing tendency to reach out to a wider global audience, making moral pronouncements not closely tied to the faithful alone or even designed, with any precision, to mesh with missionary efforts. Fervent statements concerning conflicts such as that between Israelis and Palestinians joined impassioned (usually abortive) efforts to press American officials to commute death penalties. For the papal staff the line between clearly Catholic moral promptings, about sexual restraint or opposition to abortion, and these broader moral efforts may well have blurred. But the implications of the wider campaigns in terms of world opinion were fascinating, since they clearly prompted Catholics to participate and sometimes to lead in the kinds of moral outrage more often, in the past, spurred by Protestants, and since they also reflected the growing importance of world opinion with which Catholic outreach could now conjoin.

Aside from the mutual benefits from a juncture of two powerful forces, the papal role in world opinion reflected many of the wider postwar trends. There was a clear attempt to compensate for deficiencies in moral leadership during the World War II period, and particularly the failure fully to attack the Holocaust. The recent papacy has frankly admitted the lapse, and the provision of papal sanctions against more contemporary advocates of racial hatred, even where Catholics were not directly involved, clearly follows from the reaction to past mistakes. The Cold War obviously entered in, a firmly anti-Communist papacy being eager to build a larger but non-Communist world opinion on the basis of ethical and not merely sectarian leadership. For the Church, decolonization was coupled, particularly in Africa, with growing Catholic dependency on non-Western populations; without detracting from papal sincerity, the association with wider moral causes encouraged this linkage as well. Papal leadership in global morality, with no sectarian strings, could promote a favorable context for Third World Catholicism. There was even a technology component, as improved air travel facilitated more sweeping and frequent global visits, which in turn reinforced the association of the papacy with expressions of world opinion.

The specific conversion to an effort both to utilize and to enhance world opinion occurred in the 1960s, when under Popes John XXIII and Paul VI and with the Second Vatican Council of 1962–65, the Church dramatically altered its approach to Communism and, to an extent, the whole modern world. The older strategy, of anathematizing Communism and other uncongenial forces in the modern world, gave way to an emphasis on leadership in defense of human rights. In 1963 the Vatican Council issued the Declaration of Religious Freedom, which treated the topic in moral terms similar to those already common in other world opinion campaigns: "the human person has a right to religious freedom," which "has its foundation in the very dignity of the human person." This approach encouraged not only a new kind of offensive against Communist policy, but also associated the Church with other human rights campaigns against economic injustice and the excesses of capitalism (not a brand new theme), the dangers of nuclear armaments, many impositions of the death penalty, and many kinds of war. John XXIII had already intoned against the dangers of modern war ("it is contrary to reason to hold that war is now . . . suitable"), and the Church began to take an active role in pronouncements against conflicts that did not necessarily involve Catholics. The Church began to speak not only as a religious institution but also on behalf of humanity, and this was a tremendous addition to the world opinion movement. The transition included elaborate apologies not only for Catholic silence during the Holocaust but also (in 1993) for Church complicity in slavery and the slave trade in centuries past. Papal efforts were enhanced by similar campaigns by other church officials, such as the American bishops. Catholic definitions of human rights, particularly in the abortion area, did not always mesh with world opinion more generally (though they could complicate any attempt to claim global standards). Overall, however, the transition was both revealing and important in the promotion of world opinion.[8]

Another, even broader element took shape around the Cold War and decolonization. The new context for world opinion also followed from changing European needs, in some ways unexpectedly. Enhanced emphasis on world opinion, from its conventional European base, fit a deteriorating, or at least increasingly complex, diplomatic context in several respects, besides helping Europeans feel they were reversing interwar apathy in the face of injustice. European military and diplomatic power declined in relation to the two superpowers of the Cold War. Asserting leadership in world opinion provided an alternative channel for expression, sometimes in protest against superpower abuses, particularly on the American side. Loss of colonies, and an increasing acceptance of anti-colonialism, was another blow to European power. But the use of world opinion, for example to protest human rights abuses in Africa or Asia, gave Europeans a new, entirely respectable way to attempt to intervene in the wider world, including many former colonies. Such an approach had not been as necessary previously, either because abuses could be directly tackled by imperial governments or, more commonly, because it was these governments that perpetrated the abuses. World opinion was by no means exclusively Western, and its gradual though inconsistent broadening was a legitimate postwar theme. But strong elements of its Western origins persisted, and without accusing Europeans of insincerity or hypocrisy, it is possible to see some special service to European interests in world opinion's new force. This raises some complex issues about the impact of world opinion on parts of the non-Western world, and on non-Western reactions to it. That is, hostile reactions may reflect disagreements in principle, but a resentment against particular neo-colonial aspersions may also be involved. The Eurasian interest in world opinion also informed the still complicated topic of world opinion and the United States, with the mixture of American involvement but also European targeting of the United States that this relationship has long involved.

Two final factors in the shaping of world opinion in recent decades, both closely linked, involve relationships to trade and the interaction of world opinion and globalization. The middle decades of the twentieth century saw a number of societies attempt to isolate themselves from undue dependence on international trade: Stalin's Soviet Union, Hitler's Germany, and Mao's China are key examples. From the 1970s onward, however, most societies decided that involvement and openness provided the better option. China reversed its position on international trade from 1978 onward, with impressive results; Gorbachev's policies, beginning in 1985, had similar implications though less striking economic outcomes. Levels of trade and global economic interpenetration increased steadily, and only a few countries (notably North Korea and Burma) stayed outside. There were several implications for world opinion. First, the formation of foreign businesses and the involvement of international merchants provided additional means of knowing about practices in certain societies which could provoke outrage (though economic agents are not usually in the outrage-reporting mode). More important were new motivations for societies like China to be sensitive to world opinion, in the interests of avoiding embarrassment or economic disadvantage because of reported practices that repelled a larger international community. World opinion gained new leverage through the possibility of economic boycotts, not only against offending nations but also against global corporations – and this was a significant new dimension in the whole world opinion movement. On the more positive side, new carrots could be offered for compliance with world opinion, when the decline of the Cold War reduced alliance options and advancing globalization created additional reasons to wish to please the West. Membership in the World Trade Organization could be an important spur, extending well beyond trade policies to human rights issues; the same applied to potential gains from American or European Union aid and, for some countries, membership in or alignment with the European Union itself. However, the same global commercial network provided reasons for some of the leaders of world opinion to soft-pedal certain concerns, in the interest of avoiding trade disruptions. The strange decline of international movements against child labor was one example of how growing dependence on globalism created constraints as well as opportunities.

The phenomenon of globalization provoked diverse reactions, with economics again in the forefront (along with environmental concerns), though with cultural issues attached as well. The intensification of international contacts, and particularly the growing role of powerful multinational companies in organizing working conditions and seeking maximum economic advantage, provoked increasingly articulate movements against globalization. These movements, in turn, sought opportunities to disrupt global economic gatherings and, even more, to influence a wider world opinion. Beginning with a World Bank meeting in 1999, in Seattle, protesters took to the streets to dramatize their concerns about globalization's impact on the world's poorer regions, on labor, on the environment, and on cultural identity (with particular attention to symbols of cultural homogenization such as McDonalds). Here was another twist in the relationship between world opinion and the intensification of international linkages, in which protest leaders in essence asked for a global movement against presumably excessive global connections. It was not clear that world opinion would rally as asked; the jury is still out on this subject, since full-scale anti-globalization movements have enlisted only small minorities. But the complexity of the forces involved in facilitating and generating world opinion, has in recent decades been highlighted.

Growing international linkages provided the context for a resurgence of expressions of world opinion in the decades after World War II, and particularly from the 1970s onward with the cooling of the worst tensions of the Cold War and the completion of the most extensive decolonization efforts. These linkages did not erase barriers to the formation or implementation of world opinion, particularly where deep power interests or economic advantages were involved; world opinion still often failed or simply fell silent. But the linkages did promote greater knowledge of exceptions to presumed global standards, and they did provide some new means not only for rallying world opinion but for driving it home through diplomatic or commercial pressures. Key players, notably the Europeans but also some leaders in the Third World, found new reasons to utilize world opinion to articulate vital interests in a post-imperial context. The United Nations, though sometimes beleaguered, on the whole provided a far more effective outlet for world opinion than the League of Nations had done. But growing international linkages could also complicate world opinion. Some regions, forced into contacts they found threatening, rebelled against expressions of world opinion as one way to salvage identity. Growing international knowledge could generate a new awareness that the world was not united on some key issues, particularly on certain social issues involving deep familial commitments; here, world opinion might have to retreat. Even as the concept of world opinion received growing recognition in this new phase of its deployment, contests persisted over its definition.

For all the complexities, it's important not to lose sight of the key points. In contrast to the decades of hesitancy before World War II, when opportunities for effective international opinion seemed to shatter after the promising nineteenth-century beginning, by the 1970s more people, in more different places, and on a wider array of issues found voice to express concern or outrage through what came increasingly to be known as "world opinion." The trend built on new opportunities for expression. It also reflected new worries and, for many, an urgent need to use global opinion to combat powerlessness in a world that often seemed to be spinning out of human control. World opinion in this sense represented a renewed effort to use high emotion and massed voice to counter the less savory activities of sundry great powers, multinational corporations, and abusive dictators.

As we move into greater detail, about world opinion and some of the great issues of the past half-century, the existence of a new period for world opinion generates key themes to monitor amid the mix of specific stories: To what extent did world opinion globalize, moving beyond its largely Western roots? What new methods were enlisted to bolster world opinion. With what new issues did world opinion most successfully engage? And the big one: to what extent did world opinion come to embody not only moral outrage, its traditional staple, but also a new need to gain expression and assert control amid growing dominance by faceless agencies and otherwise unaccountable authorities?

7

THE SURGE OF WORLD OPINION ORGANIZATIONS

Beginning with Amnesty International, in 1961, a series of organizations emerged – non-governmental organizations, or NGOs, in the common jargon – that existed on the basis of world opinion and related pressures, and little beyond. They stimulated world opinion on a foundation of beliefs in universal rights, and equally universal disgust and outrage when these rights were abused. Fact-finding missions and subsequent dramatizations and wide publicity became their stock in trade. The organizations channeled this opinion into specific pressures to correct the abuses discovered.

These groups differed from the associational thrusts common in areas like women's rights in that they depended more directly on grassroots expressions and passions, though they also adopted resolutions that sought to codify global criteria in areas such as human rights or environmental standards. They closely resembled the groups that had sprung up against slavery, almost two centuries before, though they were more formally organized and more carefully global. Amnesty International plausibly claimed to be the second-oldest human rights organization, after Anti-Slavery International. Organizations like Amnesty International involved many of the same intellectual precedents as had the antislavery movement and used grassroots techniques that, with due regard to changes in technology and reporting speed, had similarities as well. Even basic geography echoed the earlier movement, with Western Europe and particularly Britain at the core, the United States and then other parts of the world chiming in as significant ancillaries. After an interlude of almost a century, a massive expansion of global conscience accompanied this new surge of organized world opinion, with significant results to match.

❖❖❖

Amnesty International's formation is revealing, since it showed the growing potential of world opinion in the context of decolonization and the Cold War, and it expanded the range of targets for world opinion while calling on classic ingredients. A British socialist lawyer, Peter Benenson, launched the organization with a long article in *The Observer*: "Open your newspaper any day of the week, and you will find a report from somewhere in the world of someone being imprisoned, tortured or executed because his opinions or religion are unacceptable to his government . . . The newspaper reader feels a sickening sense of impotence. Yet if these feelings of disgust all over the world could be united into common action, something effective could be done."

Here were the vital components of world opinion: a belief that many voices could be raised against injustice, a sense of passionate outrage, and a conviction that global standards of political behavior could be defined. Benenson himself was a Catholic convert – another sign that Catholicism was being added to the roster of doctrines that could generate world opinion. He was aided by several colleagues, including Eric Baker, a prominent Quaker who had been heavily involved in nuclear disarmament campaigns – an even more direct religious link to past world opinion campaigns that had also started in Britain.

Benenson established a London office to collect information about the names and conditions of what his group called "prisoners of conscience," defined in terms of global criteria of justice: "Any person who is physically restrained (by imprisonment or otherwise) from expressing (in any form of words or symbols) an opinion which he honestly holds and which does not advocate or condone personal violence." Members of the new organization were actively recruited during the following year as the group conducted "fact-finding" missions in various parts of the world. Amnesty's efforts were partly inspired by the concerns about Communist repression, and an early mission was sent to Czechoslovakia. But from the outset there was an attempt to achieve political balance and neutrality, with a trinity of coordinated campaigns in the Eastern bloc, the West, and the developing world. Unlike antislavery, world opinion was now advancing to a realization that the West harbored its own internal faults, beyond abuses like slavery that it might inflict elsewhere which global standards might correct; it was not just a matter of preaching to other regions. Early campaigns thus focused on issues in places like Northern Ireland as well as the Communist bloc. Members were formed into small groups and urged to "adopt" individual prisoners and conduct active letter-writing and petition programs on their behalf, with the aim of embarrassing offending governments into remedial action. More general reports soon developed as well, such as an initial 1965 bulletin on prison conditions in Portugal, South Africa, and Romania (again, the careful geographical distribution).

By 1977, when Amnesty won the Nobel Peace Prize, it had identified over fifteen thousand political prisoners and had assisted in the release of more than half of them. A Dominican trade union leader, Julia de Pena Valdez, described the process: "When the first two hundred letters came, the guards gave me back my clothes. Then the next two hundred letters came and the prison director came to see me . . . The letters still kept arriving and the President called the prison and told them to let me go. After I was released, the President called me to his office . . . He said, 'How is it that a trade union leader like you has so many friends all over the world?'"[1] Or the simpler report by Professor Luiz Rossi, a Brazilian, in 1973: "I knew that my case had become public. I knew they could no longer kill me. Then the pressure on me decreased and conditions improved."[2] Amnesty became heavily involved with some very prestigious prisoners, like Victor Havel in Czechoslovakia, Nelson Mandela in South Africa, and Aung San Suu Kyi in Burma, but it worked on more routine cases as well. By 2004 the group could claim contributions to the release of more than forty thousand people. Its basic strategy, combining moral conviction with massive publicity and a global voice with the goal of shaming often repressive regimes and sometimes authoritarian leaders into leniency, involved the exercise of world opinion in its purest form – and it often worked. The initial focus on individual cases, each with dramatic potential, was ideally suited to the operation of world opinion, though Amnesty's ability to accumulate significant numbers of offenses and corrections was truly impressive, a tribute to a diligent staff, ample use of the media, and extensive communications.

Amnesty International was most famous for its activities in what is commonly called the Third World – in Africa, the Arab world, Central America, and so on. But the organization was no mere heir to enlightened imperialism. It devoted great effort to espousing decent treatment for prisoners in British jails in Northern Ireland, winning release for some and decrying the use of torture. Attacks on the American prison system won a bit less attention, but the growing campaign against the death penalty added an important component to the tensions between world opinion and the United States.

Amnesty International was initially greeted with some hostility by established organizations like the United Nations, which, despite its Charter, had not at that point developed an active human rights agenda. Many officials resisted the idea that a non-governmental organization could be involved in setting standards. Amnesty successfully pioneered this connection, which became established practice for a variety of NGOs and in turn facilitated the expansion of world opinion and the range of abuses world opinion targeted. Amnesty's own agenda widened steadily, from its initial concern with imprisonment for expressions of opinion, to active advocacy against the use of torture, and, more recently, against the death penalty in any form. The organization widely publicized cases of torture in Greece, in the later 1960s, again using media attention and letter-writing campaigns to press authorities to ease up on particular individuals. In this case, the effort also induced the Council of Europe to file formal charges, which raised Amnesty's profile in Europe more generally (even though, or perhaps because, Greece initially withdrew from the Council in response) and led Amnesty itself to launch a more formal "Campaign for the Abolition of Torture" in 1972.

Amnesty International worked hard to develop a large and widely distributed membership base. It depended on members for funding as well as voice, for it carefully avoided taking money from governments. National sections were established in many European countries, in the United States, and elsewhere. By 2004 the organization had over a million members, and even before that it could organize petitions – like one in the 1970s against torture – with more than a million signatures (directed to the United Nations, which adopted a resolution against torture in 1973). Amnesty went beyond antislavery efforts in regularizing wide membership rather than depending on decentralized groups and more sporadic surges of passion. At the same time, individual groups, national or regional, could go after local targets as well as participating in more global campaigns.

Geographic scope was a consistent concern. The number of countries with chapters expanded steadily, to twenty-seven countries by 1970. But Amnesty International continued to be heavily Western in membership, enthusiastic contingents in the United States, Canada, and Australia complementing the European core. As Latin American politics liberalized, by the 1980s, chapters developed there, often spearheaded by family members of former prisoners whom Amnesty had assisted. By 1984, Amnesty chapters existed in fifty countries, and by 1989, when the organization had 700,000 members, they came from 150 different nations. By this point annual council meetings were frequently staged outside the West, in Asia and Africa; and in 1992 Pierre Sané, a Senegalese, became secretary general of the organization. By 2002 Amnesty had developed an active campaign in Russia.

As its own agenda blossomed, Amnesty depended not simply on careful investigation and wide publicity for individual cases of abuse, but also on spurring its membership to expand their own range of concerns, in the process extending global standards and definitions. Thus Amnesty worked to formulate criteria that would allow action against "disappearances" of the sort that bedeviled political activists and their families in Latin America in the 1960s and 1970s. In 1980 the group listed 2,665 individuals who had "disappeared," including a twenty-day-old baby. Here again the movement stimulated the reaction of a United Nations Working Group, which depended on NGOs for most of its information.

The capacity for prompt action in specific cases was maintained. On 27 February 1981 six members of a human rights organization in Buenos Aires were arrested; the wife of one called the Amnesty representative in Argentina, who in turn notified the International Secretariat; international telegrams, mainly from Europe and the United States, began reaching the Argentine government the next day, and Amnesty cabled the nation's president directly; Amnesty issued an Urgent Action Bulletin on 3 March which appealed for more telegrams and letters. The prisoners were released on 6 March. Through the 1970s and 1980s Amnesty handled 1,500–2,000 individual cases each year. In 2001 its local groups worked on behalf of over 2,800 named individuals subject to arrest, torture, or a death sentence.

Methods expanded with technology. By the later 1990s, email began to loom large in spreading word about abuses and in soliciting expressions of outrage. The organization won an award in 2001 for its Stoptorture website.

As it developed as a major outlet for world opinion, Amnesty International encountered several revealing tensions. The first, entirely predictable, involved the balance between extensive membership and a commitment to some spontaneity, and the lures of formal organization. Particularly active volunteers and full-time officials could easily come to feel that the operation was really theirs, the members' interest and participation being a sporadic and passive component. Members, in turn, could judge that Amnesty was escaping their control, that their voice (and funds) might be called for but their capacity for spontaneous expression was being blunted. The organization was trying to remain much closer to some kind of public opinion that most of the international women's or labor associations did, to make sure that the portrayal of global standards had a real audience behind it; but the leaders did not want to lose the bureaucratic advantages of organization, and some disjunctures emerged as a result.

The second, related tension was more directly relevant to world opinion. Amnesty International began as an organization devoted to individuals subject to rights abuse, and the pain and drama their cases generated. It retains this flavor. Increasingly, however, the leadership wanted also to participate in defining more general standards, such as those applicable to torture or disappearance. Here (as with slavery earlier) individual cases became illustrations of problems more than causes in themselves. Members, and even mid-level volunteers, might become passionately involved with particular instances of injustice and not especially sympathetic to the organization's desire not to sacrifice gains in winning approval for standards to triumphs of individual justice. This dilemma persists to this day, national branches occasionally disputing with the central body about what importance to place on a single case.

Over time, Amnesty International has become increasingly involved with broad thematic or regional campaigns, at some cost to the fight for individual prisoners that characterized its inception. Human rights abuses in the diamond trade, or in Saudi Arabia, or as part of ethnic conflict in the Balkans are characteristic of this wider effort. So are the recent attempts to create a general standard in global opinion against the death penalty, or on behalf of the International Criminal Court and its jurisdiction over war crimes and abuses of military power. By 1999, Amnesty International's Council agenda was filled with items such as the impact of economic relations on human rights, a campaign against impunity for human rights abusers, sexual attacks on women during civil wars, and the conditions of refugees. Here is a familiar dilemma in world opinion: how much depends on the power of individual injustice, with human faces attached, and how much can be mobilized on behalf of broader global principles. In moving toward the latter, Amnesty was hoping to widen its scope, in terms of the number of individuals it could protect, and to accelerate its role in expanding the standards applicable to abuses more generally – a process first illustrated by the movement from imprisonment, to torture and "disappearance," and to the death penalty. Amid these changes, Amnesty petitions were as likely to support general resolutions, like that against torture, signed in 2001 by thirty-five thousand individuals, as to target specific individuals.

The turn to wider principle also involves Amnesty in increasing collaborations with other NGOs and with formal international organizations such as the U.N. or the Organization of American States. The effort to prod individual governments through embarrassment persists, but it takes a back seat to the wider relationships.

Finally, the terrain on which Amnesty International operates has itself changed, which has encouraged some of the shifts in tactics and targets. With the end of the Cold War and the spread of formal democracy, the number of governments deeply engaged in human rights abuses of the classic types has diminished, despite the persistence of cases in parts of Central Asia and elsewhere. Many abuses now emanate from paramilitary forces or non-governmental groups. As Amnesty International increasingly turned to issues such as the mistreatment of women in civil strife, or the crimes associated with ethnic cleansing, it was dealing with individuals and groups impervious to the embarrassment that conventional world opinion seeks to generate. Hence the increasing recourse to more institutional measures, such as the International Criminal Court.

Amnesty International has played and continues to play a major role in the evolution of world opinion on a host of key issues. Although it is not immune to criticism from various vantage points, its success has helped inspire a number of similar ventures that in turn have reflected and contributed to world opinion's trajectory.

Elements of Amnesty's most recent statute, adopted in Senegal in 2001, clarify its take on what the foundations of world opinion are, in the broad human rights field, and what global standards, properly enunciated and implemented, can accomplish:

> Amnesty International's vision is of a world in which every person enjoys all of the human rights enshrined in the Universal Declaration of Human Rights and other international human rights standards . . . Amnesty International forms a global community of human rights defenders with the principles of international solidarity, effective action for the individual victim, global coverage, the universality and indivisibility of human rights, impartiality and independence, and democracy and mutual respect . . . In addition to its work on specific abuses of human rights, Amnesty International urges all governments to observe the rule of law, and to ratify and implement human rights standards . . . and it encourages intergovernmental organizations, individuals, and all organs of society to support and respect human rights.

True to its history, the organization has continued to add human rights goals. Although still emphasizing its work against torture, extrajudicial executions, and disappearances, Amnesty has launched programs to protect women's rights, citing "abuses primarily suffered by women" along with those common to people of both genders and all ages, and has begun to work against abuses of gay people.

Human Rights Watch, a younger organization that some regarded, by the early twenty-first century, as more supple than Amnesty International, differed from its older relative in several respects. It was more clearly the product of the later stages of the Cold War. It was based in the United States, though with branches in key countries around the world. It did not strive for a large membership base or massive letter-writing or petition campaigns.

Human Rights Watch began in 1978 as Helsinki Watch, a group set up, with U.S. government encouragement, to monitor rights abuses in the Soviet bloc in keeping with the Helsinki accords between the two Cold War giants. The focus was on the human rights provisions of those accords, as they applied primarily to Eastern Europe. In the 1980s the organization added an Americas Watch, because of widespread abuses in the civil conflicts in Central America. Coverage of other parts of the world ensued until, in 1988, the umbrella group gained its current name.

Like Amnesty, Human Rights Watch (H.R.W.) featured careful investigations of alleged abuses, which could then be publicized. It worked hard to balance research and advocacy. By 2003 it had a core of 150 professionals, mainly lawyers, supplemented by a "growing cadre" of volunteers. By 2003 H.R.W. was tracking situations in more than seventy countries and was adding programs about women's rights, children's rights, and arms trafficking to its central concerns. It played a major role in detailing rights abuses in the Balkans, Indonesia, Rwanda, and Israel/Palestine.

Human Rights Watch's principles rested squarely on the moral imperatives that undergirded world opinion – "international standards of human rights apply to all people equally" – while arguing that "sharp vigilance and timely protest can prevent the tragedies of the twentieth century from recurring."

With less focus on individual cases of torture and imprisonment than characterized Amnesty International, H.R.W. gathered more systematic data on abuses by individual governments, rebel groups, or corporations, hoping to use both United States government action and wider world opinion to put constructive pressure on the offenders. The organization was quite successful in winning wide publicity for its reports, particularly in the American press, which constituted a partial surrogate for world opinion. Human Rights Watch also worked for more general agreements, winning an international accord against the use of child soldiers (the agreement stipulated a minimum age for service in armed forces) and spearheading the International Campaign to Ban Landmines (which the United States refused to sign). Like Amnesty, it frequently called for international tribunals to deal with war crimes, invoking this procedure against Serbian leaders and also against leaders in Rwanda, where the group's testimony helped lead to the conviction of several "genocidaries."

Human Rights Watch strove to maintain independence from the United States government. It took no government funding and it participated in attacks on abuses within the United States, particularly in prisons and among immigrants; and it condemned the death penalty. Its women's division mounted a major project on abuses in United States prisons. As early as the 1980s H.R.W. (along with Amnesty, though in a largely separate effort) vigorously resisted assertions by the Reagan administration that human rights abuses in Central America were the doings of left-wing insurgents alone, and the organization's policies had a great deal to do with encouraging conciliation efforts in the region. In 2004 H.R.W.'s annual report took the United States to task for its arbitrary arrests and imprisonments in the "war on terror" and also rejected human rights justifications for the war against Iraq, arguing that war could be legitimate against imminent or ongoing executions of innocent civilians but not as a retroactive measure long after the worst abuses had ceased. Because its efforts relied less on grassroots opinion and more on pressure tactics, it did seek to influence U.S. policies and official definitions of abusive states, which could then be called to account and denied aid or financial backing. Yet use of press statements and reports loomed large as well, helping to mobilize a larger opinion. Human Rights Watch added to the efforts of Amnesty and other groups in creating an increasingly active and extensive set of global standards and an interaction between mixed enforcement – a public audience combined with other sources of pressure – and a sense of guilt and vulnerability on the part of some offenders.

Like Amnesty also, H.R.W. increasingly extended its range of concerns. The establishment of a Women's Rights Division led to particularly active efforts in the 1990s to argue that domestic violence against women was a criminal matter, not a cultural one. In 1993 the Division joined other groups to present a petition to the United Nations Conference, signed by 240,000 people from 120 countries, insisting on recognition that "women's rights are human rights." Human Rights Watch was also active in researching and publicizing activities in the arms trade, which could feed civil violence in parts of Africa and elsewhere which in turn typically led to horrendous rights abuses. Here was a case where H.R.W. relied heavily on implicit world opinion, arguing that many arms trades could not withstand public awareness, such that media attention was the best antidote.

On a scale smaller than that of the larger, less centralized Amnesty effort, H.R.W. steadily widened its geographic range. To its initial East European and Latin American interests, it added programs in both Africa and Asia. It played a major role in calling attention to human rights abuses in China after the rollback of the democratic movement there in 1989. While Chinese leaders characteristically dismissed efforts by H.R.W. and others as mere "noise," campaigns visibly contributed to releases of well-known political prisoners, usually timed in conjunction with negotiations with the West.

Although observers noted that H.R.W. maintained a more limited agenda than Amnesty International, it proved capable of more effective action on some issues. A 1999 campaign on behalf of the rights of former untouchables in India, for example, led to considerable attention and some policy changes, whereas a comparable Amnesty effort a few years earlier had been less compelling. On the whole, however, the two organizations worked in similar directions, their obvious competition a healthy component in furthering the vitality and reach of the NGO movement and its capacity to galvanize world opinion.

The visibility and frequent success of some of the leading mobilizers of world opinion inevitably created a growing crop of imitators. Some featured a distinctive ideological base – for example, more strictly denominational and less apologetically Western. And some added tactics to the basic arsenal of opinion, invocation of international law, and political pressure.

The International Justice Mission (I.J.M.), for example, was a strictly Christian organization whose activities accelerated in the early twenty-first century. It was United States based, with a board of directors that included only one person outside the U.S. (a Latin American). There was a wider connection to human rights activities, since some I.J.M. leaders had earlier attempted to rouse world opinion against the genocide in Rwanda and now turned to a different strategy and a somewhat different audience partly because of frustration with the substantial apathy they encountered. The I.J.M. proudly proclaimed its Christian principles, deriving from what the leaders saw as biblical imperatives. "From Scripture we learn that the Creator is a God of justice and righteousness; that He measures all individuals against an absolute standard of divine holiness. We learn that every person, without distinction, is created in the image of God and is precious in His sight." All of this was close to the statements of global moral standards common in world opinion, but the sectarian twist was fascinating. Like its sister groups, I.J.M. sought to investigate situations of injustice, calling attention to individual and collective victims and seeking to mobilize international outrage. Like its sister groups also it emphasized conveying "perpetrators" to a reckoning in courts of law. Its educational arm sought to inform a wide audience that effective justice could be brought about by international efforts. The group focused heavily on young victims of sexual abuse, in countries such as Cambodia, and had some success in dramatizing the plight of child prostitutes (and the villainy both of local pimps and of international tourists). The I.J.M. also gained some results in persuading governments to tighten legal penalties against individuals who traveled for the purpose of sexual exploitation. But efforts did not stop there: I.J.M. also organized direct rescue missions, plucking children from brothels and taking them to care facilities (from which, however, forty percent would quickly escape).

The place of distinctive programs of this sort in the larger evolution of world opinion is hard to determine. Less truly international than most world opinion programs, more sectarian in the definition of global standards, more assertive in tactics, the efforts nonetheless testified to the effectiveness of the NGO–world-opinion combination, which was now generating a series of stepchildren. The efforts did not seem clearly differentiated in the eyes of many local officials. Cambodian ministers, for example, were at pains to respond to the I.J.M. campaign with at least verbal assurances of support, lest recalcitrance weaken their standing in the international community or reduce their eligibility for economic support. It was imperative to react to the demands of Western-dominated world opinion, at least rhetorically, and difficult to make fine distinctions between specific sources and strategies.

The establishment of and support for human rights organizations, mobilizing wide public response, mirrored the contemporary evolution of world opinion more generally. The Western base and derivation were obvious, even as moral concern extended to situations in any region. Yet there was also attention to fostering local organizations as a means of providing additional support and vital information.

This process led in turn, mainly after 1985, to a host of additional regional human rights groups linked to but separate from the characteristic Western base. Literally hundreds formed, such as the influential Fundacion Rigoberta Menchu Tum, in Mexico City, concentrating on rights issues for indigenous peoples, primarily in Central America but with some broader interest as well. In 1993 over 180 Asian rights organizations gathered to seek some modifications in international standards through recognition of collective needs along with individual rights, but maintaining a moral commitment. By the early 1990s numerous organizations had formed in Africa, often to monitor the still-shaky rights pledges of newly democratic regimes. Just as the goals of world opinion expanded in the rights area, and debate expanded a bit too, so did the geographic range of the mobilizers.

The addition of environmental concerns to the lexicon of global standards and moral responsibility began to take shape in the 1960s. The obvious cause was the growing level of environmental degradation and the appearance of widely sold books, like Rachael Carson's *Silent Spring*, that publicized this fact and urged counteraction. As with human rights, most specific problems were local, but they involved more general principles and – even more than with human rights violations – much of the damage was demonstrably, and increasingly, international in scope. World opinion had to be aroused.

International environmentalism initially centered in Britain, Canada, and the United States – another overlap with earlier forms of world opinion and mobilization. Although many groups were formed, with varied specific purposes, almost all of them paid some attention to public opinion across national boundaries, attempting to educate, to provide specific cases that would draw outrage, to stimulate and then capitalize upon a real sense of environmental morality and responsibility.

The first major international environmental group, the World Wildlife Fund, originated in Britain in 1961. It grew to have a diversity of national centers, including branches in Pakistan, Malaysia, and elsewhere, with a total of six million members by the mid-1990s. The group's efforts rested mainly on direct conservation, so its role in mobilizing world opinion was a by-product at best.

The Friends of the Earth (F.O.E.) formed in 1969, an outgrowth of the American Sierra Club. The organization has focused particularly on government policy – involving both individual states and international organizations. With many regional branches in Asia and Eastern Europe (Indonesia, Estonia, and so on), F.O.E. resembled the other NGOs in carefully seeking international outreach and a dissociation from too much Westernism. The F.O.E. has sponsored an array of local campaigns against destructive environmental policies or the lack of environmentally positive policies. It has also worked on more general issues, like ozone pollution, the destruction of rain forests, and protection of Antarctica, where it has urged appropriate international conventions. The F.O.E. has gained a large membership base, of 700,000 or more by the mid-1990s. It seeks to codify and disseminate international standards of environmental behavior and protection, rather like the associations that have worked to propagate global criteria for women or labor. World opinion serves as a backdrop rather than an active principle.

It was really Greenpeace, founded in 1971, that brought the principles of world opinion more directly into the environmental movement, with a primary reliance on the force of publicity and expressions of moral outrage as a deterrent to bad behavior, whether governmental or corporate.

Its correspondence with other facets of world opinion was uncannily precise. The movement had vaguely religious underpinnings – the first meeting occurred in a Unitarian church in Vancouver. Quaker principles figured largely: the idea was to "bear witness" to environmental problems in order to force large numbers of people to feel a moral responsibility for redress, which in turn would press the parties involved to change their behavior. Dramatic individual cases played a vital role, again as in other facets of world opinion. Photographs of dead whale calves illegally killed by a Russian fleet, heart-rending pictures of Greenpeace members embracing baby seals to prevent their indiscriminate slaughter – these were the environmental equivalents of the stories of political prisoners or their torture.

Greenpeace began as an effort to stop United States nuclear testing in the Aleutian Islands. One founder, Marie Bohlen, reportedly said, as a test loomed: "Why the hell doesn't somebody just sail a boat up there and park right next to the bomb? That's something everybody can understand."[3] Two separate boats were sent, and though they did not prevent the test they achieved widespread media coverage and elicited thousands of members for the fledgling organization.

By the mid-1990s Greenpeace had active branches in thirty countries, a staff of one thousand, and over six million members worldwide. The organization focused on toxic substances, energy issues and atmospheric degradation, nuclear armaments and plants, and oceanic and terrestrial ecology. As with Amnesty International, decisions were decentralized, and individual branches organized the bulk of the campaigns depending on local targets and issues. As with the human rights NGOs, issues were distributed among Western industrial countries and the developing world.

Although Greenpeace produced a host of educational materials, seeking to shape and mobilize world opinion in terms of environmental morality, it differed from the human rights groups in its tactic of self-made news, designed to dramatize the cause and win wide publicity. Ships that directly blocked French nuclear tests or the harpoons of a whaling fleet, stuntmen who climbed the chimneys of a Dupont chemical plant to highlight its pollution of the atmosphere – these were staples for Greenpeace. They demonstrably gave it media coverage, sometimes successful in winning redress. The group of Greenpeace members who climbed the side of the Time-Life building in New York, unfurling a banner reading "take the poison out of paper," thus won an agreement to convert to non-toxic paper in the production of *Time*. Nonviolent confrontations – "to redress the assault on the natural world by using peaceful direct action" – was the order of the day. Calls for the boycott of particular products or wider petition campaigns also figured in the Greenpeace strategy, but they were secondary to the power of publicity before a global audience. The result, as Greenpeace combined with other international and local environmental groups, was a tremendous extension of the concerns that might be addressed through world opinion.

As with human rights NGOs, the big groups tended to encourage additional entrants, sometimes bent on more direct action. Earth First!, formed in the United States and the United Kingdom in the early 1980s, grew tired of what was seen as timidity and undue bureaucracy in Greenpeace. Its tactics emphasized specific attacks on corporations cutting down rainforests in Malaysia, rather than efforts to mobilize opinion. Demonstrations might seek to disrupt a Malaysian or Japanese tourist office, or a shipment of paper within the United States, as the group refused to either "condemn or condone" acts that resulted in destruction of property. Though not part of world opinion as such, these activists could both build on and fuel a wider sense of concern.

The emergence of an unprecedented armada of volunteer organizations, based on defining and attempting to enforce global standards of political and environmental behavior, and relying substantially, if not primarily, on the mobilization of world opinion, added a vigorous new ingredient to international relations. One commentator contended that Amnesty International's goals and techniques indicated "a qualitative change in transnational social activity."[4] Change or potential change operated in several directions. Reigning political leaders might worry about subsequent international prosecution for abuses – though the effectiveness of this factor to date is debatable. Both Amnesty and Human Rights Watch pushed for international tribunals and for regularization of legal proceedings, not only against ethnic cleansers but against more routine authoritarians like Pinochet of Chile. With clearer success, the groups put pressure both on established governments and on Third World regimes. Greenpeace and kindred organizations could embarrass both governments and, more readily, corporations. The NGOs gained results by urging leaders in Western Europe and the United States (and in related organizations like the Organization of American States and the European Union) to add to their foreign policy goals and their criteria for international favor due recognition of human rights and, to a lesser degree, environmental performance. At the same time, they stimulated responses from many countries in Africa, Asia, and Latin America, which were keenly aware of the downside of international embarrassment or at least eager not to lose favor with the power brokers of the industrial world. The international script was not rewritten entirely, and there were many breakdowns, but there were new actors, and world opinion provided a vigorous chorus whose voice could not be entirely ignored.

The opinion-based NGOs, whether focused on human rights or the environment, took on international issues and increasingly, despite Western origins and headquarters, developed an international constituency. All had members throughout the world. The growth of associated NGOs in Asia and Latin America was striking. Linked to the big human rights conglomerates, for example, powerful organizations like the Union for Civil Liberty, in Thailand, or the Indonesian Legal Aid Foundation supported the same basic causes, helping to develop local campaigns and adding voice to the global standards and global programs. Environmental organizations, similarly, touched base with grassroots protests against degradation, from Brazil to Africa.

All the major NGOs contributed to extending a sense of global standards and responsibilities, in the West and elsewhere. Environmental awareness surged from a minor concern to a major political preoccupation between the 1960s and the early twenty-first century, picked up by some major green parties in several countries and regularly recorded in opinion polls. Sensitivity was greatest in the West. It owed much to specific problems and to local groups, but the sense of a global movement, and the dramatics and pedagogy of Greenpeace and its companions, helped the process along. Here was a case in which local concerns easily blended with a belief in the need for international action; global warming, for example, might create effects in Jersey or New Jersey, but its causes were largely located elsewhere. Human rights, or protection of baby whales, depended more heavily on the classic moral empathy component of world opinion, but this empathy gained ground as well. Without a surge of world opinion the key groups could not have got off the ground, but as they mobilized they extended the surge immensely.

The mutuality of the relationship was the key point for world opinion. The unparalleled expansion of international NGOs and local groups with global connections created unprecedented opportunities to mobilize world opinion and to expand the number of topics on which world outrage could find expression. The diversity and divisions among the NGOs prevented fully coherent leadership (which would in any event have reduced the spontaneity on which the emotional side of world opinion depends). But there is no question that, with the principal NGOs, world opinion now had leadership as never before. The whole development was predicated on the power of world opinion, on a realization of what it had accomplished and could achieve. The NGO surge enhanced more than created. But the combination of the surge and of world opinion's growing potential opened a new chapter for world opinion's role as a forceful, independent factor in a host of policy domains.

8

WOMEN AND LABOR: CONTEMPORARY WORLD OPINION AND SOCIAL ISSUES

From the clear departures embodied in the proliferation of opinion-related NGOs, we turn now to a murkier aspect of recent world opinion: the continued effort to take on social issues, particularly those of women or workers. We have seen that some of the NGOs adopted those aspects of the women's cause that could be identified in terms of human rights abuses, which indicates both the importance of the cause and the inability of older approaches to handle it successfully. Despite important developments, it is fair to say that world opinion still did not manage to assimilate fully an expanded social agenda in the postwar decades.

The resurgence of world opinion after World War II included renewed attention to social issues, particularly the conditions of women, children, and workers. These issues were already on the world opinion agenda, as was discussed in chapter 3. But the agenda had also included some serious limitations, compared with the related question of slavery and forced labor. Domestic concerns usually overshadowed international ones. Ideological and other divisions limited the capacity to mobilize widespread opinion. It was not easy to generate widespread outrage or a sense of moral responsibility for abuses that were severe but not as dramatic as those of slavery and sometimes tended toward the routine – abuses such as lack of political voice or excessive hours of work. These constraints, combined with a highly motivated leadership, tended to push global advocates for workers and women toward a reliance on international organizations and conferences more than on world opinion per se.

Even amid renewed campaigning, many of these characteristics have persisted in the gender and labor field. The basic point is clear-cut: a definition of international standards for women or for workers still did not generate widespread emotional support, even though various international organizations steadily and in many ways successfully amplified what these standards were. Competing issues nearer home and disagreements over what the standards should be and who was really responsible for offenses retarded global opinion.

In the labor field the Cold War limited international opinion for many decades, generating competing statements about workers' rights and abuses. On the Communist side, where internationalism in principle burned bright, the Cold War tended to generate demonstrations on broader political issues, such as N.A.T.O. or other military or diplomatic programs, rather than focusing attention on working conditions per se at the global level. On the capitalist side, reformist unions gladly pointed out the lack of freedom for worker associations in Communist countries, but had more difficulty rising above these contests to an international focus on workplace abuses. In the heady 1950s, when union strengths crested in the West, purely national action often seemed adequate. Both sides in the Cold War might turn a blind eye to working conditions in Third World countries, in favor of currying their leaders' support for "free world" or Communist alignments. In this situation, the quiet, somewhat bureaucratic program of the International Labor Organization, pressing for agreement on standards for certain aspects of working life, continued to make greater headway than world opinion campaigns.

Prospects for international activity were livelier on the women's front, where Cold War issues, though not irrelevant, loomed less large. The revival of ardent feminism in the West, from the late 1960s onward, provided a new spur, similar to that which had first galvanized a world opinion effort in the decades around 1900 but had then faded somewhat. The associational thrust seemed to pay off with renewed support from agencies in the United Nations, providing a kind of world opinion that was not dependent on a great deal of grassroots organizing, at least outside the Western world.

Other developments, for labor as well as for women, gave new impetus to world opinion in the social sphere. From its inception, the United Nations and its great power supporters envisaged a more active social agenda than the League had done, though there was continuity as well. United Nations proclamations on women were more sweeping than those the League had generated. The International Labor Office was able to build on some of the basic research accomplished in the interwar years, to work for a wider range of conventions applying to workers. A second spur, beneath the surface of the Cold War, involved decolonization. A host of new nations, eager to seem respectable, turned to international agencies for help in drafting constitutional codes applying to women and workers. There was renewed interest in Latin America as well. Associational efforts often seemed to pay off with ringing assertions of commitments to equality of pay or protections for child workers. What might be called the "neo-imperialist" aspect of world opinion also came into play – the sense (in the West and in Western-dominated international organizations) that former colonies needed guidance and standards to live up to the demands of civilized society where workers and particularly women were concerned. And by the 1990s the force of globalization brought new conditions and new, or newly publicized, abuses to international attention. For women to some extent, for workers more generally, globalization provided new opportunities to dramatize certain kinds of problems and to drive home a moral responsibility that had not been easy to rouse against older abuses.

Limitations, however, remained daunting. The same globalization that spurred new concerns about working conditions also put new pressures on workers, many of them women. It was not at all clear that international attention was adequate to counterbalance the new pressures for exploitation. The associational approach could also race ahead of real change. Many conventions could be negotiated, many constitutional provisions could be celebrated, without real improvements in people's lives. The workings of world opinion were complicated in all areas, but the social agenda continued to impose great challenges. Disagreements beneath the surface of conferences and proclamations were one problem. Lack of adequate concern was another. The fact that real change had to occur in families and workplaces, and not at the level of law and formal state policy, was perhaps the most daunting. World opinion in the social realm remained a work in progress.

Reliance on international organizations to advance women's causes seemed to pay off handsomely after World War II. This enhanced enthusiasm for associational efforts more than for grassroots campaigns for women in distant lands.

The diminution of some nationalist passion in the Western nations, plus growing decolonization increased the number of countries with some feminist leadership and facilitated wholehearted stumping for global rights. During the 1950s, for example, Iranian women's leaders played a significant role in spurring international attention to gender issues. Picking up on themes evoked in the 1930s to less effect, the United Nations Charter and the Universal Declaration of Human Rights stipulated legal and political equality for women, along with equal pay for equal work. A series of conventions in the 1950s and early 1960s, under the U.N. or subsidiary groups, insisted on equality in politics, rejected inequality in work, pay, and education, and insisted on free consent to marriage, all in the name of "the equal right of men and women to the enjoyment of all civil and political rights." The principle of women's inclusion in the panoply of global human rights was now officially inscribed. As part of "International Women's Year" in 1975, an article on international law claimed a growing concern "of the larger global community" for "outlawing sex-based discrimination" in all forms. "The particular norm against sex-based discrimination finds expression in many authoritative communications, at both international and national levels, and is rapidly being defined in a way to condemn all the great historic deprivations imposed upon women as a group." The language of moral responsibility, basic in world opinion, could be increasingly assumed in the gender arena. As a U.N. spokesperson put it, "In a global community aspiring towards human dignity, a basic policy should, accordingly, be to make the social roles of the two sexes, with the notable exception of childbearing, as nearly interchangeable or equivalent as possible."[1]

The number of international women's organizations soared, particularly in the 1970s: fifty-nine new groups emerged between 1940 and 1974, then another thirteen per year between 1976 and 1985, when United Nations backing for a "Decade of the Woman" stirred wide support. Particularly interesting was the emergence of new groups in Africa, such as the African Women's Task Force (1985), continuing the expansion of the associational effort. Above all, there was now direct United Nations sponsorship for key international meetings, at five and ten year intervals beginning in 1975, with massive delegations increasingly dominated by the Third World. At the 1985 Nairobi conference, for example, sixty percent of fifteen thousand participants were from non-Western, non-industrial nations (with 157 nations represented in all). It became routine for periodic conferences, and the General Assembly, to issue proclamations against violence against women, stipulating rape as a war crime, pressing for equal access to education. Relevant non-governmental organizations were urged to advance the agendas that emerged from the larger gatherings on specific individual states and to help monitor the results. In the same vein Amnesty International launched its major campaign in 2004 on violence against women, claiming that a third of all women worldwide were subject to violence and that world opinion should construct new barriers to this abuse. The associational approach to women's issues, pioneered a century earlier, was both enshrined and vindicated.

There were rough spots. International meetings could be complicated by Cold War disputes, and the Communist International ran its own series of women's meetings in the immediate postwar years. Other tensions, like the conflicts around Israel, could distract. More relevant disputes, for example over family values, could complicate agreement on certain aspects of women's rights. A 1994 U.N. conference in Cairo, on population issues, saw delegates from Muslim nations (including Iran) plus Vatican and United States representatives resist explicit endorsements of certain birth control options because of conflicts with religious principles. Third World representatives recurrently chastised Western women's leaders for attitudes they found patronizing or irrelevant.

There were also some interesting hesitations on the part of key international agencies. The question of female circumcision in northeastern Africa, deeply ingrained in local custom, was a case in point. Most European colonial regimes had deplored the genital mutilation of women, but had not moved against it actively lest resistance be aroused: imperial stability was more important than global standards. But several colonial administrations did ban the practice in principle after World War II, in the waning days of empire. On the other hand, some African nationalist leaders defended the practice on grounds of custom and family unity (the great Kenyan leader Jomo Kenyatta noted that it was a "mere bodily mutilation"). The U.N. Social and Economic Council urged the World Health Organization (W.H.O.) to take action as early as 1958, but its requests were rejected on grounds that "the ritual operations in question arose from a social and cultural context." African women's leaders moved into action in a U.N. seminar in 1979, noting adverse consequences to women's health. Finally W.H.O. budged in 1982, asserting that international standards required a vigorous stance against female circumcision, urging governments to ban the practice, and encouraging education among women "to inform the public about the harmfulness of female circumcision."[2] By this point, global criteria were in place, but the decades of hesitation were revealing: international opinion, even through associations, could falter in face of local custom, particularly given a new liberal sensitivity to relativism in cultural standards. This hesitancy, in turn, could easily limit the later effects of global pronouncements: circumcision retreated slowly. For whatever combination of factors, there did not seem to be as many easy targets for world opinion in the gender arena as foot binding and sati had provided a century before.

What was more impressive, however, was the extent of agreement emerging from conferences, prepared for by prior decades of international collaboration among the leaders of the women's movement. The 1994 population conference, for example, ended with a ringing endorsement of the principle of expanding educational opportunities for women, on grounds that these provided a vital spur to knowledge of both purposes and methods of family planning – a result in keeping with the goals of global feminism for more than a century. Enshrined in meetings of this sort was substantial agreement on the idea that women did have transnational issues and rights, that international associations, drawing from national women's groups, were appropriate bodies to deal with these matters, and that uniform declarations could be obtained. There was, through the organizational mechanisms now embellished by United Nations sponsorship, a global world opinion on questions of gender. Historian Judith Zinsser, who participated in the 1995 Fourth Conference on the Status of Women, in Beijing, stated the claim directly: "No one can deny" that the United Nations efforts, and the networks they spawned among women's organizations, "made the rhetoric of feminism the common phrasing of national and international speeches and reports. The world community has acknowledged that women live in an inferior condition and that this situation is not acceptable."[3] Zinsser also stressed the unanimity of the "international endorsement." Given the recency and radicalism of feminism, the achievement of a definable world opinion around its principles constitutes a tremendous change.

Yet the effectiveness of this form of world opinion, heavily shaped by the leadership ranks and disproportionately Western, continues to raise questions. Even Western feminists, encouraging and enjoying the resurgence of international contacts after a decade of largely domestic concerns from the mid-1960s to the mid-1970s, often continued to concentrate on the difficult issues of work and household nearer home. Then they were further distracted by the decline of the feminist current amid conservative revival from the 1980s onward. It continued to be debatable whether the global sympathies involved in women's rights deprivations in distant lands were keen enough to support more direct and conventional manifestations of world opinion. Sympathy in principle was not in question any more: the patronizing attitude of Western feminists to "their Asian sisters" around 1900 was a thing of the past. But the priority of international outrage was still in some doubt, which helps explain the eager embrace of global conferences with rather less grassroots campaigning or careful monitoring of outcomes.

Moreover, disputes about what women need and deserve, beyond the sometimes slender ranks of feminist leadership, may well have inhibited manifestations of widespread world opinion, well into the twentieth century and even today. Western values of greater individualism, sexual openness, and more legal and informal independence from family controls have not been uniformly appealing even to the leaders of women's causes in Africa and Asia. Correspondingly, the habits of women outside the West, when not simply constrained by male domination, may have qualified active beliefs in a common sisterhood, on the part of Western feminists. It was hard not to carp, for example, when some Middle Eastern women began apparently voluntarily to resume the veil. Divisions in goals and practices, in other words, may have inhibited the formation of a genuinely global opinion and possibly even the fervor of Western sympathizers when they turned their attention worldwide to a lukewarm female audience. The same divisions also slowed the development of the kind of embarrassment about gender backwardness that would motivate reactions to global statements. Even female circumcision could find its relatively unembarrassed public defenders.

Finally, there is the question of drama. Antislavery, and the campaign against white slavery, succeeded because of gripping personal tragedies and the possibility of mixing the assertion of universal moral responsibility with deeply moving cautionary tales. Did women's rights not lend themselves to this approach, or was there a failure in leadership, an undue devotion to principles in the abstract? Lack of a vote or routine husbandly domination were, and remain, legitimate issues of human rights, but they may be inherently more difficult to dramatize save in immediate, local, or possibly national contexts. Specific rights abuses involving women have the capacity to rouse: recurrent examples include evidence of mass rape during wars or ethnic cleansings, and the powerful international reactions to verdicts of death by stoning for convicted female adulterers in Nigeria or Pakistan. The Amnesty anti-violence campaign in 2004 sought to build a new international consensus – for this would be a novel set of standards on a global basis – through vivid individual cases and images. Connections can be made, but they may fail to apply fully to key portions of the women's rights agenda. This gap makes the associational approach to world opinion, relying more heavily on committed leadership, almost unavoidable.

All this is not to say that the associational approach was ineffective. For starters, it did succeed in claiming its legitimacy as an expression of global advocacy, in asserting the mantle of world opinion as an expression of morality. And it managed this over a long period of time. This is why the approach found such ready responses in the League of Nations and the United Nations. At the level of proclamations by global organizations, world women's rights advocates have succeeded impressively well at winning acceptance of Western-derived statements of equality under the law, and rejection of traditional forms of male dominance, from violence through deprivation of schooling. Repeated, passionate assertions have won huge results when mediated through non-governmental organizations and frequent conferences. Constitutions in most new or revived nations after World War II inserted a clause on the equality of the sexes as a matter of routine, from China (1954) to Paraguay (1967) to Israel (1951) to Egypt (1972) – a remarkable, if not sometimes largely rhetorical, testimony to the power of what had been established as a global norm. It was revealing, in 2002, when the United States sought world backing for its conquest of Afghanistan, that abuses of women served as a propaganda centerpiece, reflecting doubtless sincere American belief in the importance of the issues involved but also an assumption of predictable global response. International feminist pressure has accounted for the addition of rape to the standard list of war crimes, a major innovation by the United Nations in 1993. Though the mechanisms of forming and expressing world opinion were distinctive for most women's rights issues, the results in terms of developing a widespread global consensus in principle have rivaled those of the campaign against slavery. A form of world opinion has been shaped without the apparatus of mass support, and it wins many global victories.

More practical impact is often another matter, as many feminist assessments have already established. It is not too hard to get sweeping declarations. There have been few systematic efforts to establish a definite alternative to the global rights approach, aside from the backlash of a few nations in the Islamic world. Declarations are frequently followed by widespread compliance on the part of national governments, quick to sign the latest international convention. Often, however, the chain breaks after this point.

Several African nations, for example, responded quickly to United Nations initiatives from 1975 onward. The President of the Ivory Coast claimed a Women's Year in 1975 and set up a Ministry of the Women's Conditions and for the Promotion of Women, with a commission exploring the implementation of legal and economic equality. Changes in the law did facilitate women's choosing jobs on their own and controlling wages and personal property. The Organization of African Unity (O.A.U.), in 1981, recognized "international standards of general application designed for the protection of rights of women." A new O.A.U. charter vowed elimination of "every discrimination against women . . . as stipulated in international decorations and conventions," in the name of "regulated civilized behavior and conduct toward all human beings."[4] Courts in a number of countries, including Tanzania and Botswana, ruled in women's favor when they sought control over property or their children, citing their nations' signatures on various international conventions. But, these rulings aside, the monitoring of new rights was scanty, and specific legal enforcement often fell short. The African Charter itself offered a hedge: though endorsing equality under the law, it also allowed states to take into consideration the virtues of their historical traditions and values and the need to preserve family cohesion. In the later 1990s, furthermore, many courts began to backpedal, as in Zimbabwe, ruling against women's right to inherit property in favor of an "African tradition" that only men could own. It was not clear that very much had happened in the real world of daily relations between men and women.

An exceptionally sympathetic (male) civil servant in India describes a similar mix. Sudhir Varma was greatly inspired by the Year of the Woman in 1975 and by materials resulting from the Mexico City conference. He took a leading role in helping to organize women's groups in the state of Rajasthan, encouraged also by a related federal measure that reserved a third of the seats on village councils to women. Clearly, international proclamations had impact. But Varma also conveyed his own discouragement at continued domestic violence against women and the inequity of educational opportunities in his region. Women council members there were, but they were usually chaperoned by their husbands, who openly told them what to do. Varma also noted a decline in interest by the 1990s, as the world opinion that had been mobilizable on women's issues seemed to turn to other matters. Again, the associational approach to global standards had ambiguous results.

A final example, from Africa again, may seem particularly poignant, demonstrating both that world opinion has an impact and that, because gender issues are so deeply personal, the impact is often limited. In Niumi, a village in Gambia, a number of international organizations have worked to end female circumcision. Some Gambian women's groups have taken up the issue as well, and many expatriate women have written to condemn the ritual. But many ethnic groups persist in the practice – ninety percent of Mandinka women are circumcised – on grounds that it is traditional and essential for acceptance not only into marriage but also into women's meetings. Even some highly Westernized women participate, while often opposing the practice in principle. Gambia's President spoke out against "such harmful practices" in 1997, but political resistance prompted a change of tone. In 1999 he argued that the practice "is part of our culture and we should not allow anyone to dictate to us how we should conduct ourselves." Even worse, he cautioned Gambians who spoke out against female circumcision: "There is no guarantee that after delivering their speeches they will return to their homes."[5]

Finally, there are new issues. Examination of world opinion on conditions for women frequently focuses on the interaction, or clash, between global standards and local traditions, and without question this covers a good bit of the topic. But women's situations do not stand still. Two kinds of problems were emerging around 2000 that raised new challenges for global concern. The first involved new uses of women as scapegoats amid more general social change. A series of reports from India and Pakistan revealed a modest but troubling pattern of dowry murders, in which men, disappointed with what their new wives brought by way of property, simply vented their rage by killing them. Accounts of this upsurge in the Western press brought expressions of outrage, but it was not clear that international opinion had any particular staying power against such private kinds of violence. More obvious were the problems resulting from globalization's impact on some women. Exploitation of women workers in factories producing for global markets, and the reviving international trade in women for sex were the two most obvious downsides to recent global trends where women were concerned. Could world opinion respond? The question merged with the evolving connection between world opinion and labor.

Two kinds of global standards applied in the labor field in the decades after World War II. There was the divided internationalist rhetoric emerging from the Cold War, and there were the ongoing associational efforts spearheaded by the wider-ranging efforts of the International Labor Organization and kindred international bodies.

Dominant issues for the I.L.O., as it moved forward after World War II, included complaints about lack of freedom for worker associations, and issues of racial discrimination in the workplace. Most were directed at the Communist bloc and, secondarily, at former colonies. Attacks on South African apartheid figured prominently in I.L.O. deliberations until the 1990s, conjoining the larger groundswell of world opinion. Child labor received growing attention, with complaints about the sale of children for work in Haiti, Thailand, India, and elsewhere; in Thailand, discussions included concerns about sexual exploitation. The range of accepted standards expanded. It was only in 1947 that the I.L.O. issued a convention affirming that "It shall be an aim of social policy to abolish all discrimination among workers on the grounds of race, color, sex . . . in respect of . . . wage rates, which shall be fixed according to the principle of equal pay for work of equal value."[6] Special emphasis on equal treatment for women won approval in many new national constitutions and codes – 124 countries ratified the I.L.O. convention on the subject, and many countries, from Spain to Jamaica to India and Nepal, incorporated the principle in revised labor charters, particularly in the early 1990s. As before, however, most I.L.O. measures were adopted quietly, without reference to public opinion and with great reliance on careful negotiation and the application of social science expertise. As before too, many ringing agreements proved difficult to implement, particularly amid widespread poverty in the Third World and amid adjustments to market economies in transitions from Communism. The role of the I.L.O. in promoting global standards expanded, but its ability to win real agreement on these standards, from employers or from impoverished families, remained complicated. Arguably, I.L.O. discussions – quite apart from agreement or implementation – did not keep pace with the evidence of worker exploitation emanating from the global relocation of factories.

The continuing limits of world opinion in the labor field shone through dramatically where children were concerned, despite renewed discussion in the 1990s. Observers attuned to the I.L.O., even before World War II, could confidently predict the emergence of global standards concerning the use of children for work – their age of entry, their rights to opportunities for schooling, their protection from certain kinds of dangerous or degrading jobs. Even beyond the I.L.O., it was reasonable to expect a clear movement, now that slavery was largely dealt with, on to the next most obvious form of exploitation of workers against (or at least without) their will.

By the 1920s standards for the treatment of child workers were widely agreed upon throughout the industrial world. Beginning with British measures in 1833, most industrial societies had progressively limited the hours children could work, regulated their ages, and introduced other forms of protection. Child labor reform quickly included interest in international measures, if only because it was clear that conditions in individual countries were deeply affected by competitive conditions abroad. French advocates by the 1840s, for example, were pointing to British measures as evidence that it was safe to take action nationally without loss of an edge in labor costs – while they also urged further steps throughout the industrializing world. Here, too, was promise for the future development of world opinion on the subject. To be sure, early measures were strictly national. They also were often hollow, since inspections and effective punishments were lacking. The addition of compulsory school requirements, from the 1870s onward (earlier in the northern states of the United States) contributed to more systematic work limitations. By 1900 few children younger than twelve were formally employed in the industrial societies, at least in the cities, and protective measures were beginning to spread to Eastern Europe and Japan. By the 1930s even younger adolescents were mainly removed from the labor force save in part-time capacities. A massive amount of passionate discourse, over many decades, went into the contention, not only that children should have time secured for schooling – a huge transition from the standards of agricultural society but that children had an innocence and physical vulnerability that must be protected against the harshness of excessive labor. The debate seemed over in the West and some distance beyond. Here, surely, was the basis for a larger movement of world opinion against the misuse of child workers – if not against child labor pure and simple – around the globe. Surely, a Western-based world opinion could be mobilized toward the conversion of childhood from work to schooling on a worldwide basis. It would not be surprising if implementation lagged, but at least rhetorical conventions could be established, statements of policy if not full practice.

Until the 1970s, this evolution seemed underway. Western reformers confidently assumed that their standards could apply more widely, which was after all the way much world opinion has been formed. Discussions in the I.L.O. and elsewhere seemed fruitful. But the process proved largely stillborn.

As early as 1919, in its first session, the I.L.O. established fourteen years as the minimum age for children in industry. The I.L.O. continued to discuss child labor through the 1930s and after World War II, and in 1973 proposed raising the minimum age to fifteen, noting that child labor was hazardous to the physical, mental, and moral well-being of the individual while also preventing effective schooling. Here was an associational commitment to a clear global standard that extended the experience of Western industrial nations to the world at large. But here also is where the process began to break down. This second minimum age convention, which also included measures against child soldiers and other abuses, was adopted by only 102 countries, too few to constitute international approval. And so, in terms of international legal standing, the measure died on the vine.

Objections varied. The United States displayed its recurrent dislike of binding extra-national agreements, and it had specific concerns about disruptions of the use of children among migrant workers, so vital to agriculture in many parts of the country. A variety of Asian and African countries argued that, in their poor economies, child workers were absolutely essential to family survival and to global competitiveness in labor costs. There were also a variety of specific objections to the I.L.O. convention on grounds of complexity as well as difficulties of implementation.

As this recurrent ILO campaign stalled, there was a remarkable absence of international outcry. Of course there were disappointed reformers and union leaders in many industrial countries who – whatever their level of altruism – worried about the impact of cheap foreign child labor on their own members. But no further steps were taken for almost a quarter-century, and the issue – committed advocates aside – largely disappeared from view. What had been a promising extension of world opinion dissipated: it turned out that there was no clear world opinion on child labor, a situation that remains true today.

What were the barriers? Two factors are clear. First, a number of developing countries, now free to express their opinions thanks to decolonization, simply disagreed with the effort against child labor at this point in time. Their views were shaped by the primacy of their own economic concerns, where low labor costs were essential, and by the undoubted beliefs of many families that child labor was both normal and desirable – a view encountered in the West too a century-and-a-half before, when child labor reform was just getting off the ground. The second factor was the rapid decline of the labor movement in the West, with the United States in the lead. Labor pressure counted for less, which left national politicians free to ignore issues of this sort, which might anyway seem remote and complex.

Arguably, several other developments amplified these factors. The changes in liberal sentiment, toward greater sensitivity to cultural differences, may have played a small role: was it legitimate to try to dictate standards for children to other societies? More important was the rise of multinational corporations eager to seek out cheap labor, quite willing to include child workers in this process, and hostile to international restrictions or even undue international scrutiny. Intensification of global competition not only involved direct use of teenage workers by multinationals with branches in Southeast Asia or Africa; it also pressed local firms toward even greater reliance on child labor, seeking savings on labor costs to compensate for their competitive disadvantages in technology. Growing commitment to free market economies as the motor for successful development had similar consequences. The International Monetary Fund (I.M.F.) and other agencies pressed Third World governments to reduce their social spending as a means of freeing up resources for private investment. India, for instance, reached an agreement with the I.M.F. in 1991 which slashed social spending on food subsidies, health, and even education, in favor of supporting the export industrial sector. The reduction in government services, combined with diminished economic regulation, increased the dependency of poor families on the earnings of their children while also enabling local elites, as employers, to run exploitative and unsafe businesses free from regulatory enforcement. And again, there was no global response. Despite precedents and potential, there simply is no global passion about child labor.

Interpretations vary. Children's advocates can plausibly lament the triumph of latter-day capitalism over appropriate concern for children's welfare. Many Western participants in world opinion, quick to subscribe to environmental causes, have not adopted the cause of unseen children as readily as might have been expected. (This is true even within countries: the American middle class has proved surprisingly tolerant of a rapid expansion of poverty among children in the inner cities; in this sense global neglect is part of a larger pattern of dismissal of the children of others.) Obviously, many people in many societies – including the West – are eager to take great pains for their own children in ways that have no bearing on their reactions to global concern for children. Deliberate ignorance and denial are considerable; some may explicitly prefer the lower prices they enjoy as consumers of international goods than any commitment to reform.

A more sympathetic take is possible as well. The failure of global child labor standards may constitute a salutary step in the development of world opinion, as viewpoints from outside the West gain increasing leverage. The role of international capitalism in muting child labor action complicates this judgment. But it would arguably have been premature to attempt a global statement against child labor of any sort, another hollow gesture that would have achieved little impact in the Asian and African target areas. The hesitancy also reflects a recognition of cultural differences, for example in the definition of the age of effective adulthood. It is better to advance more slowly and realistically, and to explore possible compromise, rather than to presume a glib triumph of Western standards.

It is also true that the absence of a loud global voice on subjects like child labor encourages continued reliance on an associational approach to world labor issues, and we have seen that there are pluses and minuses to this approach. Dependence on groups like the I.L.O. for global pressure may have limited the opportunity to develop more genuine world opinion and passionate outrage of the sort that has been cultivated in, for example, the environmental area. It's a tough call, and one that deserves continued attention.

What is clear is that the subject of child labor is not dead, though it has perforce been scaled back given the absence of international agreement. The United Nations Conventions on the Rights of the Child (1989; ratified by all countries except the United States and Somalia), though not addressing labor per se, did seek to assure access to schooling. Global associations returned to the charge more directly during the 1990s. The Anti-Slavery Society, still alive and well, sponsored the Global March against Child Labour in 1998. This united a number of NGOs from around the world to press for further action and included wide publicity for individual children caught in situations of tragic exploitation. Anti-Slavery also continued to campaign for greater protection of migrant workers, particularly children, producing materials, including videos shown widely on television around the world. The Federation of International Football launched a "foulball" campaign in 1996, refusing to buy or endorse soccer balls sewn by children (part of the larger movement against sweatshop labor; see chapter 9). In 1999 the I.L.O. adopted a new agreement, entitled the "Worst Forms of Child Labor Convention," by which it hoped to win wider support from member governments. Targets were use of children as soldiers, the sexual exploitation of children, and the employment of children against their will as pledges against household debt. (Debt bondage had been tackled before, by the United Nations, as part of the ongoing struggle against what amounts to forms of slavery.) The United Nations followed in 2000 with protocols against child soldiers and the use of children in prostitution and pornography. The latter protocol covered the sale of children as well. The associational apparatus directed at labor abuse, developing and voicing global standards, was reviving, now recognizing the limits of any international mandate and attacking specific problems rather than child labor in general. Individual governments pushed for change as well. American legislators recurrently threatened tariff action against countries that exploited child labor too extensively; here, the intent was more to protect labor conditions at home than anything else, and the results risked driving children in the poorest countries to even worse forms of abuse. In 2004 the papacy issued strong statements against child soldiers and sexual exploitation, contributing to what seemed to be an emerging consensus on global criteria for appropriate treatment of children.

Amid these developments the number of children at work did gradually begin to decline. Almost eighty-eight million children below fifteen were at work worldwide in 1980 – more than seventy percent of them in Asia; in 1990 the figure had dropped to seventy-eight million, with particularly dramatic declines in East Asia. Only in Africa and, even more strikingly, South Asia were rates of child labor actually rising. Overall, trends seemed to be at work, even in the absence of effective world opinion, that were transforming childhood; which raised the possibility that, in future, world opinion might coalesce not just against abuses but against child labor itself as an abuse. The jury was still out.

❖❖❖

World opinion hovers on the edges of major social issues involving women and workers, including child workers. Standards are available, associational definitions have advanced, but there is extensive disagreement and a surprising lack of widespread, mobilizable passion. Some expansion of world opinion may have occurred, as in targeting some of the worst abuses of children at work or in gaining growing awareness of physical and mental indignities inflicted on women during civil strife. The associational approach seemed to work better for women's issues than for those of labor. There is no denying the importance of the various U.N. and conference resolutions on women, despite problems of implementation and disagreement in certain parts of the world. Labor, beset even more than feminism by the weakened domestic political base, additionally faced not only disputes between traditional and reform factions but also the inroads of global capitalism.

There were obvious questions for the future, in terms of clarifying what global standards could win acceptably wide agreement and where, if at all, a sense of outrage could be generated – particularly beyond dramatic individual cases of human rights abuse, where again women seemed to draw more attention than workers or even children.

By the 1990s some observers were becoming increasingly pessimistic. Feminists bemoaned not only the implications of the resurgence of conservative strands of Islam but also the relativism that, they argued, was watering down liberal passion. Martha Nussbaum warned of a worship of difference:

> Highly intelligent people, people deeply committed to the good of women and men in developing countries, people who think of themselves as progressives and feminist and antiracist . . . are taking up positions that converge . . . with the positions of reactions, oppression and sexism. Under the banner of their radically and politically correct "anti-essentialism" march ancient religious taboos, the luxury of the pampered husband, ill health, ignorance, and death.[7]

Many labor analysts, understandably disappointed by the limitations on international standards in the past, expressed great anxiety about the apparently unstoppable march of global capitalism. They worried that trade unionists, already at a great disadvantage, would surely slide back further given the growing ease of moving industrial operations from one country to the next, seeking the lowest wages and the loosest regulation – a process some aptly termed "social dumping." Others contended, however, that international trade union solidarity was improving, thanks both to the new globalization threat and to the end of Cold War distractions. They pointed to renewed actions of solidarity, for example a successful international day of action in September 1996, when Scandinavian, Australian, Canadian, and American workers targeted ships bound to or from Liverpool, to bolster a major strike in that British port. Purely national protests and nationalist vision were on the decline. Again in 1996, the International Federation of Chemical, Energy, Mine and General Workers (a British union) formally resolved that "action has to be planned on an international basis right from the start."[8] These currents were furthered, for European labor, by the growing success of the European Union, which automatically forced a rethinking of the geography of labor organization away from separate national programs.

Problems were clear, but prospects were not clear-cut. There was some response, relevant to the mobilization of world opinion as well as associational activity, to the increasingly global challenges of capitalism. In this context, another new direction of world opinion, directed towards monitoring the activities of multinational corporations, gained growing importance. Emerging in the 1970s, closely associated with some of the opinion-based NGOs like Greenpeace, this extension provided new successes in combating abuses of labor (including attacks on local labor organization), as well as launching protests associated with product quality and, above all, environmental degradation. Women's issues were embraced in this current as well, though mainly through involvement as workers. It would be daring to argue that this new approach was yet adequate to the task, in either the environmental or the social arena, but it was an important departure for world opinion, as we will explore in the next chapter.

9

WORLD OPINION, THE CORPORATIONS, AND THE ENVIRONMENT

Two significant innovations in world opinion toward the end of the twentieth century intertwined. Global concerns began to be effectively expressed about certain aspects of international business behavior, as multinationals were added to the list of targets against which world opinion could be directed. Environmental criteria constituted a second addition, expanding the range of standards and atrocities that could rouse activity across many borders. Many environmental targets were themselves corporate, eliciting the same tactics as did other aspects of international business behavior. But the move into the environmental arena also included efforts to influence government policy, so this facet of contemporary world opinion generated further complexity. Both corporate and environmental targets depended greatly on the expanded activities of NGOs, the addition of consumers as well as environmental units to the roster of global mobilization, and an intermixture of local and international NGO operations. Characteristically, as we will see, new local mobilizers first identified problems and then called for international back-up, including the outpouring of opinion and related pressure that the larger organizations could provide, particularly as the internet accelerated both information and reactions.

Here was where world opinion – though part of globalization, indeed an early if not always effective part – began to take on, not globalization as a whole, but specific manifestations of globalization as it intensified in the later twentieth century.

The movement of world opinion into the arena of corporate activity had several spurs. Most obvious was the growing importance and visibility of corporate policies, and the internationalization of their operations. No one concerned about labor or the environment could rest content with a purely political approach, targeting the policies of governments alone. It became increasingly clear that many corporations had powers exceeding those of many states. From the 1970s onward, no one could argue that national action would suffice; indeed, national movements and opinions seemed secondary to the need for a global scale. The inclusion of corporate activities into the scope of world opinion had one decided advantage over the more conventional political targets: product boycotts, or their threat, or other disruptions of consumer attraction, could greatly amplify the force of publicity and outrage. The environmental area offered special opportunities as well to influence Third World states.

The expansion of world opinion into the corporate and environmental realms was an important change. It maintained, however, the central features of world opinion. It was based on a sense of universal rights and standards and an often passionate reaction to their abuse. It fed on individually dramatic stories, which continued to be crucial in generating focus and emotion. It maintained the recent turn to world opinion not simply as an expression of justice but as a recourse against forces that otherwise threatened to spin out of control. And the direction of world opinion against corporate excesses maintained the tension between associational activity and the mobilization of a wider public audience. Labor movements as well as many NGOs were crucial to this further extension of world opinion, but there was a larger reservoir as well.

The idea of international regulation of corporate behavior was not new. Financial criteria to govern international investment were elaborately discussed in post-1945 economic conferences such as Bretton Woods. They hardly stirred public attention, however, and interest in international codes declined in the 1950s and 1960s. The 1970s, however, saw a revival of interest, with the expanded United Nations participating in the discussion as a means of moderating the growing power of multinationals.

A crucial issue won growing international attention from the 1970s onward, as public health workers – both local and foreign – began to report higher infant mortality rates in Third World countries when mothers bottle- rather than breast-fed their childen. The timing was interesting, since the recognition of corporate targets coincided with growing economic globalization, with the increasing activities of NGOs, and with a lull (as will be discussed in the following chapter) in more conventional diplomatic and policy targets stimulating public outrage. But the key initial spur was the recognition of a new and deadly corporate behavior, compounded by initial defensiveness on the business side.

The problem turned out to be starkly simple: bottled milk was made by adding water to dried milk formulas produced and actively promoted by international companies like Nestlé. The water was typically polluted and was not properly sterilized by the families, for want of both knowledge and easy means. Hence the rising infant mortality. An initial conference on the subject, spurred by a physician running the Caribbean Food and Nutrition Institute in Jamaica, led to some articles that began to receive wider attention from the press. United Nations health groups started to warn against over-promotion of artificial infant foods in 1974, and then a variety of NGOs, both church and consumer groups, took up the cause. A British group, War on Want, produced a documentary entitled *The Baby Killers*, which a Swiss Third World Action Group translated into German under the title *Nestlé Kills Babies*. (Nestlé sued the Swiss organization, which led to still-wider media attention as the case dragged through the Swiss courts.) In 1977 a United States group formed to promote a sweeping product boycott against Nestlé. Both United States government inquiries and World Health Organization conferences sought codes of conduct for manufacturers in the infant foods industry. Ultimately an international W.H.O. code was devised, mainly restricting promotion (for example, by nurses in the field); Nestlé accepted the code and the changes began to result in substantial decreases in infant mortality.

Crucial to this resolution, completed in 1984, was the global public pressure on a company that had long fancied itself a "mother's friend." The company was also vulnerable because consumers could easily find alternatives to its vast product array, from chocolates to teas to other foods. Ironically, in a number of court cases developed around the issue of product representations in Africa and Asia, Nestlé usually prevailed. But legal victories paled before the judgments of the world community. The NGO network quickly blossomed to include over a hundred groups working in sixty-five countries: the Nestlé boycott committee itself had eighty-seven institutional members, including the National Council of Churches in the United States. The boycott, according to one mobilizer, was the "most devastating attack [ever mounted] on corporate advertising in the Third World."[1] Although organizations played a crucial role in producing dramatic pamphlets, films, and advertising, it was public passion that provided the fundamental goad to reform. The issue was widely framed as a question of ethics, with Nestlé branded as "immoral" in the best traditions of world opinion – and it turned out that corporations, as least in the consumer sector, did not like that kind of label.

The process took a while – the boycott began in 1977 and gained ground gradually – but it had clear result. Public involvement was intense. Children got into the act in the United States, pressing parents to adhere to the boycott and providing information about the surprising range of Nestlé products. Although religious organizations played an important role, as usual, the advent of consumer groups was more striking as they sought and found a genuine international voice.

Nestlé faced its own version of embarrassment, just as various states had done when confronted with world opinion. Boycotts helped immensely, as the company gradually moved from hostile defensiveness to a recognition of the need for greater accommodation to new international standards and for active interaction with leading opinion organizations.

As the controversy about infant feeding declined, thanks to acceptance of general global standards, questions arose about new targets involving product quality, for example international production and exchange of pharmaceuticals. Neither world opinion nor relevant organizations became fully engaged, however. The Nestlé campaign, directed to a lesser degree at some other corporations, showed the potential for boycott-supported world opinion in identifying and correcting multinational abuse. But this potential was soon directed toward different areas of corporate behavior.

One of the most recent extensions of world opinion to corporate behavior, developing from the late 1980s onward, has involved a new kind of attention to working conditions. The goals are novel or at least more open to global support than labor issues had been in the past, and a distinctive set of mobilizing groups is involved. But key tactics spilled over from earlier successes in cases like Nestlé, including a reliance on the power of publicity and potential boycotts to elicit corporate response. As with the infant foods campaign it has often proved easier to bring corporations to heel, at least temporarily, than to win from governments general reforms of labor policies.

During the 1990s and early 2000s, global standards were applied to labor abuses in new ways. The developments were surprising in some respects. The globalization of manufacturing created severe new pressures on working conditions around the world, as multinational corporations deliberately sought out overabundant low-wage labor in countries that had an ineffective regulatory apparatus. Many sweatshops offered exceptionally low pay and unsafe conditions and forced excessive hours on their workers as well. Conditions were compounded, in industries like textiles, by the common practice of contracting out to local factories (not always locally owned) that produced for many multinational brands, which partially disguised the involvement of the multinationals. Worker resistance frequently erupted against harsh conditions, but it was equally frequently repressed by lockouts, dismissals, and even violence.

Many observers worried that global pressure would collapse against the lure of cheap goods made by unknown workers in distant lands, that the advance of economic globalization would smash resistant voices. The concern was all the more appropriate given the checkered record of world opinion in the labor area historically: it was not clear that international standards were widely accepted in this field. Even in noting the greater engagement of world opinion in labor issues, with some positive results, there can be no claim that world opinion has kept pace with the spread of abuses. But a new relationship is being sketched, and some observers find considerable promise for the future.

Several novel factors have brought world opinion to bear on international working conditions more clearly than before. International standards are available, and here the older associational approach pays off. The International Labor Organization has a number of relevant conventions, for example on the freedom to organize, on the unacceptability of servile labor, and on unusually harsh conditions for children. Many of the exploitative factories blatantly violate the standards, which sets up exactly the kind of juxtaposition, the possibilities for defining injustice, on which world opinion thrives.

Although many consumers in the West and the Pacific Rim blithely purchase items without concern for the conditions in which they are manufactured, it is possible to feel some sense of active responsibility for the conditions of the distant, unseen producers – the same type of sentiment that has generated moral outrage in other instances, beginning with slavery. The workers may be remote, the direct employers unfamiliar, but the resultant products carry common brand names in Europe and the United States, and this means a moral implication whatever one's level of empathy with the unknown workers. Further, although not a dominant theme except among trade union participants, there can be concern as well for the impact of foreign sweatshop conditions on local workers and even national economies. An interest in elevating international standards as a means of protecting jobs at home provides another motive, of enlightened self-interest rather than moral altruism, for a new level of involvement.

The same economic globalization that helps produce or widen the new exploitation creates greater awareness of the exploitation: globalization causes problems, but it also feeds the expansion of world opinion as a partial corrective. People who know nothing of traditional working conditions in Southeast

Asia or Mexico gain new knowledge when these conditions (or sometimes even slightly better ones) characterize the activities of well-known companies: it is both easier to acquire information and more dramatic to present it when the responsible agents are themselves familiar. The new global information technology vitally complements these developments. It is now possible to transmit information about labor abuses widely and very quickly, generating global response before companies can succeed in wearing their workers down by dismissals or other retributions. World opinion can now, thanks to the internet, feed on dramatic outrage about individual cases rather than focusing simply on more general policy issues that lack immediacy or human appeal. Heart-rending accounts of worker suffering and even death have dotted the appeals for new standards of decency in labor treatment. The common use of group pictures of the workers involved provides further immediacy (even though, somewhat jarringly, the workers are usually smiling – a triumph of media protocol over suffering).

The democratization of the late twentieth century is the final ingredient. Many countries have become sufficiently open that international trade unions and other mobilization groups can win access to information about local working conditions. (Substantially closed societies like China, despite abundant exploitation, do not generate major campaigns because the necessary information is lacking.) Local support groups – like the Legal Aid Society in Indonesia – have gained enough freedom of operation to link to the new international effort. They can both provide dramatic detail and channel expressions of support. These countries also have labor laws crafted according to international criteria, as a matter of national respectability if not deep commitment. The laws are not consistently enforced and many local officials remain corrupt, but both global and domestic protest groups can point to the existence of national rules, not just abstract international standards, and ask simply that they be enforced. The factor of embarrassment can enter in quite readily.

In this new and dynamic context both established national labor movements and new NGOs began to develop strategies that closely paralleled those of Amnesty International or Human Rights Watch, with some of the same capacity to use global outrage but some distinctively effective tactics as well.

In 2003, 537 workers in a textile factory in Bandung, Indonesia (P.T. Kahatex Sweater) walked out, fed up with wages below the national legal minimum, required overtime for no pay, and other abuses. The company immediately fired them and locked them out. Either the workers informed the Legal Aid Institute of Bandung, or representatives of the Institute had been earlier involved. In either event, news of the situation quickly spread to NGOs in Europe and the United States. They, in turn, organized an active, web-based campaign for petitions both to the Indonesian government for equitable treatment and to the international purchasers from the plant – including mainline firms like Nike. German and Austrian groups were particularly active, because the plant was owned by some German capitalists. Internet solicitations included pictures of the workers and dramatic quotes from those who had been forced to work despite illness or injury. Pressure on the buyers and the European owners was the crucial component, because they were vulnerable to consumer retaliation through boycott and to more general embarrassment after more than a decade of unfavorable publicity, and because it was the Western buyers and owners who were capable of putting real pressure on the local management. In this instance justice triumphed. The workers were rehired and pledges were made to observe Indonesian law on matters such as wages and hours. The NGOs urged members immediately to change their websites in order to end all appeals for product boycotts; a reformed company, however belatedly responsive, should be rewarded.

Another campaign also involved Indonesia. The website dramatically proclaimed, in the best tradition of universal moral criteria, "Workers' legal and human rights are not respected in PT Busana" – another textile factory. Workers daily faced accidents from unprotected motorized sewing machines, which drove needles into fingers; pay was derisory, with no allowance for the required overtime, and the hours were exhausting. Yet a protest effort resulted in immediate dismissal. The global response orchestrated by the NGOs, was swift and passionate: "No one should be forced to work unpaid overtime, or be paid illegally low wages," and the right to strike was enshrined in the Universal Declaration of Human Rights. What could outsiders do? Sign the petition, which was then directed to the European and American corporations, famous brands again, that purchased the factory's product. Signatures poured in from individuals and groups, the latter including not only unions but consumer cooperatives and specialized NGOs such as the Durham Anti-Sweatshop Campaign based in the northern English city. Signatories mirrored the contemporary geographic bases of world opinion in general: mostly from Western Europe, Australia, Canada, New Zealand, the United States, and the Pacific Rim (particularly South Korea in this case, but also Japan and Hong Kong), with significant representation from Mexico and Brazil and scattered involvement from Malaysia and elsewhere, plus considerable local support from NGOs in Indonesia itself. The multinationals were publicly pressed to take responsibility for the conditions in which their wares were produced. Inquiries were pledged and the local company finally caved in, at least temporarily, to the pressure of world opinion mediated by capitalist anxiety about image and sales.[2]

Clothing workers were not the only targets of global concern. Two British NGOs, Fairtrade and Christian Aid, galvanized other European and East Asian groups to establish basic working codes in Asian toy factories, directed toward better working conditions and improved safety, after a rash of factory fires.

The role of the mobilizers was crucial in these campaigns, which involved hundreds of individual factories each year, primarily in Mexico, Southeast Asia, and increasingly parts of Africa. In addition to the large American and European unions, two new groups were particularly prominent. In Western Europe, the Dutch-based Clean Clothes Campaign, with branches in all major countries and with links to unions, consumer programs, and other organizations, served much the same function as the big NGOs in the human rights field. It issued Urgent Appeal emails focusing on the grievances of workers in individual factories and also on attacks on trade union officials, along with clear indications of ways to get involved. The American-based Students Against Sweatshops, with branches on over two hundred college campuses, concentrated on pressing university administrators to withdraw university logo patronage from sweatshop factories. The groups were closely linked to the Workers Rights Consortium, which actually provided the international researchers to investigate conditions in factories, mainly in Third World countries. Another U.S.-based group, the National Labor Committee, complemented the more systematic inquiries by generating massive public relations efforts against sweatshop operations in which particularly well known companies or public figures were involved. The Committee became famous by highlighting the involvement of celebrity Kathy Lee Gifford in ownership of Central American factories producing for K-mart amid distressingly substandard working conditions. The actress cried and vowed remediation. A more recent Committee target was hip-hop superstar and fashion designer Puff Daddy, branded with poor working conditions in his source factories in Latin America.

Campaigns against sweatshops have sensitized the multinational companies that own major clothing and shoe brands. Some, including Nike and Reebok, have formed their own Fair Labor Association, which investigates labor condition charges but faces criticisms that it is not really active in following up worker claims of abuse. The Nike story is fascinating. In 1991, when first confronted with evidence that workers in one of its plants, in Indonesia, were being beaten, the local manager claimed, "It's not within our scope to investigate." Five years later, the company acknowledged responsibility for working conditions in subcontracted factories and developed its own code of standards. Imperfect, as recurrent actions against Nike attest, but a real change.[3]

The Nike case became one of the most noted efforts of world opinion, centered in this case in the United States and Europe, against corporate foot (or shoe) dragging. The case began slowly, with efforts by a few muckraking journalists to call attention to low wages and miserable conditions in factories in Indonesia and later Vietnam. A new NGO, Global Exchange (founded in 1988 on a general human rights platform) soon adopted the cause. It took three years of agitation to generate any significant media attention, but finally the *New York Times* and soon the cartoonist Gary Trudeau took the case to heart. Church groups also picked up the cause, the American Interfaith Center on Corporate Responsibility, a significant investor in its own right, insisting on remediation of abuses. Student groups began agitating against university purchase of Nike products. These wider recognitions provided an opening for more dramatic tactics. Global Exchange brought union organizers who had been fired by their Indonesian factory to the United States and arranged a variety of media events in Nike retail outlets, some of which encountered abusive behavior from store guards, which merely enhanced the publicity. Kathy Lee Gifford, now a remorseful convert to good labor practices, embraced one of the Indonesian workers publicly, while dismissive remarks by a far greater star, corporate endorser Michael Jordan, added fuel to the fire. By 1996–97, the furor was slowing Nike sales and affecting its stock values. It became obvious that the company needed to commit, at least in principle, to closer monitoring of the labor policies of its suppliers.

The sweatshop campaigns in general have also galvanized various unions to take on international issues and widen their tactics. The American textile union U.N.I.T.E., for example, routinely organizes campaigns against globally linked sweatshops. In 2001–2 the union publicized poor working conditions in factories producing clothing for a French retail giant, Pinault-Printemps-Redoute (P.P.R.); the targets included a warehouse operation in Indiana. Tactics involved demonstrations in front of P.P.R. stores in Europe, a mock Gucci catalogue (one of the chain's brands) showing pictures of workers in the Third World, and direct solicitations of P.P.R. shareholders. At one point workers from various countries were flown to Indiana to concert strategies with their American counterparts. Ultimately, contract arrangements were made allowing American workers to bring complaints to P.P.R. on behalf of workers in sourcing factories. U.N.I.T.E. was also active, through collaboration with unions in Latin America and Indonesia, in developing programs to support workers in Lesotho, with demonstrations at Gap stores in New York and extensive press conference activity. Gap agreed to reopen a factory in Latin America that had closed in response to unionization, while improving conditions in Indonesia – though conditions in Lesotho remained untouched as local movements splintered.

All of this occurred despite, or to some extent because of, the continued weakness of the labor movement in the United States and to a degree in Western Europe. Global standards were becoming increasingly identified that allowed wide appeals to world opinion based both on morality and on international law, particularly as defined by I.L.O. conventions. The campaign to improve labor conditions relied perhaps excessively on reactions to individual cases, rather like the human rights movement in its post-1945 infancy; this reactive approach was particularly true of the Clean Clothes organization. But there were attempts as well to support trade union activities in ways that would provide some ongoing voice and improvement in developing nations, and there was some effort to enlist corporations, sometimes in concert with local governments, to stipulate acceptable basic standards in advance of opening a new plant. Always, of course, questions of impact were easier to raise than to answer. Many agreements were doubtless hollow or quickly rescinded as soon as the glare of publicity receded. Even a growing international network could hardly claim to keep pace with the expansion of the global economy. Yet it remained true that international opinion, mobilized against sweatshop labor, provided a new kind of corrective to global abuse, as moral outrage spread to new aspects of conditions for workers around the world.

The addition of environmental criteria to world opinion began in the later 1970s as evidence of global effects of local corporate and state activities began to accumulate. Even earlier, in the surge of world opinion against the nuclear arms race (discussed in the next chapter) environmental impact had loomed large; though the target was weaponry, it was the effects of nuclear testing on human health that attracted the greatest outrage and led to the clearest results. Nowhere was the combination of genuine shock over violations of sensible humane standards, and a growing fear of policies run amuck clearer than in the effort to use world opinion to correct environmental abuse.

Animal rights concerns focused some of the earliest environmental movements that crossed national boundaries – though the efforts were heavily concentrated in the West. During the 1970s a number of campaigns developed to "save the whale." Educational programs spread and petitions were circulated, though tactics concentrated on pressing national governments to negotiate new limits, plus some attempts to disrupt abusive fishing fleets as a means of calling wider attention to the issue. Activities continued into the 1990s, with some success in achieving international agreements. Similar programs were applied to ivory in the 1980s, more directly attempting to limit consumer interest as well as to promote negotiation; in this case Japan, though an extensive importer, ultimately joined in. Public and sometimes disruptive campaigns against the use of furs spanned the Atlantic in the same period.

The surge of concern about global warming and other transregional environmental impacts began to affect public opinion in many regions. Repeated reports about the enhanced greenhouse effect and its roots in tropical deforestation and carbon dioxide emissions reached the popular news magazines and became increasingly common currency. Specific disasters promoted public opinion as well. The Bhopal tragedy in India in 1984, when many people were killed and injured by spills from a Union Carbide chemical plant, prompted public agitation in India and the United States; in the latter, demonstrations affected stockholder meetings and, though corporate response was sluggish, particularly in terms of paying indemnities to those directly affected, the Union Carbide campaign drew unions and community organizations toward greater environmental responsibility. Major oil spills had similar effects.

By the mid-1980s a host of new international and also local NGOs began to develop, eager to protest environmental abuse by both corporations and national or regional governments. The combination of a periodically available world voice plus extremely active organizational activity had measurable impact on both corporate and governmental behavior.

In the late 1980s attention began to focus on the environmental impact of the McDonald's chain. In both the United States and Western Europe considerable concern was voiced about the non-biodegradability of McDonald's wrappings, particularly the ubiquitous styrofoam. Critics also noted extensive purchases of Brazilian beef, from ranchers who increasingly encroached on the Amazonian rainforest. Pickets recurrently circled McDonald's restaurants – usually small groups, but persistent. Websites were created, like McSpotlight, to detail the various environmental and labor misdeeds charged to the chain. The pressure had direct impact on reputation and sales. By 1990, after the usual initial defensiveness, the company was ready to change tactics. As a spokesperson put it, "Because of our high visibility, the environment was becoming a monumental problem for us."[4] The solution? A renunciation both of styrofoam and of the importation of Brazilian beef. Plus a loudly announced partnership with the Environmental Defense Fund. Plus, a bit later in the decade, other public relations efforts such as sponsorship of a pseudo-rainforest in the Adelaide zoo, complete with massive self-congratulatory publicity. The effort left critics cold, as they focused on the obvious window dressing; but there was serious change as well, and obvious indication of the power of mobilized world opinion when there was potential effect on sales.

Again in the 1980s, rubber tappers operating in Brazilian forests along the Amazon came to wide public attention in the United States and Western Europe. The tappers had a long history of tension with government authorities committed to more efficient development and with local landlords eager to reduce the forests in favor of more profitable agriculture. Union organizing activity developed in the late 1970s, but so did more ambitious government plans for road and dam construction that would shrink the forests. Periodic violence escalated. The Catholic Church in the region helped support the rubber tappers and to draw their cause to the attention of global groups such as the Environmental Defense Fund and the World Wildlife Fund. A leading local organizer, Chico Mendes, won a United Nations award in 1987, and a host of NGOs and wider public petitions pressed the Brazilian government to change its priorities to protect the environment and the workers who depended on it. Another rubber tapper was invited to speak in Germany. The weapon of choice, besides sheer publicity, was pressure on lending agencies, particularly the Inter-American Development Bank, which threatened to reduce investment support. Then Mendes was assassinated, presumably at the instigation of local ranchers. This was precisely the kind of tragic catalyst on which world opinion so often depends.

Outrage spread quickly on both sides of the Atlantic. Brazilian leaders, understandably annoyed by foreign insistence that an international public claimed a stake in national environmental policy, were amazed at the furor over the "very ordinary termination" of an obscure labor leader.[5] As a result the government was forced to modify its development plans; in consequence the rate of local killings dropped markedly and the government did assert more control over illegal cuttings. World opinion had another partial success to register, and its role not only in environmental protection but also in offering a voice to extremely vulnerable, otherwise isolated groups was confirmed.

Global environmental activism continued on these fronts in the 1990s, with particular focus on Southeast Asia but also, still, Latin America and parts of Africa. Success was mixed, and the impact was complicated. Associational activity often trumped public opinion. But the latter was available and its potential expression through boycotts or changes in investment policy helped sustain the campaigns of the NGOs – which also depended on the same wider commitment to global standards for their funding.

A number of multinational companies locating operations in Indonesia encountered reactions similar to those being applied to sweated labor when they proposed extensive incursions into forests or the hasty disposal of chemical wastes. Local NGOs – and there were about fifty in northern Sumatra alone by the middle of the decade, focused entirely or in part on environmental issues – frequently reported concerns to the government, even launching lawsuits against apparent violations, while also contacting international NGOs such as Greenpeace or Earth First!. These in turn would add to the commentary to governments while also holding the companies up to international scrutiny. In several cases, planned factories were either scrapped or modified, by companies that feared global public reactions (and their impact on sales and stock values) far more than the strictures of local government agents.

Pressures were also applied to governments directly when plans called for deforestation. An Indonesia rayon company gained a government license to work in the national forests, ignoring existing rules covering waste disposal. The response was an NGO lawsuit, with support from public opinion and funding from abroad, spearheaded in this case by Friends of the Earth International and the World Rainforest Movement. Another case, from Botswana in the late 1990s: a local environmental group contacted Greenpeace about a government water project. Rumors spread that the international lobby was going to call for a boycott of diamonds, similar to efforts that had been mounted against furs; this inaccurate report was enough to cause the government to drop the project.

A combination of tactics was applied to environmental issues. The myriad international groups sponsored educational efforts and tapped media coverage. They pressed United Nations agencies and conferences to formulate appropriate environmental standards, with particular attention to deforestation and climate change, but also species protection and other goals. Legal action against corporations could join in, as in a 1996 suit against Texaco, mounted in the United States on behalf of Ecuadorian victims of environmental damage in the 1980s. Wide membership in the NGOs brought both funding and the potential for public outcry. Relationships with international investment agencies, including the U.N. Development Fund as well as the World Bank, were particularly potent in motivating governments to demonstrate some responsiveness. For their part, many governments (Indonesia was again an example) were more tolerant of environmental protests than of other forms of dissent, partly because of the links to foreign investors but also because they seemed less threatening to political authority.

Third world countries provided the principal targets for world opinion and the mobilizing groups, because of the looser regulations and the constant multinational corporate pressure to seek maximum environmental advantage. But world opinion, and associated boycott efforts, could be directed at countries like Japan, for what were regarded as exploitative fishing practices, or at companies operating in the West. Tuna canners, for example, were pressed to end their acceptance of fishing practices that killed many dolphins, and public attention plus boycott threats did force some units to alter their policies and to protest their innocence as widely as possible. Finally, international and local pressures alike combined to force real changes in the environmental policies of multinational corporations. Some of the shifts centered on pious pronouncements and public relations moves, but there were some substantive results as the new relationship between public opinion and corporations placed the environment on an active agenda.

The addition of multinational corporate targets and environmental concerns to the agenda of world opinion is an important development, expanding the criteria applied to international morality – including environmental morality – and moving beyond some of the limitations of the purely associational approach that had dominated international labor standards previously. The corporate category remained distinctive in world opinion. Because corporations were usually sensitive to expressions of outrage, at least at the public relations level and sometimes beyond, world opinion often did not need the massive petitions and demonstrations required for other issues. A hundred signatures and a department store demonstration, with the potential for wider boycott, often generated some response. Volume was replaced by careful tactics, for example in withdrawing university purchasing support from certain producers. Brand name corporations and public figure investors could be moved more readily than, say, authoritarian states. In the process, however, a sense of global standards did emerge concerning the environment and sweatshops, and there was real passion behind them. A public that might be occasionally moved to reconsider their purchases on the basis of global signals, and a deeply committed group of mobilizers with their immediate supporters opened a promising new chapter in world opinion.

These were early days, reminiscent in some ways of domestic battles against corporate exploiters within Western society a hundred years before. There too, muckraking publicity drew attention and could occasionally force a real retreat. The question was whether this historical analogy would hold. For in the industrial countries, dramatic appeals ultimately broadened over time into support for regulations of labor and some environmental actions, which in turn allowed more durable progress to take hold. We simply don't know if comparable developments – the capacity to move from individual examples to larger legal developments – will emerge on the more global scale.

There were other complexities too in the environmental area. First, it was not easy (either for mobilizers or for their targets) to define clearly what precise standards world opinion was willing to uphold. How much deforestation was too much? What animal species would find particular favor with a global public? It was clear that world opinion could be roused against particularly heinous cases of environmental (or labor) abuse, particularly if accompanied by violence and intimidation against local groups, but a full definition of global environmental norms, that would be consistently supported by opinion and not simply the ever-active NGOs, had yet to emerge.

Many companies noted a related problem, familiar enough from world opinion's deployment in other areas: a somewhat whimsical selection of targets. A leading multinational chemical company pulled back from one opinion-contested enterprise in the early 1990s, in Indonesia, only to find out that several local operations were allowed to proceed with even more destructive activities with no reaction. Their conclusion, understandably enough, was to ignore the threat of outcry next time around, because undue responsiveness put them at a competitive disadvantage. The same issues will doubtless beset many of the sweatshop campaigns, where again a company-by-company approach risks dramatic inconsistency. World opinion and its mobilizers face an obvious challenge as corporate targets and environmental concerns – innovations still, in the larger scheme of things – work into the regular agenda.

Another complexity follows from the familiar Western base of the loudest global voices and the leading international NGOs. Particularly in the environmental arena, a tension has developed between the more programmatic approach of the organizations in the industrial world – the "North," as the environmentalists often put it – and the more flexible requirements of local NGOs in Southeast Asia or Africa. Asian interest adds a useful component, and some mobilization groups, like the Asia–Pacific Peoples Environmental Network, avoid the predominant Western base. But the fact remains that, confronted with environmental hazards, the interested voices in the North tend to work for maximum protection. Local groups, by contrast, often seek a compromise position that will prevent undue damage but will also accommodate the need for jobs or agricultural land. Local groups may also resent the ready threat to withhold international investment funds, again because of their dual interest in development as well as environmental protection. There have been times when local groups have simply not appealed to world opinion, for fear of its clumsy or excessive application – even when they lost ground as a result.

Partly because of these complexities, partly because of the novelty of the effort, the impact of world opinion on corporate activities and the environment has been limited. Abuses proceed more rapidly than world opinion can thus far address. Many companies yield to pressure briefly, only to resume their agenda when attention turns to another problem; or they move to a different area – China, for example, which is less open to global scrutiny. Public relations ploys rival real policy change. It is hardly surprising that this new frontier for world opinion has yet to be fully defined – and perhaps it will always escape full definition. Despite inadequacies, it is also true that the world-opinion–NGO combination constitutes one of the only counterweights against the downsides of the accelerating global economy.

10

WORLD OPINION AND STATECRAFT: A GROWING RECORD

In its decisive third, still contemporary phase, world opinion has played an increasing role in international relations and in the human rights policies of many individual states, first in addressing the most frightening features of the Cold War and then more broadly, as the Cold War began to recede from the 1970s onward. In the initial outpouring, massive demonstrations over nuclear weaponry and Vietnam provided a new basis for public involvement in international issues, surges of passionate outrage extending to many parts of the world, not just sectors in the West. The impulse to direct world opinion toward statecraft was not new: moral outrage had previously applied to real or imagined abuses by the Ottoman Empire, and it had gasped and failed in reaction to military developments in the 1930s. But past judgments had been almost entirely Western and their targets had been limited. Now, changes in the global economy and world politics gave expressions of opinion a wider base than before, and the targets multiplied as well. Success was not uniform, but there were some splendid victories in which world opinion contributed greatly to reducing inhumane or dangerous policies.

The resurgence was fueled not only by extensions of moral outrage, but by growing fears that, unchecked, world diplomacy and military policy risked spiraling out of control. Increasingly, conjoined with a more assertive United Nations policy on human rights, world opinion began to count in the diplomatic arena, and it gained a bigger appetite in the process. The revival and extension of world diplomatic opinion in the 1950s and 1960s provide the general context, and then key specific cases suggest the new dimensions and explain why global reactions emerged as inescapable factors in the political calculations of individual states.

❖❖❖

The early stages of the Cold War generated vivid responses among several publics. Developments such as Soviet seizure of states in East-Central Europe and the Berlin blockade and airlift had massive repercussions in international opinion. But a real global opinion did not form, largely because of the new gap between "East" and "West" and because of the internal political divisions, and diversities of reaction to United States dominance, within major Western European countries. The preoccupation of much of the rest of the world with issues of decolonization and national independence further complicated global reactions, though by the 1950s some voices from India, Egypt, and elsewhere began to be raised against the folly of the Cold War. Yet, amid varied moral responses, it would be hard to identify a global voice. The Korean War, for example, though diversely viewed, did not produce clear reactions in anything like a world opinion.

Pacificism had been badly damaged by World War II, when most people at least in the Western world (outside the defeated powers) decided that war could have valid goals. A few pacifist groups survived, and the early stages of the Cold War goaded some to new efforts; but there was no large international voice on the subject of war.

Reactions to the advent of the atomic bomb and then the early stages of the nuclear arms race between the United States and the Soviet Union provoked some response. Anti-war and world federation groups played a role here, as did concerned scientists in many regions. Public opinion in several Asian and Latin American countries, like India and Venezuela, expressed new fears. But widespread reaction soon receded in Third World countries, even as leaders like Nehru continued to express a vigorous anti-nuclear stance. Local issues, including decolonization, or a sense of sheer powerlessness seemed to cool any widespread response. Japan generated more consistent protest, after some initial silence. By 1948 eighty-one percent of the Japanese public was opposed to any Japanese rearmament, and hostility to atomic testing grew as well. Protest activities also surfaced in the United States and Western Europe, reflecting new anxiety. In countries like Norway, where no possibility of nuclear development existed, public demonstrations took on considerable proportions by 1948.

By that time, however, Communist parties and leaders had begun to exploit anti-nuclear sentiment, setting up a number of anti-war organizations and triggering demonstrations among the party faithful in countries such as France. Amid growing Cold War tensions, these activities soon discredited the movement and inhibited any real world opinion on the subject. By 1953, disarmament sentiment was in retreat, as several leading countries, the Soviet Union at their head, joined the nuclear club and as exhaustion or escapism predominated more generally.

This was not a permanent situation, however. The later revival of disarmament activity provided general stimulus to the vigorous re-emergence of world opinion in the diplomatic and military sphere. World opinion here reflected two vital developments: first, along with the legacy of moral responsibility, the new and palpable fear that policies of the leading powers were jeopardizing the future of humanity and that only world opinion could provide a corrective; and, second, given the global nature of the threat, the rapid and active involvement of almost every society in an unprecedentedly widespread outpouring.

The stimulus was the increasing testing of nuclear weapons and the spread of the hydrogen bomb, both taking shape by the mid-1950s. As in earlier instances of world opinion, general principles and dramatic individual events conjoined: an American nuclear test in the Marshall Islands in 1954 delivered radioactive fallout to a Japanese fishing boat, ultimately killing one crew member and hospitalizing many. Extensive outrage followed quickly. It was spurred by some conventional players, like pacifist groups and the international Society of Friends; other Church groups quickly joined in, first in Britain and then elsewhere. New players included a number of leading scientists and intellectuals, headed by the likes of Bertrand Russell and Albert Schweitzer. This group, eventually including key Soviet figures, organized widely publicized conferences, like the Pugwash series. Japan took an early lead in wider reactions, for obvious reasons; eighty-six percent of the Japanese public opposed U.S. tests. A host of meetings generated massive demonstrations and petitions; the Japanese Council against Atomic and Hydrogen Bombs (Gensuikyo) became a permanent organizer. Heavy involvement of Buddhist leaders added a significant new element to world opinion, at least in the area of peace and disarmament. Huge movements developed also in Australia and New Zealand, stimulated by the use of the Pacific for testing. An Australian spoke of the "absurd risks" of nuclear testing and the spread of weaponry, arguing that people either "reach the point of self-destruction or organize for peace."[1] Western Europe joined extensively, with marches of tens, even hundreds of thousands in countries like Germany, where a new voice was stirring amid realization that the country was particularly vulnerable. The papacy spoke out, even before its larger conversion to participation in world opinion. Considerable outcry developed also in the Middle East, particularly in Egypt against French testing in the Sahara, and leaders spoke out in Africa; India was also engaged. Only Latin America, perhaps feeling safely distant, remained relatively quiet in what was otherwise an exceptionally widespread protest from the late 1950s into the 1960s.

Geographic extent was matched by new social outreach. Many women leaders and women's organizations groups played a decisive role, particularly in grassroots efforts in, for example, Britain and Scandinavia. Youth groups and college students were also heavily involved.

Marches, petitions, sit-down strikes on potential sites, even international law suits against American policy all attempted to drive world opinion home. Though most action was national and only loosely coordinated, aside from the scientific meetings, the International Confederation for Disarmament and Peace was set up in the early 1960s to provide some linkages, representing over a hundred organizations in forty-four countries.

The governments involved initially resisted the pressure, claiming among other things a Communist plot; and there was some manipulation by the Soviets, though this was not a primary component of the movement. Gradually policymakers reacted more positively. A number of individual states, like Japan and Sweden, renounced nuclear weaponry on the strength of global standards. And the United States reconsidered. As President Eisenhower noted in 1958, in speaking to the passionate nuclear advocate and anti-Communist Edward Teller, "the new thermonuclear weapons are tremendously powerful; however they are not . . . as powerful as is world opinion today in obliging the United States to follow certain lines of policy."[2] There have been few more eloquent acknowledgements of this new diplomatic force.

And policies did change. From a moratorium on testing in 1958, the first test ban treaty was negotiated in 1963. The Soviet Union welcomed the opportunity to score points with world opinion. British policymakers shifted their orientation rapidly. Somewhat more hesitantly, under Eisenhower and then Kennedy, the United States leadership followed suit, at least with regard to the atmospheric testing that had caused such environmental peril. The thirst for ever more sophisticated weapons, proved by testing, yielded to other imperatives. As an Irish Committee on Nuclear Disarmament paper noted, "the marchers, the letter writers, the petitioners, in dozens of countries on every continent" had made their anxieties felt.[3]

This accomplished, the movement began to fade. Many advocates had hoped for outright disarmament, and world opinion was still felt in some of the later non-proliferation treaties. But with the worst abuses corrected and with acceptance of the improbability of moving the great powers to further major concessions, attention shifted elsewhere – including to the war in Vietnam. Some leaders also lamented a growing "numbness," as people became accustomed to a nuclear world in which little short-term danger seemed to emerge. The result was an ongoing inconclusiveness in the relationship between world opinion and the nuclear threat, one of many cases in which success remained in some ways incomplete. But success was undeniable, the only clear instance to date in which a global outcry forced reconsideration from the great powers on fundamental issues of peace and security.

Further efforts did follow, for example in recurrently protesting installation of new United States missiles to bases in Europe during the 1970s. A large nuclear freeze movement arose in the early 1980s, again capable of rousing hundreds of thousands of demonstrators in key cities in the industrial world. There was some link between earlier global concern about nuclear testing and the spate of national efforts protesting the uses of nuclear power, again in the 1970s.

It was the Vietnam War that most obviously replaced nuclear testing as the focus of world opinion in the diplomatic arena. Movements against the war, or at least its extension through bombing campaigns against North Vietnam and neighboring countries, stimulated wide protests in the later 1960s. By 1969 seventy-five percent of the Japanese public opposed United States tactics. Substantial Buddhist opposition developed in many Asian countries, including South Vietnam. Along with many American Jewish organizations, opposition groups gained ground in Israel, sometimes arguing that an active voice was essential to avoid the kind of silence that had facilitated the Holocaust. Considerable moral passion was generated as the war dragged on and pictures of civilian deaths and injuries gained wide dissemination. Waves of anti-American demonstrations occurred in Western Europe. One march ended in stoning the United States embassy in London, in what one observer called the "worst riot in memory." Cultural outposts such as the Amerika Haus in Heidelberg, Germany were turned into fortresses against the possibility of mob attack. Revulsion grew particularly among younger Europeans, for whom the war brought a loss of faith in American leadership.

In Europe and the United States, the global voice against the war joined the larger currents of youth protest, making it easy to identify the high emotional pitch but less easy to pinpoint the precise diplomatic criteria world opinion was seeking to advance. Although it was true that suspicion about United States policy began to inform world opinion (influencing American participants in it as well as Asians and Europeans), other elements of the youth outburst proved powerful but transitory, beginning to recede by 1973. The impact of global protest against the Vietnam War was also hard to trace. The intractabilities of the war itself plus domestic unrest within the United States had far more influence on the U.S. government than did global concern; Lyndon Johnson and Richard Nixon did not display the sensitivity that Eisenhower had shown toward anti-nuclear sentiment a decade earlier. Other non-Communist governments also largely bypassed the protest in favor of support for United States policy. Japan, for example, actively facilitated United States supply operations despite public hostility to the war.

After the war drew to a close, several years passed without a major eruption of world opinion on the diplomatic front. New issues, like the oil shortages of the 1970s, provided distractions. The expanding activities of the human rights NGOs focused attention on a series of individual incidents, and the new corporate targeting attracted global attention. Perhaps, in the wake of the youth movements, a certain fatigue set in where high-stakes policy issues were concerned; it is not always easy to explain periods of quiet or retreat in world opinion. The pause was brief, however, and world opinion roared back on a number of policy fronts in the early 1980s.

Along perhaps with its success in contributing to the ending of nuclear testing, the greatest single triumph of world opinion in the twentieth century was its role, along with strong internal pressures, in unseating the system of apartheid in South Africa. The ingredients were ideal: a morally unjustifiable policy that also produced dramatic individual atrocities, plus enough Western involvement, through the European origins of apartheid's architects and corporate investment in the resource-rich nation, to stimulate a sense of responsibility as well as outrage in the West European and North American seats of world opinion. But effective world opinion – and particularly its still-essential Western component – was slow to form. In this case much of the initial movement took shape in Africa and Asia as part of the larger anti-imperialist current. Even with greater Western involvement, spurred by dramatic specific atrocities, observers long argued that the mobilizers' tactics would prove ineffective, which made the ultimate success all the more intriguing.

The apartheid system took shape from 1948 onward, after the Nationalist (Afrikaner) triumph in South African politics. International reaction formed early among many new Asian and, soon, African nations. Each African and Asian conference from the 1950s onward expressed outrage at the apartheid system, and representatives made vigorous presentations at the United Nations.

The argument was simple: the apartheid system contradicted established global standards concerning human rights and fundamental freedoms for all, as U.N. Article 55 specified, "without distinction of race." This was not exactly public opinion, but the moral content and geographical range were striking. In the 1950s spokesmen from nations such as Pakistan carried the international argument. In the face of opposition to U.N. action from the West, a few nations, like Japan, Turkey, and much of Latin America, held back. A massacre of South African protesters in Sharpeville in 1960 spurred additional resolutions. By this time the emergence of new states in Africa had relocated the centers of Third World agitation on the subject. Frustration with Western-led equivocation mounted. In the 1960s the United Nations became willing to discuss economic sanctions, but the deliberations were meaningless without explicit support from the industrialized sector.

Though not initially very potent, movements against apartheid began in the West during the 1950s. They called forth many components familiar from earlier world opinion struggles: Church groups, specific new NGOs, and individual leaders with a high moral profile. In the United States, this was enhanced by vigorous sentiment among African Americans and civil rights activists, and the surge of agitation for racial equality within the nation during the 1960s provided increasing fodder for petitions and efforts to establish boycott actions against apartheid. The earliest anti-apartheid organization in the United States, the American Committee on Africa (A.C.O.A.), formed in 1953, brought together a coalition of black and white civil rights leaders. It organized educational programs and a variety of demonstrations, while raising money for relief projects in South Africa. Its activities accelerated during the 1960s, and the A.C.O.A. opened a Washington office at the end of the decade (at a time when the U.S. government, under Nixon, was insisting on conciliation of the white regimes in Southern Africa). Joining with several mainstream Protestant denominations – Episcopalians, Presbyterians, and the United Church of Christ – the A.C.O.A. created an Office on Africa as a permanent lobbying arm, hoping to persuade Congress to press the South African government.[4]

During the 1970s a variety of African American activist groups stimulated public discussion of apartheid, which joined national legislators with community action organizations. African Liberation Day marches occurred in 1972 and 1973, bringing over ten thousand people to Washington – a noticeable number but, as skeptics also noted, well short of a meaningful proportion of the population by the criteria employed to evaluate demonstrations. A variety of academics, many interested in education and research about Africa, sponsored their own petitions and forums, while Church groups expanded their activities as well. Labor movements and a lawyers' organization (the Lawyers Committee for Civil Rights Under Law) also organized educational efforts, local petitions, and congressional testimony. The collapse of the Portuguese empire in Africa and the political turmoil after Nixon's resignation spurred more intense discussion in the mid-1970s. By this point also, the Cold War seemed less omnipresent, creating more opportunities to consider putting pressure on putative allies like South Africa whose policies in other respects were so unappetizing. African American politicians gained new prominence in the Carter administration (1976–80). Beginning in the 1970s also, a number of American cities began to pass laws divesting their investment funds from corporations that maintained activities in South Africa, a crucial new tactic that greatly magnified the impact of public opinion while helping to create additional targets more vulnerable than the South African government itself. A new NGO, TransAfrica, was formed in 1977, led by African American politicians, and bent on accelerating the anti-apartheid campaign.

The election of Ronald Reagan in 1980 and the rightward tilt of American politics on the surface set the campaign back within the United States, but in fact this larger complexity served as a further goad. Church groups redoubled their efforts against apartheid. The issue spread to university campuses, where student groups, recalling some of the milder sit-in tactics of the 1960s, strenuously pressed administrations and boards of trustees to divest their endowment funds of South African connections. A Campaign against Investment in South Africa formed in 1981, joining the established NGOs in the field, as did the American Friends Service Committee, the leading Quaker outreach organization (a connection to world opinion's past). National meetings coordinated tactics on college campuses, among trade unions, and among city councils and state legislatures. Marches on Washington in 1982 and 1983 were larger than before, and many of the same activists also participated in anti-nuclear demonstrations.

Public opinion pressure also developed in Europe and elsewhere during the same period. As in the United States, the Sharpeville massacre spurred growing international awareness. The Commonwealth expelled South Africa in 1961 because of its racial policies; the move was primarily prompted by the concerns of the Commonwealth's new Asian and African members, but it stemmed also from the growing outcry in Canada and elsewhere. Even though British policy held back, because of economic and security interests, public concern mounted from many traditional sources along with advocacy from South African exiles in London. The British Council of Churches urged economic disengagement from South Africa from 1979 onward. The Trade Union Congress forged agreement with nine retail chains to remove South African goods in 1985. By this point a substantial segment of British opinion favored economic sanctions; by 1986 a majority (fifty-six percent) of the public believed that the nation's policy was not strong enough. The pace and size of public demonstrations against apartheid accelerated.

Amid growing unrest in South Africa, breakthrough occurred between 1984 and 1986. Domestic agitation increased greatly, culminating the long campaign of the African National Congress and its allies and causing some to worry about violent protest. It is vital to keep this internal agitation and attendant police brutality in mind, for without its pressure on the apartheid system, world opinion could not have been roused; and it was in this domestic arena, of course, that the real courage lay. But the global contribution was essential as well. For many African Americans, apartheid served as a surrogate for racial grievances within the United States whose expression was not likely to garner such wide support. Many college students, sincerely appalled by apartheid, also enjoyed the opportunity to chide academic administrations and nudge American capitalism. All of this was in the context of a conservative, inflexible national administration, which was too popular to challenge outright.

The Free South Africa Movement was founded in 1984 and immediately launched a series of more confrontational demonstrations, resulting in many arrests (over three thousand within a five-month period, including members of Congress). Massive demonstrations surrounded the South African embassy, and others pressed the United States government and key corporations. Growing numbers of universities pledged disinvestment. Prestigious leaders, including children of Jimmy Carter and Robert Kennedy along with university presidents, the well-known Yale chaplain William Sloan Coffin, and Jesse Jackson, bore public witness on many occasions. Public opinion solidified; by 1986 a majority favored official United States pressure against Pretoria. A South African ban on news dissemination in 1985, though successful in reducing the number of stories about apartheid, protest, and retaliatory police violence, did not dent U.S. public opinion, which maintained its high levels of hostility to the system. Polled sympathies for the black South African population, at fifty-nine percent in the United States before the ban, rose to sixty-four percent a few months later, showing that outrage had become self-sustaining and no longer depended on consistent nutrition from the media. By this point almost a thousand organizations were working against apartheid in the United States, almost four hundred of them primarily focused on the issue. As always, moral outrage spurred mobilization, which in turn furthered the expression of outrage.

Opinion now translated into decisive pressure, again along with movements elsewhere and with the courageous protests in South Africa itself. By 1986 twenty-one states, sixty-eight cities, and ten of the largest counties in the United States had adopted divestment policies, and over a hundred universities, including the most prestigious, had withdrawn nearly a half-billion dollars from firms doing business in South Africa. United States investments in the nation were more than halved between 1983 and 1985. Several major companies pulled out entirely. In 1986, against the wishes of the Reagan administration, Congress officially acted to encourage companies to withdraw, leading a number of major corporations to cease activities in South Africa. The American contribution to world opinion had found teeth, particularly in corporate action but now in national policy as well.

Much of the public pressure rested on corporations, generating many of the same considerations that direct campaigns had evoked over product quality or the environment. Reluctantly, multinational corporations calculated the value of a South African portfolio – in most instances three percent or less of total investments and earnings – versus a global loss of customer confidence and more systematic boycotts. The costs from global opinion outweighed those of divestment, so divestment occurred. Direct pressure from shareholders, themselves participant in this swell of outrage, factored in as well, as did the economic sanctions act passed by Congress in 1986.

The United States played an unusually important role in world opinion against South Africa. The crucial position of American-based corporations like General Motors, and even more the relationship of apartheid to racial issues and audiences in the United States are the reasons for this. Correlations between anti-apartheid outrage and views on racial justice within the nation were unusually tight, overriding more general political affiliation or foreign policy stance. But the United States was hardly alone. Canadian opinion rallied at about the same time, and in similar ways, putting pressures on the government to sanction South Africa and to spur British action as well. A Canadian academic articulated the standard but compelling basis for active participation in world opinion: "In few other cases of political repression is the situation so morally unambiguous."[5] Many industrial countries, buffeted by internal opinion and frequent demonstrations, acted economically against South Africa along lines similar to those which had developed in the United States. Thus Japan banned certain exports in 1985, asked its citizens not to purchase South

African currency, and then expanded the economic measures considerably in the following year with a long series of prohibited imports. The British government, more reluctant because of extensive traditional involvement, bowed to pressure in 1986, prescribing an extensive list of banned imports and an embargo on arms sales and pleading for voluntary cessation of new investment by British corporations. The European Union was more forceful, stopping new investment by members other than Great Britain in 1984 and then issuing extensive import prohibitions along with diplomatic and cultural disengagement in 1986.

All this became an international crusade, slow in germinating but then bursting forth with irresistible force. Corporations yielded. Governments, almost uniformly resistant because of Cold War fears about losing a strategic ally and a real reluctance to risk economic assets or put pressure on powerful economic units, caved as well. World opinion became a strategic factor on its own account, trumping more conventional criteria. The resultant pressure on South Africa finally prompted rethinking, aided by some courageous statesmanship on the part of the new Nationalist leader de Klerk. Nelson Mandela, the head of the African National Congress, was released from long imprisonment in 1900. The apartheid system was entirely dismantled with the democratic elections of 1994. The massive problems remaining in South Africa failed to sustain their presence on the global radar screen, but on the crucial issue world opinion had won.

World opinion developed a somewhat similar focus on the Palestinian cause. The parallels to South Africa were numerous, with the huge exception of the predominant outlook in the United States and as a result with much less decisive impact. Arab opinion was by the late 1940s, hostile to Israeli seizure of territory regarded as Palestinian and it hardened further in ensuing decades. As with apartheid, the origins of larger-scale opinion started outside the West, nearer the affected peoples, and as part of the larger rising against Western or Western-backed imperialism. Arab publics were far more consistently committed than were many of their governments. Communist regimes and media supported the Palestinian cause from the 1960s onward, including active involvement from China. By the 1970s, after long disinterest, Japanese opinion was also roused. The 1973 war and the oil embargo sparked attention and growing hostility to Israeli policies. Public attitudes and government policies alike became increasingly pro-Palestinian, blaming terrorism on Israeli intransigence.

A Citizen Congress to Seek Peace in the Middle East organized a teach-in in 1982 to protest Israeli invasion of Lebanon, and a variety of other NGOs formed in Japan. Victims of Nagasaki and Hiroshima atomic attacks expressed their solidarity in a striking gesture. Calls and letters from the public flooded Palestinian offices in Japan, offering support. Indian opinion was also sympathetic, again on shared grounds of anti-colonialism and self-determination.

Opinion in Europe was slower to form, conditioned among other things by profound regrets over the Holocaust. Palestinian officials assiduously courted the European press. The Israeli invasion of Lebanon and subsequent massacres in refugee camps finally turned the tide toward more active outrage. Media coverage of extensive destruction and human suffering could not easily be ignored. German opinion, for example, turned from guilt-laden support for Israel, to increasing favor to the Palestinians. France and, more gradually, Britain moved in the same direction, after long favoring Israel as a democratic bastion in the region. In an interesting variant on moral universalism, one British paper noted how Israel was formed by refugees unfairly forced from Europe, who made refugees of the Palestinians in turn: "Israel visits the sins of generations of Europeans upon the children of Palestine's Arabs."[6] Southern European countries and the Vatican were increasingly emphatic as well. A few European countries held out, at least until the revival of mutual atrocities after 2000: Sweden, Denmark, and The Netherlands were particular cases in point. The United States and Canada, however, were the big abstainers. Polls noted occasional blips of opinion against Israel, as following the 1982 atrocities, but there were no consistent currents or large expressions of outrage.

There was, in sum, a real world opinion favoring better treatment of the Palestinians, including a right to statehood. Its origins outside the West, amid a kind of moral reaction identical to world opinion in other cases where the West took a lead, show the increasing range of global standards and a global voice. But in contrast to the apartheid case, this was world opinion divided, with crucial allies largely uninvolved. Though encouraging to Palestinians and influential on Israeli peace factions, world opinion generated no decisive outcome. The governments most involved, Israel and the United States, were not fundamentally swayed, and global passions never quite cohered amid this resistance.

There were, however, other important victories, some of them overlapping in time the application of world opinion to apartheid and to Palestine, some developing a bit later. In one key instance the organizers of the global voice successfully pressed a reluctant United States, a global David against a hesitant Goliath.

World opinion had a great deal to do with changes in the repressive policies of several Central American regimes during the 1980s, particularly in El Salvador. This involved both pressure on conservative militants in Central America, responsible for many brutalities amid civil strife, and pressure on the United States to wean itself from support for the militants, a challenging task during the Reagan years. Wide publicity given to assassinations of civilians by right-wing "death squads," and to political imprisonments and torture played a vital role in what became a constructive process of change.

There were many players. Human rights NGOs took a lead role, including Amnesty International, which published a number of telling reports; and H.R.W.'s Americas Watch division formed expressly over the issues involved. Latin American opinion mobilized in the human rights area from 1973 onward, with the brutalities of the Pinochet regime in Chile. A number of Latin American NGOs spearheaded publicity campaigns. Catholic organizations and pronouncements played an important role, another sign of Catholicism's growing place in world opinion. Brutalities against foreign Catholics in Central America provided some of the most dramatic fodder for global mobilization. Labor organizations, including United States groups, chimed in strongly, spurred by attacks on local union leaders. Immigrants from the region to the United States and Canada were able to provide an additional voice, an interesting twist to the participant list in world opinion. All this added up to an international outcry against human rights abuse, reaching a crescendo by the mid-1980s. The United Nations became increasingly involved, both a result of and spur to further world opinion. The European Commission also played an active role. The result was a series of regime changes, in El Salvador, Guatemala, and Nicaragua, between 1984 and 1990 and the increasing democratization of the region. That all this occurred despite rearguard action by the United States was a particularly impressive demonstration of the effectiveness of the alliance between world opinion and transnational organizations.

A Guatemalan human rights activist summed it all up:

> If it were not for that international assistance, principally from Americas Watch, Amnesty International, the World Council of Churches, solidarity organizations from democratic countries, Canadian organizations, organizations of Guatemalans working in the US, Canada or Europe, without the moral and political help of those organizations, I believe that we would have been dead

many years ago, the army would not have permitted our organization to develop ... If you don't have the contacts, if the people who are doing the killing know that nobody is going to do anything if you disappear, then you disappear ... It was vital to have contacts so that information could go outside.[7]

One other point is crucial in this pattern of success: the existence of local groups and leaders brave enough to venture opposition and provide information to the outside world, aware of world opinion, bolstered by it but also actively contributing to it. Less happy cases in the same period, particularly in Cambodia, where massive violence occurred with far less world opinion reaction and certainly far less remediation, resulted in part from the lack of this factor.

The fundamental force that created the essential about-face in Central America was world opinion, or the threat of its involvement, with the attendant capacity to generate embarrassment if not remorse. European economic aid added to incentives, but it was the power of publicity – the world watching – that really turned the tide within Central America and among United States policymakers. Boycotts and military threats, concomitants of world opinion elsewhere (key factors a bit later in the Balkans), were not in play. Organizations were vital in articulating moral standards and bringing abuses to light, but their strength rested on public outrage. This was world opinion at work.

The surge of world opinion in the 1970s and 1980s, with apartheid, Israel–Palestine, and Central America as key foci, was an extraordinary outburst. It owed much to some of the fears and passions roused by the Cold War, particularly through the disarmament movement – which had stimulated many of the concerns and organizations later active on other causes. But it was also the decline of Cold War polarities that encouraged various mobilizers to envisage other issues and to urge that moral imperatives might override Cold War alignments. By this point also the decolonization movement was in full force, but with many of the big issues resolved, which allowed focus on particular sticking points, with South Africa at the top of the list.

The surge, and its several obvious successes, demonstrated among other things that global outrage could induce even great powers like the United States to shift gear in policy areas seen as significant but not fundamental to the national interest: hence the changes of mind on Central America and South Africa, though not on Israel. By the early 1990s a Democratic Congress and Republican administration were even prone to anticipate American outrage on international issues before it actually took shape: hence a worried intervention against human rights abuses in Somalia, which aborted in part because opinion was not fully engaged.[8]

World opinion backpedaled in the diplomatic arena, however, in the 1990s. It is not easy to say why. Some fatigue may have set in. The end of the Cold War provided new distractions that did not call for outrage so much as self-satisfaction, particularly in the West; and some sectors of the public and the media turned away from international issues. News coverage measurably declined in the United States. By this point also, human rights offenders, aware of public reactions, became more resistant: the global voice, combined perhaps with a bit of corporate pressure, was not enough to win response. In this context, effective mobilization required more effort than before, and much of the relevant public turned away from the challenge. For a time also the Israeli–Palestinian conflict took a more hopeful turn, which reduced the apparent need for monitoring through public opinion. Whatever the reasons, a lull set in. The bloody confrontation between Tutsis and Hutus in Rwanda largely passed without great reaction, despite earnest attempts by some NGOs to mobilize response: here was a notable failure of global nerve, after the stirring advances of the two previous decades in South Africa and Central America. Human rights repression in Burma (Myanmar) was largely ignored. It was hard not to recall the 1930s, when world opinion had failed in articulation against dreadful events.

There was one successful application of world opinion during the decade, though it also illustrates new complexities. World opinion roused slowly to new crises in the former Yugoslavia. Mere expressions of dismay proved inadequate, and there were few corporate pressures relevant in this recently Communist region. Genuine public concern had to interact with military decisions by several key states to produce anything like a meaningful response. Yugoslavia was followed by a similarly hesitant role of global opinion in East Timor, half a world away.

After 1990 much attention turned to the former Yugoslavia, where Serbian military aggression and policies of ethnic cleansing ultimately provoked substantial outcry. The campaign was halting initially, since the region was not widely known and there was a considerable inclination to hope that, with the Cold War over, international problems would go away. In Europe and North America a sense of responsibility (along with capacity for intervention) was most fully engaged. Circumstances varied within the West, opinion in Canada, The

Netherlands, and France being prompt and vigorous, Germany and Britain active, Italy and particularly the United States more reticent. National distinctions reflected different leadership stances: the Italian army's opposition to military involvement helped complicate public reactions. In the United States a sense that Europe should take care of its own mess was heightened by recent costs and losses in the Gulf War and the intervention in Somalia; national policymakers ultimately decided on a more active stance in advance of a clear mandate in the opinion polls. Russia's adoption of a pro-Serbian policy may have reflected a more nationalist public opinion, though the leadership took the key decisions regardless of wider input. The papacy was also hesitant, conscious of Catholic interests in a divided region, but ultimately it helped shape a need for action.

The atrocities in the Balkans increasingly stimulated broadly based moral outrage. A widely publicized mortar attack on a marketplace in Sarajevo in 1994, which killed sixty-eight people, was especially moving. The media provided graphic imagery, though this was truer in Britain, where a B.B.C. channel at one point offered fifteen hours straight of prime-time coverage, than in the United States, where poignant scenes of women, children, and streams of refugees alternated with long periods of relative silence in a post-Cold-War media setting in which international news was being scaled back. There was no dearth of the kind of dramatic personal evidence that so often plays a role in world opinion. Demonstrations and polling majorities clearly reflected a universalistic compassion, directed toward a Muslim minority under attack by supposed Christians. (A failure by Dutch troops to protect Muslim civilians ultimately toppled a government in The Netherlands.) Public pressure was complicated – in contrast to the earlier situation in Central America – by the defiant resistance of the Serbian regime: the glare of publicity alone would accomplish nothing. Certainly by 1994, if not before, it was clear that many segments of the Western public were pushing for military intervention, despite hesitancy about possible casualties. Given Serbian impediments to purely humanitarian assistance, only military action could protect global standards of decency. Canadian opinion, backing the military option, reflected a national self-image of involvement in defending human rights. French activity stemmed in part from the early lead of influential intellectuals, through speeches and editorials, denouncing atrocities being committed just "two hours from Paris." This in turn stimulated a dramatic visit to Sarajevo by President Mitterand, in 1992, which further roused a wider public. In many countries men were more assertive than women, given the military implications involved, though there was more uniform support for measures such as accepting additional refugees and providing humanitarian aid. West Germans were far more likely to express a sense of responsibility than their new East German co-nationals, which doubtless reflected their greater prosperity but also a different contemporary history of involvement with global issues.

Despite the complexity, then, a strong international strain in public opinion, committed to human rights, played a significant role in helping to shape an interventionist policy in the Balkans, first in Bosnia and later, in 1999 amid similar problems and pressures, in Kosovo. The international link was crucial: many national publics conditioned their concern upon insistence that action should take place only on a multinational basis. The pressure was applied to Western governments for direct intervention in the absence of any concessions from the Serbian military. But the same outrage, once successful action occurred, carried on to insist on war crimes trials for the officials who had led the ethnic cleansing. The Balkans provided a messier instance of world opinion than Central America or apartheid had, because of the need for military enforcement, but on the whole it generated somewhat comparable success. Scholars debate the role of public opinion in actually influencing policy decisions, and the Bosnia and Kosovo cases certainly warrant discussion, with due regard to national variations in outlook and urgency and to different sensitivities among relevant national leaders. Still, public opinion was engaged on behalf of distant victims, and military action resulted at least in part from this engagement.

At the same time, there were a few peculiarities in world opinion's involvement in this newest Balkan crisis, including the facts that the glare of publicity did not suffice to change local conditions and that military policy had to be motivated. Considerable interventionist argument applied to the Balkan victims as Europeans rather than as human beings. This was true of French comment and also surfaced in the United States. It was widely noted that world opinion did not muster the same level of outrage in the contemporaneous, and far more horrible, massacres in Rwanda. In this more distant place, media coverage was less pervasive, which reduced the confrontation with visual imagery. A variety of NGOs worked to bring wider attention to the massive slaughter, but without great effect. Military intervention – mere expressions of outrage seemed to have no short-term impact on the forces involved – was seen as more difficult and more problematic than in the Balkans. There was, nevertheless, a legitimate question about world opinion's consistency and some probable racist blindspots. The role of world opinion in responding to mass killings remained checkered in the 1990s.

During the 1990s world opinion also became involved in East Timor, a former Portuguese colony forcibly taken over by Indonesia in 1975, though here too the record was less than glorious. Media attention to evidence of brutal repression between 1975 and 1991 was limited. The authoritarian Indonesian government impeded foreign reporters and issued a great deal of misleading information about local resistance. Western powers, including neighboring Australia, were far more concerned with conciliating the Indonesian government as a Cold War ally than paying attention to human rights niceties, though Portugal consistently attempted to place the issue on the international agenda and Church backing for the large Catholic minority in East Timor provided further stimulus. The Australian media generated horror stories occasionally, and there was recurrent public pressure on a reluctant government to develop a more vigorous policy, but world opinion was not engaged. This situation changed in 1991. Cold War constraints were gone, though established governments maintained their impulse to stick to the status quo in Indonesia. A bloody military massacre of independence demonstrators, in Dili in 1991, caught media attention around the world – one observer compared the event to South Africa's Sharpeville. East Timorese refugees and independence spokesmen could become more effective, in this context, in rousing media attention abroad. Amnesty International stepped up its critique of Indonesian policy, claiming that more than 200,000 East Timorese had been killed in less than two decades. Refugees demonstrated near Western government buildings, seeking a firmer policy. The groups were small but persistent and they spurred both moral commitment and some postcolonial guilt, particularly in The Netherlands, Indonesia's former colonial overlord. Canada, Denmark, The Netherlands, and the United States all began to modify their foreign aid policies in light of Indonesian repression. Ploughshares, a nonviolent disarmament group centered in Britain, undertook direct action against British warplanes being sold to Indonesia in 1994, again capturing considerable public attention. The two leading East Timorese advocates shared the Nobel Peace Prize in 1996, a reflection of and spur to greater international pressure. The Irish President of the European Commission took the East Timorese case as an independence movement analogous to Ireland's own historic struggles, amid considerable media attention. Finally, elections were permitted in 1999 under United Nations auspices with Australian military backing, though this did not prevent one last massacre. Global pressure had undoubtedly counted, polls in the West strongly favoring East Timor by the mid-1990s. The pressure was applied more through media outrage, and the availability of graphic images of repression, than by a full mobilization of world opinion. But public outrage was directly involved, in a somewhat confused decade, as it became clear even to the Indonesian government that that amorphous entity, "the world community" – an amalgam of media, opinion polls, and diplomatic and United Nations promptings – had decided to support a remote and little-known people.

Issues of consistency were again obvious. Why even the belated global commitment to East Timor and not to other minorities struggling against military repression? Why even a belated surge of global pressure on behalf of 200,000 killed while the two million being killed in strife in Sudan were virtually ignored? Western responsibility through prior colonial involvement, plus the connection to the Catholic minority, formed part of the answer – contrasting, for example, with the situation of the Kurds in Turkey, which was also a more significant and long-standing Western ally.[9] The East Timorese leadership proved both courageous and skillful; Bishop Carlos Belo, one of the Nobel Prize laureates, gained growing international attention. The generally nonviolent nature of East Timorese protest doubtless helped conciliate world opinion, particularly when compared with Indonesian government response; here was a contrast with, for example, the Chechen minority in Russia. But a strong dose of fickleness could not be denied. The American media were accused of fitful interest in these kinds of problems until something really dramatic happened, and other elements of world opinion shared some responsibility as well. The lesson of the 1990s was clear: world opinion could be a potent international force, but not every major tragedy could rouse it.

The 1990s also saw a major international effort against the death penalty, spearheaded by organizations like Amnesty International and strongly backed by the papacy. Massive educational efforts emphasized the non-utility of the death penalty against crime and its fundamental inhumanity; cases of wrongful conviction were highlighted, the United States being prominent in the literature. Here was a deeply felt instance of human rights abuse, newly discovered on the international scene though long discussed within individual Western countries. World opinion targets included general policies, particularly in China, Iran, and the United States, collectively responsible for eighty percent of the death penalties administered worldwide by the late 1990s, and imminent individual executions, particularly in the United States, where information was relatively available. American state governors were frequently bombarded with petitions, email systems being increasingly deployed to accelerate and multiply the pressure. A host of websites were organized to direct petitions, again both on policy matters and on individual cases. United Nations units passed resolutions against the death penalty, and a growing number of countries – seventy-six outright and another thirty-six with minor qualifications – took action.

A host of ad hoc groups formed in Britain, Canada, France, Denmark, Slovenia, Italy, and elsewhere. A Europe-wide organization arose, headquartered in Norway. It campaigned actively but also made direct contact with condemned prisoners to offer emotional and legal support. A Swiss branch even produced hip-hop music generated by American prisoners. Canadian unions, such as the Union of Public Employees, participated in the effort, blasting the treatment of several prisoners (some of them mentally impaired) by the Texas parole board. Many religious organizations, including groups in the United States, joined the campaign. As in past mobilizations, prominent people like Lloyd Axworthy, Madeleine Allbright, and Bishop Desmond Tutu helped highlight support either for general abolition of the penalty or for clemency for particular individuals. From various corners, organizations generated visits to parliamentary leaders in countries still committed to the death penalty. For example, a group called Hands Off Cain combined with Italian parliamentarians to press officials of a number of Caribbean countries in 1999. In an echo of the battle against apartheid, proposals surfaced to restrict investment in states like Texas or to boycott tourism, though there was little impact despite the increasingly inescapable assertions of a new international standard that found the death penalty abhorrent. The whole effort constituted another significant extension of world opinion, and demonstrated some interesting innovations in technique, particularly through the use of the internet. At base was the kind of moral fervor always attached to world opinion, a sense that the death penalty offended the conscience of humanity.

On 15 February 2003 the largest anti-war demonstration in the history of the world took place, protesting the imminent invasion of Iraq by the United States and some allies. Hundreds of thousands of people marched in London – some estimates claimed two million – in what may have been the biggest demonstration ever in the United Kingdom. Scottish protest was equally vigorous, centering in Glasgow. Many marchers carried pots, drums, or whistles to make what was called a "Jericho rumpus" around the site where Prime Minister Tony Blair was due to speak. Protests in Germany and Italy were also massive. Huge

marches occurred in Spain and 300,000 paraded in Athens. Many American cities were involved, with hundreds of thousands of protesters. The same was true in Australia, with marches against the government that had committed to send a contingent of troops. Large demonstrations took place in Japan and South Korea. In Seoul two thousand Buddhists said prayers for the Iraqis who would be killed. Significant protests also occurred in Indonesia, Turkey, Russia, and Mexico. Pretending to venture an overall tally would imply more precision than is possible, but clearly well over twenty-five million people voted with their feet, around the world, in a magnificently coordinated action. Not only an impressive variety of nations but also impressive arrays of humanity within those nations were deeply involved. Youth elements loomed large, but there were also large contingents of older people. Families brought children, believing despite some trepidation that bearing witness would be important for them. Anti-war union locals mobilized many workers, particularly in Western Europe and Australia, but middle-class presence was strong as well, with hosts of university students at the core. Masses of people truly found the prospect of this war repellent.

Global outrage had been building for some time, as American intentions became increasingly apparent and a gap opened between the United States and many members of the United Nations. Large demonstrations began in October 2002. Over 100,000 people marched in Florence, for example. In subsequent months, Japanese and Australian protesters camped outside the American embassies. Over fifteen thousand marched in Calcutta. In Switzerland twenty thousand gathered to press their parliament to protest the move toward war. Marchers in Paris emptied bottles of Coca-Cola, a symbolic gesture meant to imply possible economic repercussions of unilateral American action (a tactic that in the end was not widely deployed). Large groups gathered in cities throughout the Middle East, Muslim South Asia, and Indonesia.

The furor flowed from an intricate mixture of mass opinion and deliberate mobilization. Polls showed up to ninety percent of many publics opposed to the war, at least a war without United Nations sanction. The figures of eighty percent in Japan and ninety percent Russia were almost matched in many parts of Western Europe. Polls in East–Central Europe were also strongly unfavorable. The outpouring was huge.

At the same time, mobilization was exceptionally active and effective, as in all the major manifestations of world opinion since antislavery. Established groups were joined by ad hoc organizations specifically focused on Iraq. In Britain alone, there were at least twenty-five organizations. They included older efforts, including nuclear disarmament organizations born in the 1960s but also Greenpeace and the Society of Friends. International connections were quickly forged even among the many newcomers. The goal was to distribute informational materials, develop petitions, and above all mobilize and coordinate the mass demonstrations, including the rising on 15 February.

Again in a familiar pattern, many high-profile individuals participated publicly in the movement. This included a number of Hollywood stars (who formed a group, Artists United to Win without War), figures like Jesse Jackson, and British rock idols.

The role of the internet was fundamental, helping to explain how a campaign could mushroom so quickly and take on a global identity, easily eclipsing the 1960s surge against the Vietnam War in extent if not necessarily in passion. In the United States many new associations, including the dynamic MoveOn, organized "virtual marches," flooding congressional email addresses with messages from members. The organizations also used the new medium to collect funds for further efforts, while also acknowledging that, by using email to communicate and petition, and to advertise the basic message, costs could be kept quite low. An American organizer noted, "E-mail is a blessing. That's how I get in touch with most of our organizing centers and with a lot of students. We get a lot of e-mails, just simple questions with students from other campuses going, 'How can I help?' And they just sat down and wrote out three words, and then I get to send back – you know, I'll send them links to fliers, information. And it's really, really, really powerful in terms of getting them started."[10]

The greatest challenge in assessing this outburst of world opinion involves determining its meaning beyond the obvious point that hundreds of millions of people did not want unilateral United States action against Iraq. Was a new criterion being added to the list of concerns that could generate a global voice in protest? Signals were mixed. Many people were not opposed to war but merely to unilateral war: this was the clearest overall point, building on conclusions that probably began to take shape in opposition to the Vietnam conflict. Majorities in many countries (though not all – for example in Islamic regions and in Eastern and Southeastern Europe) were willing to consider war if the United Nations provided explicit sanction. Another criterion was almost as clear as the point about unilateralism, and equally important for the future: world opinion did not condone war against a state because of claims of possession of weapons of mass destruction.

Other motives entered in for some. Several veterans' groups from the earlier Gulf War argued not necessarily against war in general but against a war to be waged with massive bombing attacks likely to kill civilians. An American tank crewman, a decorated veteran, noted, "Sept. 11 was nothing compared to the destruction that we visited on Iraq 12 years ago and even more so for what will probably happen this time." Many others, again open to certain kinds of war, were particularly repelled by American arrogance and aggressive posturing. A Scottish bishop: "There are many of us who are not pacifists but who have felt increasingly concerned by the rhetoric which seems to be leading us into war in Iraq." But there were also contributions from people opposed to war in general. An Italian woman who traveled from the port city of Ancona to march in Rome phrased a common if vague thought: "We want to demonstrate that a different world is possible." After the war began, the Pope urged that "When war, like the one in Iraq, threatens the fate of humanity, it is even more urgent for us to proclaim, with a firm and decisive voice, that only peace is the way of building a more just and caring society." And many historically pacifist groups, long a component in world opinion, chimed in vigorously. But the most consistent message involved an effort to distinguish among types of wars, world opinion now being available to protest wars that involved great-power aggression without adequate justification. As a British demonstrator put it, trying to distinguish his concerns from pacifism, "The people who will be attending on Saturday are from way beyond that [pacifist] group. People who say they're not normally interested in demonstrating are saying they're anxious, angry and upset at what seems to be an unjust war."[11]

Like every extension of world opinion, since the antislavery campaign, the furor against the possibility of war in Iraq was a mixture of old and new elements. The new were most obvious. This was the first time significant world opinion mobilized in advance of an event rather than after being spurred by news of atrocities. Recollection of the civilian casualties in the previous Gulf War helps explain this departure, along with the growing concern about Israeli actions against Palestinians from 2000 onward, which stimulated sensitivities to issues in the region. Deep suspicions of the United States, fed by several recent American withdrawals from international proposals concerning the environment, land mines, and war crimes, nourished the quick response. And the Bush administration was hardly coy about its intentions, some months before the most vigorous global outcry. Nevertheless, the idea of using world opinion before the fact was an important enhancement of the incorporation of global outlook into diplomatic calculations – even though, in this instance, the massive protest failed in its immediate purpose. The idea of measuring the justice of war in advance, at least when a great power was involved, added a new element.

The geographic span of the anti-war sentiment was striking, though it built clearly on developments in world opinion since the 1950s. Agitation in the Muslim world was significant if predictable, given long-standing resentments of Western interference in the region. The concern in Japan and South Korea was a vivid reminder of their centrality to contemporary world opinion. The Japanese public felt a mission to minimize armed conflict, built from their own experiences in world war. Russian opinion was also vigorous. Despite some national variations, participation in Latin America, North America, and Western Europe continued the typical involvement of these regions in global movements.

The incorporation of new technology, and particularly the use of the internet for petitions and for coordination of demonstrations, was unprecedented. This technology was already employed in applying world opinion to individual crises, like people subjected to dreadful punishments in Muslim Africa or exposed to the death penalty in the United States. But now the full force of rapid-fire mass communication was deployed for world opinion in the diplomatic sphere, and the results were impressive. Active participation in world opinion depended on access to the internet, which continued to vary widely. The resultant audience was far wider than the West alone, but it downplayed many parts of Africa and some other regions. Worldwide, in 2002, there were about 600 million internet users in a total population of over six billion, with growth rates projected at about ten percent per year.

Familiar elements were vital as well. There was the common core of moral outrage and a need to use world opinion in hopes of harnessing policies whose ramifications otherwise risked spinning out of control. The outrage was no less keen for anticipating abuses rather than responding to abuses in fact. The proliferation of associations was another standard feature. Ad hoc groups joined well-established opinion centers, including as always many religious organizations (of all major faiths), in galvanizing world opinion and helping to organize its manifestations. This was, in sum, the latest step in a long history of world opinion, not an entirely radical departure.

The size and scope of the protest against war, and its short-term failure, are the most striking features of this latest intervention of global opinion in the diplomatic arena. There was also a significant tension. Although justifications for war centered on Iraq's supposed weapons program and the danger it posed – arguments that world opinion rejected even before the absence of significant weaponary became known – it was also true that Iraq's regime was extremely oppressive. Some proponents of war, including Britain's Prime Minister Tony Blair, whose outlook some compared to that of Gladstone over a century before, were moved in part by human rights concerns. Clearly, world opinion at this point rejects the idea that a handful of nations can unilaterally decide on military intervention even when rights issues are involved; a point left unresolved in the issue of how to balance rights concerns with the harmful effects of war, should larger international sponsorship be available.

Protest against the Iraq action contrasts with the earlier efforts against United States involvement in Vietnam. The greater scope of the Iraq effort stands out, and the fact that it was generated not in response to searing images of war, but in anticipation; world opinion seems to learn from the past. Though strong passions did not deter some governments from collaborating with the United States, they had more influence on individual state policy than in the Vietnam conflict, for some governments resisted intense U.S. pressure in part because of the potential political cost at home. The end of the Cold War helped free the decisions of individual governments, but opinion itself had gained stature in many places.

The jury is still out on the degree of prescience embodied in the global concern about war in Iraq, as opposed to the more belligerent British–American policy, but it is clear that the accumulation of global opinion interventions in diplomacy and statecraft since the 1960s leaves a vital legacy for the future.[12] There is a geographically extensive, morally sensitive global concern for others which can readily mobilize against suppressions of human rights or safety, including suppressions caused or threatened by war. Neither entirely consistent nor entirely predictable, this concern has become an inescapable factor in the diplomatic calculations of even the greatest great powers. Its importance is likely to mount. Frustrated despite its unprecedented proportions in 2003, it looms as a constraint on American adventures in the near future, whatever the rhetorical bluster in Washington. The massive if futile protest on Iraq was a culmination of several decades of growing global attention to aspects of policy and diplomacy. It also had some new features that carried interesting implications for the future. It is conceivable that American military policy, which produced a much less bloody contest than many anticipated and which could end up improving the human rights situation in Iraq (possibilities that became more debatable as the occupation wore on), will turn out to defuse the just war concern that defined world opinion in 2003; but it is equally likely the ongoing anger plus the war's messy aftermath will keep world opinion on alert.

The rich history of world opinion and diplomacy since the mid-1950s raises a more general point that is applicable to the recent experience with Iraq. Not all the targets of world opinion have involved the United States – the apartheid struggle for example involved American policy only as an ancillary issue – but the conjuncture has been frequent. From nuclear policy to Vietnam to Central America and now to the Middle East, world opinion has frequently spotlighted the exercise of American power. World opinion has sometimes held the United States to a stricter standard than it has applied to other states. Anti-nuclear protests, for example, acknowledged Soviet, British, and French policy but turned particularly on American testing. Outrage against Soviet intervention in Hungary, in 1956, or Czechoslovakia, in 1968, or even Afghanistan later on certainly roused a segment of world opinion, but it did not match the passion devoted to American involvement in Vietnam. Many Americans today see a disparity between world opinion's condemnation of U.S. action in Iraq and the willingness to vigorously condemn acts of terrorism, though this judgment can be disputed. Several points are obvious. First, expectations of what principles should guide the United States are relatively high, in part because of the nation's democratic tradition and moralistic rhetoric. Second, in contrast for example to the more impervious Soviet Union, the mobilizers of world opinion have some hope that the United States will heed global outrage – that there is some point in organizing – and at times they have been correct. But there is no gainsaying that world opinion has evolved in part in response to the expansion of American power, as a counterweight in the absence of effective power politics constraints. This component, whether justified or not, has increased in salience with the end of the Cold War and the further reduction of constraints. It adds to the complexity of American reactions as the only remaining superpower decides how to confront an undeniably skeptical undercurrent in global reactions. It underlines as well how world opinion has emerged as a diplomatic factor in its own right.

11

WORLD OPINION AND CLASHING
CIVILIZATIONS: THE CASE OF ISLAM

The key complexity of contemporary world opinion, becoming more obvious as the phenomenon advanced as a factor in international relations, involves tensions with regional standards and interests. Global pronouncements, from anti-slavery onward, frequently bumped up against different standards in particular places. When Western dominance was assumed (at least by Westerners) these variants might be shrugged off as temporary, but with decolonization they took on greater importance. The fact was that ordinary people and leaders in many places might disagree with what the self-proclaimed bearers of world opinion sought. As world opinion widened, taking on more social and environmental issues, opportunities for conflict automatically increased.

Western scholars have sometimes criticized the Western bias of most world opinion. We have noted that hesitancies over global application of feminist standards involve Western-liberal awareness of cultural diversity and a certain amount of confusion over where diversity ends and injustice begins. Even before Iraq and the accusations about new American imperialism, some maverick diplomatic specialists criticized human rights efforts – their focus was on well-meaning NGOs, not world opinion per se – for attacking certain regimes in ways that could later justify neo-imperialistic Western intervention, however great the gap in principle between moral objections and big-stick diplomacy.[1]

At times, world opinion has faltered amid disparities among the values of major societies. The clash of civilizations idea, as a vision for the world's post-Cold-War future, runs counter to the validity and growth of world opinion: world opinion could collapse again if there were unresolvable disputes about just wars, human rights, or environmental standards. Evaluating the global–regional tension is a test both of world opinion and of the clash of civilizations model. Conclusions offer support for both sides of the equation: there is contest over world opinion, and efforts to form counterthrusts based on the interests and values of different regions; but, to date, these efforts have not succeeded in overwhelming or fully redefining world opinion.

We have seen that world opinion often breaks down against contrary values in particular places, sometimes even when regional leaders offer rhetorical support for the global standards involved. Conflicts are particularly acute in the social domain, as when world opinion pushes for equal rights for women, but local judges, husbands, and fathers reassert traditional prerogatives, or when United Nations agencies advertise Western-style suggestions for children and childrearing in areas that continue to emphasize more customary family obligations.[2] Incomplete agreement on global environmental standards, and their interaction with development needs, also raises some ongoing issues.

More sweeping attempts to counter world opinion emerged for several decades in the Cold War. The Communist bloc sought to insulate itself from Western-dominated world opinion with a massive system of censorship and propaganda. Separate news organizations formed, in essence alternative opinions, which claimed equal universality and global validity and which persuaded significant minorities in other places of their superiority, in accuracy and righteousness, over world opinion as defined in the so-called free world. For its part the West, and particularly the United States, shunned the Communist voice. The struggle of competing claims for global opinion is not new.

An intriguing effort to dispute key assumptions in world opinion emerged more recently, in the mid-1990s. As human rights advocates sought to isolate the regime of Myanmar (Burma) for its extensive rights abuses, including imprisonment and torture of political dissidents, a neo-Confucian protest emerged, particularly in Singapore and Malaysia. Leaders in these countries asserted a set of "Asian values" that, they said, ran counter to world opinion but were equally valid and indeed in Asia deserved greater credence. As Lee Kuan Yew, the Prime Minister of Singapore, put it, "The expansion of the rights of the individual to behave or misbehave as he pleases has come often at the expense of orderly society. In the East, the main object is to have a well-ordered society so that everybody can have maximum enjoyment of his freedoms."[3]

For several years, discussion of an East Asian alternative (or alternatives) to world opinion stoked the larger idea of a new clash of civilization. It was spiced by some dramatic cases, most notably the arrest and ritual beating of an

American teenager in Singapore for what (by Western standards) was minor vandalism, in which Western opinion proved powerless to win clemency. Continued tension between the Chinese government, bent on considerable political repression and opening a new offensive against a powerful dissident religious movement, the Falun Gong, and orthodox world opinion suggests that the implicit debate is far from over. But direct confrontation between an "Asian values" camp and world opinion has declined. Many Asian groups, in Indonesia, Thailand, and India, for example, immediately disputed the attack on human rights campaigns. New economic troubles in Asia and the passage of leadership to a newer generation have quieted comment as well. The overlap between Buddhist values and Western-emanating world opinion, at least on key peace and armaments topics, also bridges some gaps. There may be conflicts here, as Asian–Western relations evolve, but their vigor is unclear. Asian contributions to world opinion in recent decades, in the diplomatic, labor rights, and environmental arenas, have thus far outweighed any alternative definitions of values, providing important new vigor to contemporary world opinion.

The great tension between world opinion and an alternative system now focuses on the Islamic world – and a degree of tension here is almost as old as world opinion itself. By the middle of the nineteenth century it was clear that Western-based world opinion was eager to find fault with Islam. Old Christian standards and prejudices combined with a host of new images of the Middle East: politically cruel and repressive, sexually depraved, abusive of women. Mobilization of outrage against Ottoman treatment of minorities, again particularly Christian minorities, both reflected and furthered the sour disposition of many world opinion leaders toward behavior in the Islamic parts of the world. By the late nineteenth century, as the debate over veiling revealed, world opinion was making its own impact on Muslims. Some accepted global standards and used them as a spur to reform. Others, equally aware of the standards, resisted, claiming that Islamic traditions were preferable and vital to identity, or that Western observers had it all wrong (the Ottoman reaction to atrocity claims), or both.

Relations between world opinion and Islam improved in some ways after World War II. World opinion became less exclusively Christian. Even the Catholic embrace of world opinion included a new interest in tolerance and ecumenism. Links between world opinion and decolonization opened sympathies for Muslims as oppressed peoples. Outside the United States, as we have seen, world opinion for the most part sided with the Palestinian cause against

Israeli policies, and world opinion rallied somewhat more effectively on behalf of Muslim minorities in the former Yugoslavia. Most notably, the explosion of world opinion against the American war against Iraq revealed new opportunities for Muslim activists to join a larger global current.

Despite obvious tensions, particularly over Israel, many Islamic countries periodically moved to accommodate aspects of world – predominantly Western – opinion, in order to ease diplomatic and economic relations. As with China, occasional releases of political prisoners were designed to appease human rights concerns. In 2002 Saudi Arabia revamped its legal code, allowing prisoners to consult attorneys and banning torture, changes designed to promote the nation's case for joining the World Trade Organization. Turkey, an aspirant to the European Union, made even more sweeping changes in its criminal codes in order to measure up, though considerable distrust remained. World opinion did not transform the Middle East, but it did strike some reformist chords, particularly when bolstered by interests in joining global organizations.

Rifts continued, however. Amnesty International and other rights organizations frequently found reason to criticize political repression under the authoritarian regimes of the Middle East. Gaps between the global standards urged for women and, occasionally, homosexuals, and dominant values in many parts of the Islamic world widened. Individual cases where women were slated for harsh punishments for adultery in Muslim regions were among the most striking in the world opinion arsenal in the years around 2000. Extreme applications of the sharia, for example in death sentences for adulterers, drew thousands of petitions and massive outcry in the world press. In one Nigerian case, even contestants in a Miss World competition voiced their shock, moving the competition from Lagos to London in protest. A number of governments, including those of Austria and Australia, also weighed in against an "inhumane form of punishment which violated the most fundamental human right: the right to life."[4] Non-governmental organizations in other parts of Africa, as well as Nigeria, joined in. World opinion, though often hesitant on certain women's issues, starkly disapproved of a number of common social and political practices in the Islamic world. Although it was predominantly Western in orientation, which made it all the more galling for many Muslim observers, it embraced other voices as well.

It was also true that where world opinion did conjoin with outrage within Islam, it typically proved ineffective. Repeated polls and recurrent demonstrations in Europe or Japan blasting Israeli treatment of the Palestinians accomplished nothing. By 2004 the situation seemed to be deteriorating steadily. The massive protest against the war in Iraq did not prevent the war, and increasing hostility to the United States in global opinion polls did little or nothing to improve the troubled regime-building effort in Iraq. It was not hard for a Muslim to dismiss world opinion as hostile and biased, or criminally ineffective, or both. There were a number of reasons to seek alternatives.

Elements of the idea of a distinct Arab voice were born with Arab nationalism in the nineteenth century, though public opinion hardly drew explicit comment at that point. Already a tension existed between the older concept of Islamic opinion and the newer nationalist project, which might be respectful of religious traditions but gave higher priority to secular loyalties. Widespread restiveness against Western imperialism, after hopes raised during World War I, further promoted the interest in identifying and promoting Arab demands. But it was the post-1945 decolonization and the growing conflict with Israel that really focused attention not just on Arab concerns but on the need for distinctive activities involving public opinion.

The advent of a nationalist regime in Egypt under Gamel Nasser, in 1952, ushered in the next stage in the development of Arab opinion. Claiming some involvement with the Arab world in general, Nasser promoted the idea of an "information response" to what he and others saw as undue Jewish influence in world media. Nasser, an active participant in the Third World Bandung conference, asserted the Arab commitment to fighting imperialism in any quarter. But he was particularly active concerning the various remnants of imperialism in the Middle East and North Africa, and the mutual hostility with Israel. The Egyptians established the Voice of the Arabs in 1953, a radio facility with recurrently enhanced range, designed to present the Arab version of developments in the region and to promote a unified point of view. The initial focus involved the struggle with the French in Algeria, and remaining British influence in the Persian Gulf. The Voice of the Arabs was seen as an alternative to what was regarded as Zionist propaganda that distorted Israeli violence against the Palestinians, and also to Western (particularly British) efforts to spread distorting propaganda. (A radio operation in Cyprus, the Near East Broadcasting Station, was a particular target, as an outlet of British intelligence.) Along with the effort to rally Arabs, however, came a systematic attempt to woo French and British opinion, after the end of the Suez Canal crisis in 1956. Claiming that Arab news agencies emphasized objective facts and an absence of passion, advocates registered steady gains in European (and Japanese) reactions during the conflicts with Israel in the 1960s and 1970s. In 1971 an Egyptian weekly,

Al-Mossawen, ran an article entitled "How Did We Gain the Confidence of World Opinion?" By this point, unifying regional opinion was not seen as running counter to alignment with global views. Only the United States stood apart, being much harder to wean from Israeli partisanship, and even here there were some hopes of influence. What was clear, however, was that an organized effort was essential, given the political disunity in the region, the traditional disparagement of Arabs in the wider world, and the potency of Israeli propaganda. As one authority put it in the mid-1970s, "it is to be hoped that the countries of the Arab world will collectively apply a unified information policy."[5]

Subsequent developments were not encouraging. Egypt's leadership of the Arab world, always partly an assertion rather than a fact, faded. The lack of an Arab great power had the simultaneous effect of complicating any claim to a dominant Arab opinion and creating growing anxieties about vulnerabilities to outside news media and other influences. This latter concern was enhanced by ongoing changes in media technology. More and more Muslims purchased satellite dishes during the 1980s and 1990s, and conservatives, particularly within Islam, were quick to react. As one fundamentalist put it in 1992, "The West has directed these dishes at us;" or another from Iran: "The satellites are exactly against the honorable Prophet, exactly against the Qur'an."[6] Governments and religious leaders alike had great concerns about media, including the internet, that could not be readily controlled.

These developments combined with what could easily seem a steady diet of bad news. Apart from the open sore with Israel, Muslims were under attack in Afghanistan in the 1970s and later in the former Yugoslavia and Chechnya, several regimes suffered retaliatory raids from the United States, and then Iraq was defeated and subsequently isolated, at no small cost in human suffering, in the Gulf War. Many of these attacks could be justified, and certain Muslims and Muslim groups were by no means blameless, but the sense of powerlessness was very real. Sensitivities were acute, and sometimes almost incomprehensible to outsiders. President Clinton meets Salman Rushdie, the British author who had criticized Islam and been threatened in response; and a Palestinian newspaper reacts, "The United States behaves as though it wants to subdue and force the Islamic nation to its knees. It is raging real war against us."[7]

In this context, there was interest in renewing the effort to establish an independent voice, separate from that of the West. Modern technology could help. Islamic texts began to be digitized, which in principle not only provided wider access to the Muslim community but also more standardized guidance. Globalization meant increasing outside pressures and influences but also created new means of linking up the Muslim faithful, along with more conventional means such as scholarly exchanges and sending students to foreign religious centers. Indonesia and Malaysia, witnessing a revival of Islamic activity from the 1980s onward, found new and more active connections to the Middle East. The ability to communicate more authoritative religious pronouncements grew with technology. So did the ability to disseminate some standard, unifying images, most obviously of Israeli attacks on Palestinians but also of American actions in Iraq. The formation in 1996 of a new, independent Islamic television station in Qatar, al-Jazeera, promised still more widespread capacity to establish an Islamic, or at least, Arab view of the world, in contradistinction to the pervasive Western news media.

Some Western observers, noting correctly a widespread desire not to be captured by the (to them) conventional sources of information and Western-centered world opinion, talked of an Islamic iron curtain. This discussion was part of the clash of civilization model proposed in the 1990s by a few scholars and interested American politicians, with Islam as the new Soviet empire, just as bent on separation from global views and standards, and just as menacing to the West.[8]

Yet, though there was a gap, and a real challenge to those who sought an increasingly global defense of rights and principles, it is important not to press the case too far. Islamic media and views, aside from some core agreements particularly on the Palestinian cause, were highly divided. The lively Egyptian press routinely entertained both sides of the debate over whether or not Islamic resurgence was a good thing. The internet offered chances for global Islam but also for a host of dissident religious views to propagate – one reason that Islamic leaders remained wary of the medium (not granting authority, for example, to electronically issued fatwas). Most Middle Eastern governments, in classic authoritarian fashion, sought to control the news and were frequently hostile to larger statements. Al-Jazeera gained attention partly because it was outside government control and often critical of established regimes. It was in fact hailed as a move toward more liberal and professional standards – and it has never been accused of inaccuracy, even when it chose stories with priorities different from Western-oriented global rivals like C.N.N.

The bottom line, for the moment, was this: Islam fitted uncomfortably in broader world opinion, though the estrangement was not total. There was an Arab or Muslim view on certain issues – common references to the "Arab street" on issues such as the American invasion of Iraq, were not off the mark. An edginess about if not outright rejection of Western-dominated world opinion was unquestionable. But there was also serious contention over what the alternative voice should be, a few standard targets aside. World opinion faced a serious challenge but not a complete rebellion either from a key, and troubled, region or from the second-largest religion.

World opinion is by nature intolerant, even when it works for toleration. It has always involved moral judgments that assume righteousness pitted against injustice. This is a fundamental source of its strength and frequent effectiveness. Where participants in world opinion cannot agree on some common ethical concerns, there is no world opinion. (World opinion can form amid silence from certain regions, or lack of full voice, but it cannot form amid outright and open dispute among major regions.) But the intolerance of world opinion and its checkered history with Islam make for an uncomfortable relationship. It is tempting to argue that world opinion might ease up in certain areas, for example its attacks on traditional Muslim dress for women, which may, everything considered, be a rather superficial though certainly provocative target, in favor of a more accommodating stance accompanied by insistence on certain essentials in the area of human rights and protest tactics.

But this pious hope must also encounter the elusive qualities of world opinion. There is no central office for the global voice, no world opinion managers to whom suggestions for a degree of new flexibility might be submitted. Nongovernmental organizations serve this function to a degree, and some of the leading ones could usefully sponsor some extended dialogues on a more inclusive approach toward Islam that would not do away with the kinds of core standards that have produced positive results in the past. United Nations bodies have discussed criteria for women's rights or minimal working conditions. They have not always managed to get beyond an assumption that Western standards serve as the only logical reference points. What often results are pronouncements that are agreed to but then partly ignored, or acceptance of accords (such as the children's rights document of 1989) with a host of nation-by-nation exceptions that express hesitation but do not add up to a more collective expression of alternative outlook. New initiatives would be highly appropriate around the idea of testing levels of agreement but also opportunities for genuine but less purely Western standards. More opportunities for multilateral discussion of global criteria might not only narrow disagreements among major cultures around some combination of clarification and compromise but permit some advance in areas, like children's rights, that have so strangely fallen through the international cracks.

It is important to note that, since 2001, the United Nations Educational, Scientific and Cultural Organization (U.N.E.S.C.O.) and other organizations have been convening a "dialogue among civilizations," and the Pew Charitable Trust has been trying to probe the views of different parts of the world on key policy issues with a new level of detail and clarity. These are attempts to organize a better basis for world opinion, particularly around the inclusion of Islam. Whether the efforts can overcome the complex historical relationship between world opinion and Islam, and the recent failure of world opinion to win through on points, notably on Palestine and Iraq, where it lines up with Muslim sentiment, remains to be seen.

There is every reason to encourage more interchange among major news agencies, not to eliminate competition or to presume a single version of events, but to combat troubling parochialisms.

Steps should be encouraged from the Islamic side as well as that of world opinion. Discussion of participation in versus isolation from world opinion could add to the (admittedly crowded) agenda of debate within the Islamic world over issues of reform and resistance. The absence of many identifiable Islamic voices from recent iterations of world opinion, except where specific Muslim populations are involved, is troubling, at least from the world opinion standpoint and possibly in terms of the longer-term interests of Islam as well. Efforts to find ways to join, and to help shape, larger global efforts concerning situations that are neither Islamic nor Western could benefit all concerned. The Islamic world is vast, understandably producing many needs and goals; and events in recent decades make considerable self-preoccupation understandable. But there may be opportunities, without neglecting regional concerns, to branch out.

Two or three points justify, if not optimism, at least something other than resignation before an unbridgeable gap. First, the recent history of world opinion provides welcome reminders of a capacity to extend inclusion, from what was originally an Enlightenment–Protestant base. Jewish participation has been included on a range of key issues. The African disapora has become an active player. Active collaboration with Catholicism – not a full adoption of mutual agendas, but substantial cooperation possibilities – constituted a significant shift. Buddhist initiatives have created considerable overlap as well. There is precedent, in other words, for the kind of accommodation that could at some point embrace more voices from Islam.

There is precedent, as well, from Islam itself. Overshadowed in recent decades by anti-Western hostility and the more general self-preoccupation, earlier efforts from the Islamic world should not be forgotten. These include the leadership provided to international women's rights programs from Iran, in the 1950s, and Egyptian participation in campaigns against nuclear testing. Current Muslim reform groups often speak in a global rights language that could well promote greater use of, but also greater involvement in, world opinion. An Egyptian advocate, pushing against the current authoritarian regime, wonders about the quest for democracy as a potentially slavish adherence to Western standards – but then he pulls back, noting that the goals involve "universal rights."[9] Here is an invitation to invoke a larger voice and also the capacity to contribute to it. The challenge is considerable, but there is no reason to assume it cannot be met. Were anyone authorized to set the world opinion agenda, this should be item number one.

12

CONCLUSION: THE PROMISE AND PERILS OF WORLD OPINION

In 2003 the United Arab Emirates, increasingly successful as a major center for world trade, host to a growing number of Western and other visitors, and eager for further gains in international standing, abolished the use of young boys as drivers in camel races. Previously, boys as young as six had been tied to camels, often terrified, their service desirable because of their light weight in a popular and otherwise highly entertaining regional sport. A modest change, in the larger scheme of things, but of vital importance to a few children and revealing of the extent to which global standards have become a force to be reckoned with.

World opinion not only exists, but has a persistent historical record and has become a real factor in international relations and in the policies of states and corporations. The phenomenon is little more than two centuries old, despite some precedents in earlier outreach from several of the major religions. Its core has remained consistent, even as tactics and results have varied: a belief that common standards should be applied to the basic treatment of human beings and that when these standards are violated a surge of outrage is available across national boundaries – an outrage that should be heard.

Despite early success in the antislavery campaign, it took some time for world opinion to coalesce. Ambitions for its range of applicability exceeded reality in the later nineteenth century, though there were a few victories. But in the past fifty years the capacity to rouse world opinion has improved as that opinion itself has become more global. Experience in combining the force of world opinion with the policies and favors of specific governments, with international organizations, and with tactics such as boycotts has improved as well. The range of associations eager to use world opinion, and not simply to proclaim global standards in hopes that an implication of global approval will suffice, has swelled. The record of successful applications has also expanded. World opinion matters, on a significant spectrum of political, diplomatic, and social topics.

This book has ventured a history of world opinion, as a means of providing a more coherent context for understanding and assessing the whole phenomenon. Part of the intent was to establish a record, so the subject could be related more clearly to other aspects of modern and contemporary history. A second goal was to use historical case studies to spark further interest in global opinion as a living and, on the whole, essential and healthy force in the world today and in the future. But the same historical record provides opportunities for evaluation, and we turn to this in conclusion.

There are several vantage points for drawing lessons from world opinion's history. I will first discuss what the historical experience suggests as key strengths and weaknesses. This includes the world opinion's prospects for the future. I then turn, more briefly, to evaluation in terms of related social science theories, including globalization. Evaluation of world opinion as a partisan issue comes next, and then a discussion of the relationship with and prospects for American policy. Finally, some guidelines on what to hope for in future.

Characteristic limitations are obvious in world opinion; recent developments have merely confirmed some of them. Constraints on world opinion proved nearly overwhelming in the 1920s and 1930s and may accumulate again in the future. Fickleness in world opinion cannot be denied. This derives partly from media coverage, partly from the overwhelming volume of causes to which global outrage might be applied, and partly from more troubling flaws. It is hard to avoid the conclusion that the failure of global opinion to mobilize during some of the bloodbaths of Africa – in Uganda under Idi Amin, amid the genocide between Hutus and Tutsis in Rwanda, and today amid ongoing devastation in the Congo and Sudan – suggests a degree of racist resignation to tragedies in Africa, at least where Africans seem to be responsible for the harm done to other Africans. News is available, attempts to rouse a passionate response have been made, but scant outcry results. Partly, the hesitation reflects the unwillingness of great powers – particularly the United States – to become involved. But world opinion at its strongest has preceded policy, not waited for it. The deficiency stands.

History reveals several other pervasive constraints. First, world opinion may falter because the standards in question do not elicit as wide an agreement as organizers, or world culture scholars, might hope. Although the agenda open to world opinion has expanded, there are still some shortfalls, despite the apparent availability of global criteria. We have seen that, within the West as well as in other parts of the world, hesitations have arisen about many issues relating to conditions of women and children. Efforts to use world opinion to affect situations that are personal, and not just political, are complex at best, stillborn at worst. There are other specific factors. The decline in feminist fervor in the West, amid conservative resurgence, has combined with doubts among liberals about the legitimacy of imposing Western standards on varied cultures to limit the range of gender abuses over which world opinion can be aroused. Too many people either don't care much, sometimes wondering if the feminist cause has gone too far even at home, or worry about insensitivity to legitimate cultural diversity to support potent campaigns – often despite global pronouncements from international organizations. The same applies to aspects of labor conditions amid a declining labor movement in the leading capitalist societies. Consumer self-interest in lower wage costs and therefore prices competes with fairness standards. Over-reliance on associations and their rhetorical capacity may also have retarded global mobilization in some of these areas. It's important to recognize that there is no clear or effective world opinion on certain subjects where it might be expected.

World opinion has also displayed a tension between reliance on dramatic personal examples and a capacity to mobilize behind broader principles. The storms of petitions and emails that greet news of a particular Muslim woman condemned to brutal death because of a sexual offense – often winning reprieve – are not matched by opinion campaigns against wider movements of oppression, such as the activities of the Taliban regime in Afghanistan until it was brought down by its association with anti-American terrorism. Targeting is an issue for world opinion. Organizations like Amnesty International, heavily dependent on world opinion, struggle with a balance between individual cases and wider principles. The tension is not constant. There have been extensions of world opinion's range of operation, for example in the human rights area, with the addition of torture and the death penalty to the kinds of outrages over which world opinion could be roused in 1900 or even 1960. But a dilemma remains.

Mobilization of world opinion for individual tragedies relates to another issue: the sheer magnitude of the abuses that cry out for response. Even professionals in organizations like Amnesty International struggle with an enormous case load, which expands with every new application of global standards that seems imperative. The kind of people available for petitioning and funding, not themselves professional mobilizers, can be pardoned for feeling at times overwhelmed. Some of the lapses in global response to horrors in Africa surely result from sheer fatigue, and the same may apply to other inconsistencies, for example concerning child labor. World opinion is a valuable resource but it is not inexhaustible, and despite the importance of mobilizing groups like Amnesty International there is no agency available to prioritize the array of available issues for world opinion.

Other limitations are more predictable, though the recent historical record adds detail. It is no surprise that world opinion typically falls flat when it comes up against a great power resolved to carry on with an offensive policy regardless. We will turn to the specific application of this comment to the United States later. But the same incapacity to influence powerful states that showed so tragically in the 1930s against Germany, Japan, and Italy has persisted even as world opinion has surged and solidified in recent decades. There's little question that substantial global revulsion has applied to Russian policies in Chechnya, often echoed, if politely, by various governments. The result has encouraged some additional concealment and various rhetorical twists by the Russian leadership, but no real concessions. China resisted global reactions in suppressing its internal democratic movement in 1989. Eager more recently for international support to enter the World Trade Organization and to host the 2008 Olympics, China has shown a willingness periodically to release political or religious prisoners – but without systematic changes in policy thus far. Whether the subject is the United States in Iraq or attacks on the Falun Gong religious movement in China, world opinion's limits seem clear. Even France may weather the interesting global reactions to its 2004 policy to ban religious symbols – particularly, Islamic symbols – in public schools. The question always, when world opinion butts against an established government, is: what's to lose by defiance? Occasionally, with a mid-level power, there is a positive answer, as South Africa discovered in an extraordinary application of sustained world critique combined with economic leverage; but usually there is not.

The relationship between world opinion and war remains ambiguous, for some similar reasons. Since the early twentieth century, efforts to mobilize world opinion against war in general have usually aborted, often weakening the groups involved. Feminist and partial socialist association with anti-war stances not only failed to rouse global outrage more generally, but hampered efforts to win support for women's or labor causes. Too many people, in various parts of the world, open to global programs in other respects, do not yet believe that war in general should be condemned, as opposed to certain kinds of unjust wars or some of the concomitants of war that abuse individual human rights. Further, many of the anti-war campaigns, like the powerful surge against nuclear armaments, have bumped up against the kind of great power resistance that has not yet proved assailable. Participants in world opinion, at least since the 1920s, have known that something should be done about limiting war or defining the legitimacy of war. The recent effort by Human Rights Watch to argue that war is justifiable, to prevent imminent or ongoing slaughter but not to remedy past slaughter is an interesting proposal, and world opinion is grappling with more precise criteria, as the Iraq case demonstrated. Although there are tensions over war, definitions have advanced over time, to include agreement that certain acts of war are morally repugnant and that certain pretexts for war, such as pre-emption against the real or imagined existence of certain kinds of weapons, are unacceptable. The agreement against nuclear testing was another related advance. The relationship with war is a work in progress, but not a vacuum, for world opinion. The issue of adjusting the behavior of states to the standards of world opinion is the most obvious ongoing issue.

There are circumstances in which world opinion often works quite well. The admission of troubling limitations should not detract from the stature that world opinion has achieved. Optimal situations for effective world opinion embrace injustices that generate personal tragedies that can be widely and effectively dramatized, but which then encourage mobilization against the root causes because the injustice itself seems so obvious and so horrible. They apply to situations for which Westerners may feel some responsibility, despite geographic distance – like slavery, earlier on, or lynching by people of European origin in the United States or apartheid as practiced by the same in South Africa. Situations of extreme physical harm or threat (torture, environmental damage) are the most widely condemned, in part a legacy of the new hostility to pain that accompanied the rise of humanitarian sentiment in the Enlightenment. Responsibility here can be defined in terms of targets, rather than issues.

Another optimal setting involves countries (usually middling powers or less) that are particularly eager for international approval, open to embarrassment, sometimes because they depend on international admission to markets or economic aid; or corporations dependent on international consumer response and therefore vulnerable to criticism backed by boycott potential. In certain cases these situations produce concessions more rhetorical than real, but there can be real change.

Different goals have different potentials for successful impact. The ideal cause is one for which global standards – Western oriented as they still often are – seem firmly established and preclude widely recognized dissent or alternatives. Slavery remains the classic case, but systematic racial abuse or political torture (when it can be documented and publicized) have been added to the list. The explosion of world opinion in 2004 against American prison atrocities in Iraq, and the quick American retreat, despite some rhetorical seesawing, as United States leaders realized their vulnerability on this issue whatever their real thoughts about torture, is an intriguing example of world opinion's expanded range and in this case its effectiveness even against the superpower. The ability to join opinion and publicity with other sanctions – such as criteria of entry into global or regional agreements, or boycotting – enhances potential impact immensely. The challenge, for individuals and groups eager to use world opinion in a wider range of situations, is to expand upon these ingredients.

Successful impact goes beyond the victories recorded in specific campaigns, whether these target individuals or larger policies. Some moves are designed to anticipate world opinion before it is fully mobilized. The decision on camel drivers is a case in point – criticisms could be expected, as international contacts increased, so reform reflected an anticipatory recognition of world opinion's standards and power. In other instances, world opinion contributes to a context in which policies are revised. In 2003–4, for example, several American states began to modify the application of the death penalty (eliminating the possibility of sentencing minors, for example, whose inclusion made the United States virtually unique in the world). A number of factors entered in. But unease about world reactions, at a time when the United States hardly enjoyed great global favor, was one ingredient and encouraged the efforts of domestic reform groups. There is no question that world opinion is often ignored or rejected; there is no question that minor concessions – a prisoner release or two, or the formation of an in-house labor standards group – are in some cases designed to deflect attention from larger deviations; but the impact remains considerable over a range of targets.

Two larger questions apply, though one may be impossible to answer and the other certainly difficult. First, can world opinion keep pace with the level of abuses that humans and human institutions can perpetrate on each other? And, second, are the limitations on world opinion increasing relative to the opportunities for positive results? Both questions, though particularly the second, relate to the most obvious issue for the future: whether world opinion can develop further.

The balance sheet is challenging. World opinion in the twentieth century failed to prevent major and disastrous wars and a scale of genocide – from the Holocaust to Cambodia and Rwanda – without precedent in modern history. It failed to prevent many new or extended forms of labor exploitation, or even a new round in the international sex trade of women and girls. Despite some individual victories, it has hardly checked a host of environmental depredations. Greenpeace and kindred groups have made an unquestionable contribution, but global warming and other problems have overrun their efforts to date. On the other hand, world opinion has made it more difficult – not, unfortunately, impossible – to enslave and literally impossible to create large systems of slavery. It has for the moment contributed to the reduction of political imprisonment and torture in a number of places, including much of Latin America. Despite its many limitations and hesitations, it has encouraged (along with other factors) a widespread expansion of political rights and educational opportunities for women in varied parts of the world, just as, earlier, global reactions helped end specific abuses such as Chinese foot-binding.

We have just emerged from a complex century in which people's inhumanity to people has seldom been so evident, but in which a number of measurable improvements occurred in aspects of the human condition. World opinion was relevant to most of the cases of inhumanity but too often failed either to mobilize at all or to have impact. But world opinion was also relevant to some of the gains.

Some pundits have suggested that world opinion may encounter additional limitations in future. First, they note the emergence of movements that simply are immune to global outrage. Warring bands in Africa either do not hear world reactions, since they operate in a fairly closed environment, or do not care, for they lack the considerations that promote embarrassment, including any desire to be admitted to international organizations or trade arrangements. The latter applied to the Taliban in Afghanistan. Here a movement arose explicitly defiant of world opinion, excited by its ability to thumb its nose at global standards without (for some time) apparent consequence. Will movements of this sort proliferate? The obvious moralism and fairly obvious Westernism of world opinion creates its own backlash, and it is possible that barriers will increase.

Other predictions suggest that support for world opinion will decline as the Western world – and particularly the United States – pulls away from humanitarian internationalism in response to terror.[1] If the world is increasingly viewed as a hostile environment, the capacity to care actively about distant others could diminish substantially. Here, despite well-intentioned warnings, the prospects seem less bleak. There is good reason to worry, at least short term, about the growing defensiveness and suspiciousness of the United States in the international arena. Barriers to travel and study in the United States have increased, and the temptation toward further isolationism is real. But the United States has never been the center of effective world opinion, and European reactions – despite or because of a longer experience with terror – are visibly different. Despite some new unilateralism, even the United States remains actively involved in international monitoring in many areas. Its human rights organizations continue to seek out abuse, and increasing activities against targets like the sex trade or American mistreatment of foreign political prisoners hardly suggest declining involvement. Response to humanitarian disasters like the 2004 Iranian earthquake, from genuine compassion plus an awareness of diplomatic potential, is also encouraging. If there are legitimate questions about a possible increase of resistance to world opinion, doubts about the durability of both a substantial commitment to global standards and a capacity for sympathy and outrage are misplaced.

We noted in the introduction the relationship between a study of world opinion and several existing lines of theory and research. Briefly returning to the relationship provides another way to define what world opinion, past and present, is all about.

Sociologists who have sought to define what they call global culture have necessarily covered key aspects of world opinion, though they've paid far more attention to the pronouncements of non-governmental organizations and other international bodies than to world opinion per se. They fail to make the distinction between associational pronouncements and wider participation that this study has emphasized. Even so, the focus on definable world opinion confirms that a number of global standards have indeed emerged that can, properly mobilized, spark a powerful international audience. World opinion is, however, more fickle and more limited than the definitions of global culture have usually allowed. Not every major abuse generates the expected outburst. Some extensions of world opinion, for example concerning women or children, have simply not found a reliable constituency outside the world of the reform-minded NGOs. Some resistance calls attention to the continued Western orientation of many aspects of world opinion and its leadership – a complexity that global culture scholarship tends to play down. The study of world opinion, in sum, overlaps with but differs from the effort to define a world culture. It suggests important issues and complexities that will enrich world culture research.

We have explored the links between realistic assessment of world opinion and the clash of civilizations argument, particularly in chapter 11. World opinion is often constrained by bitterly competing values. At times, world opinion has indeed enhanced the vigorous expression of these values, as regions seek to maintain their identity against the often preachy assertions of global standards. The existence, force, and continued expansion of global opinion argue against glib acceptance of a clash of civilizations model for the world's future. But world opinion is undeniably limited by clash, and the problems here may grow.

World opinion, finally, both complements and conflicts with the broader theories of globalization. The emergence of a recognizable, if not fully mature, world opinion more than two centuries ago reminds us that the origins of globalization may not be as recent as some advocates maintain. Moreover, world opinion provides a significant extension to the claim that international interactions are not only accelerating but are seriously changing the way people live. Less significant than global economic ties or even the diffusion of consumer culture, world opinion nevertheless deserves a place in the globalization lexicon. Its influence on political decisions, corporate behavior, and some social policies, and its intensification since the 1950s, deserve inclusion in any definition of globalization and global forces.

Yet world opinion, particularly in recent decades, has sought to counterbalance aspects of globalization. The need to find new ways to dispute forces beyond the control not just of individuals but of national governments or labor unions or feminist movements has been a vital spur to contemporary world opinion. World opinion is not, to date, anti-globalization. It is not, yet, mobilizable against global consumerism. The explicitly anti-globalization protests that began in Seattle in 1999, directed against the World Bank and other agencies of international capitalism, are interesting and significant but they have not captured a global audience. The groups involved have more limited constituencies, even aside from those anarchist elements that seek primarily to disrupt for disruption's sake. But world opinion has lined up behind some of the environmentalist concerns that were being expressed in the anti-globalization risings. And there is a partial embrace of the attacks on abuses of labor which formed part of the same current.

The relationship between world opinion and globalization is thus ambiguous and is likely to remain so. World opinion depends on globalization, including linkage technologies such as the internet and the lessening of national barriers. It is part of globalization and has directly contributed to it. Yet it is also a partially opposing force to key features of globalization, a counterbalance whose importance may increase. Whether world opinion or regional identities will best serve to restrain the excesses of globalization is an interesting question. Regional resistance offers the more dramatic tactics and the more flamboyant statements, but world opinion has a role as well.

Looking at world opinion as a partisan issue or an American problem – the subject of this section and the next – involves different measurements from those applied to the interaction with globalization. Most critiques of world opinion, like those of public opinion in general, have focused on limitations to effectiveness. They note the fickleness of world opinion and worry that it has inadequate impact on policy, at least in the arena of great power relations and military action. They seek generalizations to explain where and how it works or doesn't work. But the same critics admit that world opinion is usually a force for reasonableness and peace, so they worry more about its constraints and blindspots than about the quality of its standards.[2] This book has, similarly, assumed that world opinion is in the main a positive force, and we return to this claim later on. The book has raised some questions about undue reliance on Western standards and on a disproportionately Western audience which at times can verge on a kind of moral imperialism even as territorial imperialism has declined. (World opinion's role in correcting global institutions and processes caused by the West must also be noted.) The fact remains that we should be worrying far more about making world opinion more effective than about its validity.

This statement should of course rouse debate, though I would love to believe that this book has provided convincing arguments on its behalf. Two issues, beyond Westernism, must be acknowledged. One, on why Americans should accept world opinion's utility at a time when they are under scrutiny, we take up in the next section. The other, though related, involves more general issues of partisanship. Is the embrace of world opinion simply another example of liberal academese? We live at a time of vigorous debate between what Americans call liberals and conservatives, and there is no way to duck some evaluation of world opinion as a "good thing" amid considerable conservative suspicion. The issues are not as partisan as they might appear, but some judgment calls are essential.

World opinion has often challenged conservative commitments. Insofar as world opinion has characteristically involved the application of Western standards against traditional practices in other societies, it has run foul of Chinese or Islamic or African conservatism in defense of familiar standards. The campaigns against slavery raised conservative concerns closer to home about the sanctity of property. More recently, the commitment of many Western conservatives, particularly in America, to relatively unfettered capitalism, has raised tensions between some of the concerns embraced by global opinion and the conservative impulse.

As political leaders Western conservatives have frequently made their peace with regimes that do not live up to asserted global standards, because of supposed national interest. When world opinion attacked apparent Ottoman abuses against Bulgarians, it also had to attack the conservative leader Benjamin Disraeli, who was eager to conciliate the Ottomans in the interests of keeping other great powers out of the Middle East and preserving a buffer for British India. Clashes of this sort continue, now most often involving American commitment to regimes widely condemned in world opinion, from Israel to Central Asia (or in the recent past Central America). Pragmatic diplomats have frequently found world opinion a nuisance, and there is no reason to expect their annoyance to diminish.

Western conservatism also allied fiercely with nationalism, from the later nineteenth century onward. Defense of nationalism facilitated other aspects of defense of the status quo and also proved a fertile source of votes for conservative causes. Liberals, once the staunch allies of nationalism, did not systematically reject that commitment, but they lost ground in the nationalist camp and were in any event more open to internationalist appeals of the sort that could also rouse world opinion. Increasingly, much of the passion that went into global protests has been matched, in the conservative camp, by equally fervent defense of national autonomy and a host of domestic positions. For American conservatives, staunchly wedded to national sovereignty against any outside intrusion, these tensions have multiplied in recent years with globalist efforts to establish new international treaties, on subjects ranging from abuses by soldiers to environmental degradation, and with the growing opposition of world opinion to the death penalty.

There is no need to exaggerate the gulf. The origins of world opinion embrace a strong dose of Enlightenment, or liberal, humanitarianism, but also an infusion of Christian moral responsibility extended beyond the bounds of the religion. Many conservatives have resonated with the latter component of world opinion, and many resonate still. This can complicate the conservative–world-opinion divide, and not only in the West.

Over time, conservatives in most societies have assimilated many of the causes espoused by world opinion. No systematic defense of slavery is currently part of any conservative agenda. Although some European and American conservatives might argue about the priority of the issue, and certainly about definitions and latitudes, open advocacy of torture has disappeared as well. Conservatives can also contribute to global condemnations of many oppressive regimes or of violations of women's rights. It was after all a conservative American regime that played up global standards for women in relation to campaigns in Afghanistan, and this was not entirely window dressing. Except for extremist movements, European and Canadian conservatives since World War II have not differed markedly from liberals and socialists in their commitment to global standards – another sign that, whatever the initial tensions, a constructive evolution can occur. The major shift toward participation in world opinion by the Catholic Church, from the mid-1960s onward, was a huge step in reducing any automatic clash between world opinion and the principles of contemporary conservatism.

World opinion, in sum, has partisan overtones, from both past and present. Some of its targets and claims mesh with the larger clash between conservatives and their opponents in the United States, whether these opponents dare to claim the maligned mantle of liberalism or not. Political views color any assessment of the quality and value of world opinion. The American context is, however, distinctive, and even in this context the clash between world opinion and conservative positions is not complete. Many conservatives can and do find value in supporting many global standards, and world opinion need not stand or fall as a creature of partisan debate. Issues there are, but they are nuanced and depend heavily on specific times and places – including, of course, the United States today. The fact remains that most people in numerous regions – the West, the Americas, much of East Asia – and many elsewhere would agree that the goals of world opinion have usually been just, even if they provoked resistance at the time, and that problems have emanated far more from ineffective reach or tactics than from intent.

The relationship between world opinion and the United States is even more significant today than that between world opinion and conservatism. For many people, world opinion, in seeking to constrain the United States, is another means of voicing a larger need to find some way to harness forces that are outpacing human control – in this case, the forces embodied in a single dominant superpower. The need is as palpable in Europe, the traditional center of world opinion, as in developing regions. And the result poses a challenge to American policy well beyond the vagaries of any single presidential administration, even one as bent on compounding the challenge as that of George W. Bush.

The United States has long maintained an ambiguous role in world opinion – far more ambiguous than many Americans, often somewhat parochial while also convinced of the global validity of national standards, have recognized. (One of the reasons Americans are shocked when world opinion opposes them is an assumption that the United States and world opinion are one and the same; but they are not and never have been.) Although Americans have participated fully in many currents of world opinion, sharing international leadership in some efforts, such as the women's movement or the campaign against apartheid, world opinion has been more commonly centered in Western Europe than in the United States. From slavery onward, world opinion has also recurrently targeted issues in the United States, particularly though not exclusively in the racial area. Americans have sometimes responded, but at other times have displayed shock or resistance. The Human Rights Watch efforts to point out abuses in American women's prisons, for example, tended to encounter denial: rights movements were for other parts of the world, not the United States. On crucial recent issues, such as responses to global population pressure, American policymakers have staked out a distinctive line – rejecting the dissemination of birth control devices, in contrast to European and most Asian domestic and international policy; here, the United States has not so much defied world opinion as contributed to preventing its formation, while bolstering its national position as maverick on the global stage.

The United States also has a long tradition of anxious defense of national sovereignty and immunity from foreign pressures, the heritage of isolation plus nervousness about demographic dilution through immigration. This impulse, recently visible in the spate of rejections of international treaties, further complicates reactions to world opinion. Even campaigns in which many Americans have amply shared, like that against land mines, frequently run up against the unwillingness to yield any national prerogatives. And on other issues, like the death penalty, on which American majorities disagree with global standards, resistance can be stubborn indeed. Europeans, who have their own problems with some global influences – more nervous about immigrants, for example, than their United States counterparts – have painfully learned the need to modify national sovereignty in the interests of effective action, and in this sense too participate more smoothly in world opinion.

United States leadership in the Cold War also complicated its relationship with aspects of world opinion. American espousal of human rights against

Communist oppression could facilitate alignment between U.S. officialdom and long-standing traditions of world opinion. On the other hand, American suspicions of left-leaning regimes, and national willingness to support authoritarians who cooperated in the Cold War, could put the nation at odds with global standards and global advocates. Here again is a gap still not entirely healed, indeed perhaps reviving in the American preoccupation with a friend-or-foe policy toward terrorism.

Finally, the end of the Cold War left the United States as the world's only superpower and as such the target of particularly sensitive global scrutiny. Considerable envy and ambivalence had earlier dogged reactions to the United States, resented for its wealth and its tendency to throw its weight around; to these reactions was added the new sense of powerlessness, recognition that there was no easy resistance to arbitrary American action. It was almost inevitable that the United States' standing in world opinion would suffer as a result, and this condition will prevail for the foreseeable future. The deterioration has been hard for many Americans to fathom, convinced of their benevolence, or uninterested in the wider world, or both. Ironically, during the 1990s, even as American supremacy increased, American interest in and knowledge of the wider world diminished, with less coverage in newscasts and with the media closing many foreign offices. Television viewers are much more likely to know about the latest device to check for prostate cancer than to know what's going on in China or India. With American prosperity at an all-time peak, riding the high-tech wave, it was easy to assume that the rest of the world was becoming less relevant or that it should be approached by insistence on the global validity of American standards. This was not a mood in which divergent world opinion could be readily recognized.

Into this setting came unprecedented, bloody terrorist attacks in 2001, which convinced many American leaders that any national action might be justified as a matter of self-defense. Into this setting came also a presidential administration with a particularly unilateral global agenda, a defiant unwillingness to conciliate world opinion in any significant area, and an apparent proclivity to attempt to mislead about the real motivations for national action. Even before 9/11, the eagerness to defy international opinion with rejection of the Kyoto environmental accord – exacerbated by the lack of effort to discuss alternatives – suggested a growing rupture. The breaking point came with Iraq, where the United States acted despite the massive demonstrations of opposition in most parts of the world and despite the pleas of allies whose views many United States leaders seemed to delight in ridiculing.

Americans themselves hesitated. Before the Iraq war was launched, about a third of all Americans simply opposed the war; another third favored it, in some cases partly because of their resentment against international disapproval; and the other third wanted to wait until international backing could be obtained. Once the war was launched, however, the majority lined up behind the President, and even a year later, despite many indications of deceit and disappointment, many have remained relatively solid in their commitment. The gulf between national sentiment and international opinion widened. Majorities in many countries (even a number whose governments backed the war) viewed the United States as out of control, even as the bulk of the American people maintained their commitment to war and occupation. For some Americans, opposition to the war became a sign of enmity – near-treason within the United States, betrayal from quondam friends abroad. Even sources of news began to diverge dramatically. Coverage of the Iraq war varied greatly when American newscasts were compared even with those of its ally, Great Britain, and this merely enhanced the gap between national reactions and prevailing world opinion. Americans did not even know the same things, for example about the impact of bombing raids on Iraqi civilians, as the rest of the world thought it knew.

So here is a nation with a surprisingly complex history in terms of its relationships with world opinion, almost inevitably on the hot seat because of unprecedented power, which has recently exacerbated tensions through a series of defiant actions and with stated policies that claim a national right to unilateral action in future. Precisely because world opinion has become a real player in international relations, this new clash looms large in any assessment of the future.

In the short run, world opinion failed and demonstrations died down in face of the application of military force in Iraq. The lesson was familiar: world opinion cannot stare down a determined great power. There were Americans, including some in the administration, who found world opinion not only irrelevant but a goad to further assertiveness, an insult to a national conviction that American policies were not only vital to self-interest but beneficial to the wider world whether this world realized it or not. As some former allies began to make conciliatory noises, it was possible to believe that the United States had succeeded in overriding global hostility.

Yet the gap between world opinion and the United States had not really closed. International polls revealed unprecedented suspicion and hostility. This gap is unacceptable for the longer run, for at least three reasons.

One: Americans, despite their divergences from global standards, and despite current partisan debate over the global voice, are not collectively comfortable with international disdain. The disdain can be ignored for a time, concealed for a while through bellicose rhetoric; and it can goad a minority to proclaim more durable defiance. But most Americans will find that they want some degree of reconciliation with world opinion. Sensitivity goes well back in the national tradition: the preamble of the Declaration of Independence specifically refers to the framers' concern for "a decent respect to the opinions of mankind" – accurately suggesting the link between the emerging national political culture and the early phases of world opinion. To be sure, change is always possible. A nation long known, and sometimes criticized, for its sensitivity to global (and particularly European) disapproval, its perhaps naïve desire to be everyone's friend, could alter its stripes. To date, however, the American tradition assumes that the nation should operate with some degree of global approval – if not outright admiration. Many Americans are already uncomfortable with their nation's low international standing and, despite defiance or denial or sheer ignorance, more will become so.

The question of different national degrees of receptivity to and participation in world opinion is an intriguing one. We've noted that Canada has developed something of a commitment to leadership in human rights activity, as Japan has on peace issues. France may have a particularly sensitive interest in world opinion because of the self-image of its intellectuals and their role in mobilizing a broader public (certainly not the situation in the United States). An astute observer in contrast rates Russians – and not just their leaders – as characteristically recalcitrant about world opinion, despite or perhaps because of a historical experience of sensitivity to Western criticism. Though seeking approval, so this analysis runs, Russians are so accustomed to the effect of sheer power, and so tolerant of unfairness, that pressure from public opinion is likely to be noticed but shrugged off.[3] Americans have their own ambivalences and divisions. Until recently, they have tended to ignore international concerns about the death penalty, or even to stiffen their commitment on grounds that the subject is no one else's business. On balance, however, even on internal matters such as race relations, Americans have usually registered global criticism and have sought to conciliate it. Opinion counts strongly in American political culture, and global opinion is seen as a relevant measure of national standing. Long-term estrangement over foreign policy will have domestic ramifications, among other things weakening any internal support for forceful action. It was not just the complications in the occupation of Iraq but discomfort amid hostile world opinion that prompted a growth in open American doubts about the war during 2004.

Two: As members of the Bush administration have increasingly realized, deliberate defiance of international opinion has unacceptable short-run costs, whatever the demands of self-image over the longer haul. It turned out, predictably enough, that though conciliation of world opinion was unnecessary to the military effort in Iraq, it proved increasingly essential in the aftermath of apparent victory. There was the cost factor: in a complex task of reconstruction, the United States soon turned to former allies for financial contributions, and faced rough going because of its earlier unilateral stance and its continued unwillingness to accept allies or the United Nations as participants in policymaking for Iraq. There was the political factor: faced with unexpected Iraqi resistance, American leadership made recurrent gestures toward eliciting more international backing and forming a more international occupation force. Whether real internationalization would have lessened postwar violence is not clear, but it is possible. Ironically, lack of global support made the United States more vulnerable to short-term Iraqi demands, so it agreed to a political transition more quickly than some observers found sensible. The lesson is clear: American power is not great enough to allow the nation to shoulder burdens such as those in Iraq single-handedly, but if it wants world support it has to pay attention to world opinion before the fact.

Richard Haass, a former State Department official and president of the Council of Foreign Relations, argues that the Iraq war falls into a clear category of a "war of choice" – not essential as a matter of national defense (whatever the Bush administration's arguments) and not so regarded in the world at large.[4] Precisely because the motives for such wars are complex – not necessarily wrong, but not clear-cut – and because the results of wars against nations as large and diverse as Iraq are always difficult, wars of choice require careful cultivation of international support. They should be postponed until such support is won – until world opinion is lined up or at least clearly muddled, such that genuine international participation is possible, with all that means for American unity, financial assistance, and political cover both globally and in the target state. The postwar complexities of Iraq strongly suggest that American sensitivity to world opinion needs to be part of any comparable effort in the future – as had been the case in the earlier Gulf War.

Three: Finally, there is the future itself. American foreign policy will be constrained by the legacy of international bitterness the Iraq war has generated. Comparable action in future will be massively more difficult. When a majority of people in an entity like the European Union – fifty-three percent in a late 2003 poll – believe that the United States is at least as great a threat to world peace as North Korea, and greater than any other major power, American policy has reduced its own freedom of action for some time to come. National self-interest demands a massive repair job.

For several reasons, then, from national self-comfort to simple diplomatic self-interest the national good requires a more careful approach to world opinion, one that recognizes it as a serious factor in key areas of national policy – perhaps including even criminal justice policy – and shows greater willingness to acknowledge, compromise, and conciliate. This is not just a partisan issue, certainly not an abstract debate over morality (though that might be salutary as well). It compels change, even beyond the current presidential administration, and it demands attention from American leaders and all but the most hardened parochial minority.

How quickly and successfully the United States will revise its relationship to world opinion is anybody's guess. Conservative reactions to any constraints on national sovereignty must be reckoned with, though hopefully reminders of successful conciliations, such as Eisenhower's on nuclear testing, could open new discussion. Any process of harmonization will be complicated and imperfect, as the longer historical record as well as the explicit legacy of Iraq suggest. Preoccupied with domestic issues, the majority of the American people are not yet deeply concerned about global hostility; it may be some time before any new leadership takes the problem firmly in hand. Annoying and constraining as world opinion can be for a power like the United States, it has to be attended to, and interactions will change in the future.

It is also vital to remember that while the relationship between world opinion and the United States is complicated, world opinion is not (or was not until very recently) systematically anti-American. World opinion rallied smartly to the United States after the 2001 terrorist attacks, and there is wide attraction to many aspects of American life. A reconciliation effort almost certainly has to begin from the American side, but it does not require starting from scratch.

Here, then, is a huge agenda item, wrapped in some bitterly partisan issues within the United States. World opinion could continue to evolve as a largely anti-American force, while trying to pursue other targets that have nothing to do with this tension. Its effectiveness would surely suffer, and the complications for the many internationally sensitive Americans, and American-dominated groups like Human Rights Watch, that play key roles in many facets of world opinion would be intriguing. But the bigger challenge by far is to American leadership. World opinion is strong enough to persist even with United States defiance; the current tension may even increase the participation in world opinion of parts of Asia, Africa, and the Middle East. It is difficult to imagine continuing superpower success for the United States on a collision course with world opinion. The United States' military potential might not be dented, but its application would become increasingly constrained and internal support for great power operations would become steadily more confused and divided. Remedial action is essential. A valid test for American statesmanship is its success in confronting this challenge, despite the short-run temptations of playing up nationalist defiance.

The history of world opinion offers lessons but not prediction. No history says what will happen next, though it may guess, and the history of global opinion is no exception. Nor is there a governing world opinion agency to which suggestions can be directed. World opinion has always been amorphous, led by a variety of media outlets and advocacy organizations, and this is not likely to change.

There are, however, a few developments to hope for. One would not be hard to achieve, though it requires leadership: it would be very useful periodically to review world opinion on major current issues, noting where it does not cohere as well as where it does, and to publicize the reviews as widely as possible beyond scholarly ranks. Polling compilations are available – Gallup issues its international polling results on an annual basis. But these polls apply to an almost random array of issues, not all of which call forth world opinion. They are taken nationally, and though the results can be combined this falls short of world opinion as well. A more recent venture, the Pew Global Attitudes project (supported by the Pew Charitable Trusts), goes a bit further in identifying more fundamental issues, including key aspects of globalization. Thus in 2004 a significant poll was issued on generational attitudes toward global contacts, finding a wide gap in the United States and Western Europe (younger people far more likely than their elders to welcome global influences and not to claim cultural superiority), but more uniformity in Eastern Europe and particularly Asia, Africa, and the Middle East, where greater overall wariness about foreign influences remains. Another poll looked at deepening European suspicion of the United States a year after the Iraq war. This new polling approach is terrific stuff, and it is regional rather than purely national. It does tend, however, to look for global differences rather than overlaps (partly because global differences remain very real). It does not measure depth of commitment or passion, not to mention outrage, key components of world opinion. The Global Attitudes project does not, in fact, identify a dominant world opinion.[5] Any effort to pretend to define world opinion beyond polling would of course be contestable – the debate itself could be informative – but it should be undertaken. This would also facilitate the definition of world opinion (again, recognizing that it will not always exist) on the kinds of social issues that do not necessarily generate dramatic individual tragedies.

We need to know, not annually but every decade or so, whether world opinion has expanded or not – in its international base as well as its agenda. Will global evolution generate greater involvement in world opinion from Russia or China, as it has already from the Pacific Rim and Latin America? When will African voices (beyond those of inspired leaders like Mandela) enter in? Will world opinion solidify over at least some of the more extreme aspects of child labor, as very recent international conventions suggest? Will the NGOs so vital to the mobilization of world opinion successfully add to their own agendas (for example, more clearly than thus far over women's issues), as they have in the recent past? Again, it is not easy to capture world opinion in process, and hard to define what world opinion agenda can be stipulated as opposed to hoped for. The history of world opinion demonstrates, however, that expansion is recurrent, as agreement on human and environmental rights expands. We need to capture the process as it moves into the future. Creative scholarship can respond to this kind of need.

It is to be hoped that global opinion can reconcile with two of the leading forces in the contemporary world with which it is currently out of harmony. We've already tackled the question of the United States, where considerable responsibility rests with yet-to-be introduced American leadership. The question of Islam is more complicated, for world opinion has never readily embraced Islamic elements. Clearer inclusion of appropriate and available Islamic voices in the mobilization of world opinion, including extension of existing efforts by relevant NGOs, is one path. Islamic opinion should expand to include pronouncements on global issues, beyond endless soul searching about Islam itself. Clarification of what's vital and what's not is another path. Is it either necessary or useful for world opinion to press about every aspect of traditional costumes for women? What is the relationship between global labor standards and Islamic law? The historical record displays several crucial reconciliations between traditional religious forces and world opinion. Though more difficult for obvious historical reasons, an accommodation between an adjusted Islam and a more careful world opinion is not impossible to envisage.

The history of world opinion provides depth to the definition of the phenomenon. By singling out alternative tactics and periods of change, it improves the grasp of how world opinion works and what its current trends are in relation to past patterns. History enriches our understanding of blindspots, failures of omission, and incomplete consensus. It reveals the recurrent trend toward expansion of the kinds of issues world opinion can embrace, and though it does not describe the future it may suggest additional targets to be added to the agenda.

The most striking conclusion from world opinion's history is both simple and dramatic: for all intents and purposes, world opinion has always been right when roused. The historical record, including recent history, supports the claim that was simply asserted in the preface.

Aside from current controversies, world opinion has supported the right side in disputes from antislavery through the sweatshop campaigns, and East Timor – that is, for at least two hundred years. Resistance is common at the time of first expression; it is sometimes prolonged and sometimes successful; but it has always been proved wrong. World opinion has expressed one of the best and most constructive sides of modern humanity. Combined with local protest and the bridging efforts of mobilizing groups, it has allowed segments of the world's most vulnerable groups to gain occasional voice. One can debate a few interactions, like the accuracy of the manipulated data that led to attacks on Ottoman policies in the late nineteenth century or the apparently exaggerated anxiety about white slavery in the same time period. Media mistakes can lead to distorted definitions of problems. Many Americans would currently contest global standards concerning the death penalty, and Israeli leaders defy world opinion's tilt toward the Palestinian cause. Various societies can legitimately note the Western bias that world opinion frequently conveys. There have also been cases, for example during the Cold War, when divisions of world opinion on key issues such as the power balance or capitalism precluded tidy judgments about which set of standards offered greater validity.

Yet the basic argument stands. The force has been immensely salutary; the most obvious problems in its history have involved ineffectiveness, failure to articulate, or lapses in the global attention span, not goals. The principles world opinion has advocated have been sound, and this has held true even as the range of issues open to global scrutiny has expanded. Though Americans may debate world opinion's validity on the death penalty, it is pretty clear that world opinion was right about Iraq. The considerable record of moral accuracy continues.

Furthermore, the validity of world opinion is not accidental. Three factors are worth considering here.

First, wide audiences may have a built-in capacity to render accurate judgments. Over the past two centuries there's been recurrent effort to locate truth in large groups – this was once an argument for nationalism – and though some of this line of argument is abstract, or nonsensical, or at times downright scary, there may be a kernel of truth. Recent studies have emphasized the importance of canvassing wide audiences as a market-based means of finding out more about likely developments in the future than individual experts can themselves predict. Broad-based opinion may in and of itself develop criteria for predictive accuracy as well as, as argued here, moral judgments, which would provide some explanation for the historical as well as contemporary findings and could also establish political neutrality for the basic validity claim.[6]

More concretely, by the later twentieth century world opinion was sometimes becoming right because it wielded sufficient force to press its point home. In my opinion, world opinion was morally correct about apartheid. Its effectiveness, once fully engaged and backed by appropriate tactics, gave its partisans the upper hand in evaluation, and in the history books. Increasingly – and this could be a factor in Iraq – world opinion is often right because it so complicates the policy implementations of powers that disagree.

Most important, however, is the fact the world opinion's validity stems from its own basic components. When a cause is clear enough to stir world opinion, to rouse moral outrage across national and cultural boundaries, increasingly not just in the West, it has passed a crucial litmus test. Both the depths of passion and the international conviction meet standards that favor moral accuracy. The judgment of history so far uniformly supports the criteria world opinion has defined in the past and the resultant definition of atrocities that must be stopped. World opinion may err in future, and there will always be debate about new applications. Past performance does not assure the future. But the historical record is important and should give serious pause to policymakers who seek to ignore international judgment. They may succeed in the short run, but they are unlikely to be vindicated over time.

The validity of world opinion is at best half the story where the future is concerned. Amid current debate about a possible retreat of world opinion, at least in the human rights area, in the face of terrorism and renewed division, the optimists are probably right: the global voice will continue, even if there are new challenges. The effectiveness of this voice is another matter. World opinion has won major triumphs over a two-century span. But it has often failed in basic tests, or ignored vital issues, or won merely passing or rhetorical adherence – aside from important areas in which it has not coalesced at all. World opinion has become a factor in diplomacy but has not uniformly rolled back the dark forces of torture, rape, or even genocide. Here, optimism would be misplaced.

We can call for a greater appreciation of world opinion, understood now as a historical phenomenon of real importance, and we can urge additional mobilization and greater range. But we cannot assume that world opinion will sustain its momentum toward greater impact and more ambitious scope.[7]

Human Rights Watch recently issued a timely appeal urging humanity to preserve the twenty-first century from some of the horrors that shrouded the twentieth. World opinion, mobilized and heeded, is one of the key forces that might allow this challenge to be met. It deserves systematic attention and respect because of the values it can add to the global human condition.[8]

NOTES

Chapter 1

1. Donald Rumsfeld, *Pieces of Intelligence: The Existential Poetry of Donald H. Rumsfeld*, Hart Seely, ed. (New York: Villerd, 2003), p. 29.
2. For one recent, largely contemporary effort, see Frank Rusciano, ed., *World Opinion and the Emerging International Order* (Westport, CT: Greenwood, 1998).
3. Samuel Huntington, *The Clash of Civilization and the Remaking of World Order* (New York: Simon & Schuster, 1996); Jacques Baudo, ed., *Building a World Community: Globalization and the Common Good* (Seattle: University of Washington Press, 2001); Richard Langhorne, *Coming of Globalization* (New York: Palgrave MacMillan, 2001); John Gray, *False Dawn* (New York: New Press, 1998).
4. John Boli and George Thomas, eds., *Constructing World Culture* (Stanford: Stanford University Press, 1999): p. 35; John Meyer, J. Boli, G. Thomas, and F. Ramirez, "World Society and the Nation State," *American Journal of Sociology*, 103 (1997), p. 152.
5. David Weeks, "The Armenian Question and British Policy in Turkey, 1894–1896," M.A. thesis, University of London, 1950; see also Akaby Nassibian, *Britain and the Armenian Question* (New York: Palgrave Macmillan, 1984).
6. Weeks, *The Armenian Question*.
7. Ocna Holloway "Do Human Rights Treaties Make a Difference," *Yale Law Journal*, 111 (2002), pp. 1395–2042; David Rieff, *A Bed for the Night: Humanitarianism in Crisis* (New York: Simon & Schuster, 2002).

Chapter 2

1. The pilgrimage to Mecca, for example, was a terrific opportunity for exchanges of views with Muslims from around the Islamic world on political and other issues, discussions that could be continued by groups of pilgrims when they returned home.

2. The most important theoretical statements on the emergence and impact of public opinion, particularly in Western bourgeois society, come from Jurgen Habermas: see *Communications and the Evolution of Society*, trans. T. McCarthy (Boston: Beacon Press, 1979); *Moral Consciousness and Communicative Action*, trans. C. Lenhardt and S. Nicholsen (Cambridge, MA: MIT Press, 1990); and *Between Fact and Norms: Contributions to a Discourse Theory of Law and Democracy*, trans. W. Rehg (Cambridge, MA: MIT Press, 1996). For a recent study, see Jacob and Michael Shamir, *The Anatomy of Public Opinion* (Ann Arbor: University of Michigan, 2000). For history, see William Mackinnon, *On the Past, Progress and Present State of Public Opinion in Great Britain* (Shannon, Ireland, Irish University Press, 1971); and Melou Small, *Public Opinion and Historians* (Detroit: Wayne State University, 1970).

3. Thomas Haskell, "Capitalism and the Origins of the Humanitarian Sensibility," *American Historical Review*, 90 (1985), p. 359.

4. Cited in James Walvin, *English Slaves and Freedom* (Jackson: University Press of Mississippi, 1986). There is substantial debate about how much humanitarian sentiment counted in actual abolition, versus cruder economic factors. Currently the balance leans toward attributing considerable significance to the humanitarian factor; but the debate is not central to consideration of the origins of world opinion otherwise, for no one denies that international humanitarianism was present or that it was a new factor.

5. From the World Anti-Slavery Convention, cited in Suzanne Miers, *Britain and the Ending of the Slave Trade* (New York: Holmes & Meier, 1975), p. 364.

6. "The World's Convention of Friends of Emancipation, Held in London in 1840," *The Complete Works of Whittier* (Boston: Beacon, 1894), p. 284.

7. Cited in Lawrence Jennings, *French Reaction to British Slave Emancipation* (Baton Rouge: Louisiana State University, 1989).

8. Cited in Seymour Drescher, *From Slavery to Freedom* (New York: New York University Press, 1989), p. 235.

9. George Thompson, speech to the "Ladies of Glasgow," 1833, cited in Miers, *Britain.*

10. Cited in Drescher, *From Slavery*, p. 66.

11. Joaquim Nabuco, cited in Ethan Nadelmann, "Global Prohibition Regimes: The Evolution of Norms in International Society" *International Organization*, 44 (1990), p. 496.

12. Adam Hochschild, *King Leopold's Ghost: A Story of Greed, Terror and Heroism in Colonial Africa* (Boston: Houghton Mifflin, 1998).

Chapter 3

1. Kumkum Sangari and Dudesh Vaid, eds., *Recasting Women: Essays on Indian Colonial History* (New Delhi: Kali, 1989); Peter N. Stearns, *Gender in World History* (London: Routledge, 2000), chapter 7.

2. Antoinette Burton, *Burdens of History: British Feminists, Indian Women and Imperial Culture* (Chapel Hill: University of North Carolina, 1994), p. 120.

3. Cited in Geoffrey Hosking, *Russia and the Russians: A History* (Cambridge, MA: Harvard University Press, 2001), p. 276.

4. Donna Guy, *Sex and Danger in Buenos Aires* (Lincoln, NE: University of Nebraska Press, 1991), p. 24.

5. Donna Guy, "White Slavery, Public Health and the Socialist Position on Legalized Prostitution in Argentina," *Latin American Research Review*, 23 (1988), p. 68.

6. Brian Owensby, *Intimate Ironies: Modernity and the Making of Middle-Class Lives in Brazil* (Stanford: Stanford University Press, 1999), p. 60.

7. For superb discussion of Amin and other reactions, see Leila Ahmed, *Women and Gender in Islam* (New Haven: Yale University Press, 1992), chapter 8.

8. Note that Ataturk, like Peter the Great before him, could also attack men's attire in the name of civilized standards. Efforts to get Turks to replace the traditional fez with the Western-style hat had exactly the same overtones of outrage and embarrassment in face of the apparently obvious requirements of civilization.

9. Fan Hong, *Footbinding, Feminism and Freedom* (London: Frank Cass, 1997), pp. 57, 62.

10. Ibid., p. 63.

11. Quotes from Fumiko Sakashita, "Lynching across the Pacific: Japanese Discourse of Lynching before World War II," paper presented to

Organization of American Historians annual meeting, Boston, 26 March 2004. My thanks to Dr. Sakashita for a copy of her paper.

12. Mary Jane Brown, *Eradicating This Evil: Women in the American Anti-lynching Movement* (New York: Garland, 2000), p. 71.

13. Philip Dray, *At the Hands of Persons Unknown: The Lynching of Black America* (New York: Random House, 2002), p. 235.

Chapter 4

1. Natza Berkovitch, *From Motherhood to Citizenship: Women's Rights and International Organizations* (Baltimore: Johns Hopkins University Press, 1999).

2. Ibid., p. 25.

3. Leila J. Rupp, "Constructing Internationalism: The Case of Transnational Women's Organizations, 1888–1945," *American Historical Review*, 99 (1994), p. 1578.

4. Mark Thomas Connelly, *The Response to Prostitution in the Progressive Era* (Chapel Hill: University of North Carolina Press, 1980), p. 132.

5. Rupp, "Constructing Internationalism," p. 1583.

6. Ibid., p. 1585.

7. International Woman Suffrage Alliance, cited in ibid.

8. Rupp, "Constructing Internationalism," p. 1592.

9. Ibid., p. 1597.

10. Susan Pederson, "The Maternalist Movement in British Colonial Policy: The Controversy over 'Child Slavery' in Hong Kong 1917–1941," *Past and Present*, 17 (2001), pp. 161–202.

11. Statement by Edward Amseele, cited in James Joll, *The Second International* (London: Routledge Kegan & Paul, 1955), pp. 153–154.

12. Hector Bartolomei da la Cruz, Geraldo von Potobsky, and Lee Sweptson, *The International Labor Organization* (Boulder, CO: Westview, 1996).

Chapter 5

1. Cited in Mercia Macdermott, *A History of Bulgaria, 1393–1885* (London: Allen & Unwin, 1962), pp. 278–281.

2. Antony Wohl, "'Dizzy-Ben Dizzi': Disraeli as Alien," *Journal of British Studies*, 34 (1995), p. 383.

3. Cited in Ann P. Saab, *Reluctant Icon: Gladstone, Bulgaria and the Working Classes, 1856–1878* (Cambridge, MA: Harvard University Press, 1991).

4. Macdermott, *History*, p. 281.

5. Something of the power of world opinion shows in the lingering effects of the Armenian and other episodes. A century later, Turks and Armenians still quarrel bitterly over the facts of the matter – as part of identity issues but also because justifying one's cause before the court of global opinion matters, even within the historical record. Suspicions of the Turks in Europe, which help to block Turkey's entry into the European Union, reflect traces of earlier world opinion as well as more contemporary issues. Pondering the after-effects of world opinion verdicts is an interesting sidebar of the general topic.

6. James Robertson, "Sanctions and Security: The League of Nations and the Italian–Ethiopian War, 1935–36," *International Organization*, 27 (1973), p. 168, citing note from British Foreign Minister Hoore to the French Prime Minister.

7. Joseph Harris, "A Global Approach to African Diaspora Studies," paper presented to conference of the World History Association, George Mason University, Fairfax, VA, June 2004.

Chapter 6

1. Mark Philip Bradley, "Trans National Reporting and Global Human Rights Talk in the Twentieth Century," paper delivered to the American Historical Association Annual Convention, Washington, January 2004.

2. Stephen C. Schlesinger, *Act of Creation: The Founding of the United Nations* (Boulder, CO: Westview, 2003), p. 269.

3. For specific links between the Holocaust and later human rights efforts, see Howard Ball, *Prosecuting War Crimes and Genocide: The Twentieth-Century Experience* (Lawrence: University of Kansas Press, 1999).

4. Carol Anderson, *Eyes off the Prize: The United Nations and the African American Struggle for Human Rights, 1944–1955* (New York: Cambridge University Press, 2003).

5. David Caute, *The Dancer Defects: The Struggle for Cultural Supremacy during the Cold War* (New York: Oxford University Press, 2003).

6. For more on the Cold War's ironic encouragement of currents in world opinion, see Matthew Evangelista, *Unarmed Forces: The Transnational Movement to End the Cold War* (Ithaca, NY: Cornell University Press, 1999). See also chapter 10 of the present volume on the disarmament campaigns.

7. For an example of efforts to rouse international opinion against colonialism, see Matthew Connolly, *A Diplomatic Revolution: Algeria's Fight for Independence and the Origins of the Post Cold War Era* (New York: New York University Press, 2002).

8.   George Weigel, *The Final Revolution: The Resistance Church and the Collapse of Communism* (Oxford: Oxford University Press, 1992), pp. 71–72; Eric O. Hanson, *The Catholic Church in World Politics* (Princeton: Princeton University Press, 1987), p. 283. See also Frank Coppa, *The Modern Papacy since 1789* (London: Longman, 1998) (including important notes on earlier papal denunciations of social injustice in the 1890s); Oliver Williams and John Houck, eds., *Catholic Social Thought and the New World Order: Building on One Hundred Years* (Notre Dame, IN: University of Notre Dame Press, 1993); Michael Phayer, *The Catholic Church and the Holocaust, 1930–1965* (Bloomington: Indiana University Press, 2000).

Chapter 7

1.   Cited in William Korey, *NGOs and the Universal Declaration of Human Rights: A Curious Grapevine* (New York: St. Martin's Press, 1998).
2.   <http://web/amnesty.org/web/web/.nsf/printpages/AboutAI_time-line_1973>.
3.   Bron Raymond Taylor, ed., *Ecological Resistance Movements: The Global Emergence of Radical and Popular Environmentalism* (Albany: State University of New York Press, 1995), p. 315
4.   Ann Marie Clark, *Diplomacy of Conscience: Amnesty International and Changing Human Rights Norms* (Princeton: Princeton University Press, 2001), p. 10.

Chapter 8

1.   Myres McDougal, Harold Lasswell, and Lung-chu Chen, "Human Rights for Women and World Public Order: The Outlawing of Sex-Based Discrimination," *American Journal of International Law*, 69 (1975): pp. 511–16; see also United Nations, *United Nations and the Advancement of Women, 1945–1996* (New York, 1996).
2.   Bolanle Awe et al., eds., *Women, Family, State and Economy in Africa* (Chicago: University of Chicago Press, 1991).
3.   Judith Zinsser, "The United Nations Decade for Women: Quiet Revolution," *The History Teacher*, 24 (1990), p. 24.
4.   Awe et al., eds., *Women*.
5.   Donald R. Wright, *The World and a Very Small Place in Africa: A History of Globalization in Niumi, the Gambia* (Armonk, NY: M. E. Sharpe, 2004), pp. 267–268.

6. Cited in Hector Bartolomei de la Cruz, Geraldo von Potobsky, and Lee Sweptson, *The International Labor Organization: The International Standards System and Basic Human Rights* (Boulder, CO: Westview, 1999), p. 235.

7. Martha Nussbaum, "Human Functioning and Social Justice," *Political Theory*, 20 (1992), p. 204. See also Susan Okin, "Gender Inequality and Cultural Difference," *Political Theory*, 22 (1994), pp. 5–24.

8. Cited in Jane Wills, "Taking on the CosmoCorps? Experiments in Transnational Labor Organization," *Economic Geography*, 74 (1998), p. 117.

Chapter 9

1. Douglas Johnson, executive director of the Infant Formula Action Coalition, cited in Kathryn Sikkink, "Codes of Conduct for Transnational Corporations," *International Organization*, 40 (1986), p. 828.

2. <http://www.cleanclothes.org>, accessed 21 February 2004.

3. Andrew Ross, ed., *No Sweat: Fashion, Free Trade, and the Rights of Garment Workers* (New York: Verso, 1997), p. 39.

4. John F. Love, *McDonald's: Behind the Arches*, rev. edn. (New York: Bantam Books, 1995), p. 454.

5. Susanna B. Hecht and Alexander Cockburn, *The Fate of the Forest: Developers, Destroyers and Defenders of the Amazon* (New York: Verso, 1989), p. 186.

Chapter 10

1. Quoted in Lawrence S. Wittner, *The Struggle against the Bomb: Resisting the Bomb* (Stanford: Stanford University Press, 1998), p. 76.

2. Quoted in ibid., p. 182.

3. Quoted in ibid., p. 462.

4. For an excellent description and analysis, see Donald Culverson, "The Politics of the Anti-apartheid Movement in the United States, 1969–1986," *Political Science Quarterly*, 111 (1996), pp. 127–149.

5. "The Black Paper: An Alternative Policy for Canada towards Southern Africa," *Canadian Journal of African Studies*, 4 (1970), pp. 363–394.

6. *Daily Express*, 9 June 1982, cited in Michael Suleiman, "Development of Public Opinion on the Palestine Question," *Journal of Palestine Studies*, 13 (1984), p. 103.

7. Cited in Susan Burgerman, *Moral Victories: How Activists Provoke Multilateral Action* (Ithaca, NY: Cornell University Press, 2001), pp. 70–71.

8. Jonathan Mermin, "Television News and American Intervention in Somalia: The Myth of a Media-Driven Foreign Policy," *Political Science Quarterly*, 112 (1997), pp. 385–403.

9. The gradations of religions linkage with the West are intriguing. The Catholic connection helped call more attention to East Timor than did the more diffuse Christianity of a large minority in Southern Sudan. But this Christian link helped draw more interest from the West to Sudan than to the ever greater massacres in Congo.

10. <http://mutex.gmu.edu:2123/universe>.

11. <http://news.bbc.co.uk/2/low/europe/2429123.stm> and <http://new-svote.bbc.co.uk/mpapps/pagetools/print/news.bbc.co.uk/2/hi/in_depgth/2875555.stm>.

12. On the relatively consistent emergence of world opinion as a policy factor, if somewhat optimistically rendered, see Frank Rusciano, *World Opinion and the New International Order* (Westport, CT.: Greenwood, 1998).

Chapter 11

1. Michael Hardt and Antonio Negri, *Empire* (Cambridge, MA: Harvard University Press, 2000), e.g. pp. 36–37.

2. Suad Joseph, "Childhood, Citizenship & Globalization in Lebanon," *Journal of Social History* (forthcoming).

3. Cited in William Korey, *NGO's and the Universal Declaration of Human Rights* (New York: St. Martin's Press, 1998), p. 473.

4. B.B.C. Monitoring Original Source, 24 August 2002.

5. M. Abdel-Kader Hatem, *Information and the Arab Cause* (London: Longman, 1974), pp. 95, 276.

6. Daniel Pipes, *The Hidden Hand: Middle Eastern Fears of Conspiracy* (New York: St. Martin's Press, 1996), p. 92.

7. Ibid., p. 96.

8. Elle Kedourie, "Feature Article: Islam Resurgent," *Encyclopedia Britannica Book of the Year* (1980).

9. *Washington Post*, 23 March 2004.

Chapter 12

1. W. R. Smyser, *The Humanitarian Conscience: Caring for Others in the Age of Terror* (New York: Palgrave Macmillan, 2003).
2. Philip Everts and Pierangelo Isernia, eds., *Public Opinion and the International Use of Force* (London: Routledge, 2001); this is also the focus of Frank Rusciano, ed., *World Opinion and the Emerging International Order* (Westport, CT: Greenwood, 1998).
3. This argument is pursued in Douglas Coulter, "Miracle, Mystery, Authority: Teaching in Russia 1989–1994," manuscript from the author.
4. Richard Haass, "Wars of Choice," *Washington Post*, 23 November 2003.
5. Pew Charitable Trust, "Public Opinion and the Polls," <http://www.pew-charitabletrusts.org>. This issue is also taken up in Rusciano, *World Opinion*, appendix II.
6. Work by Robin Hanson serves as an entrée here: see <http://hanson.gmu.edu/decisionmarkets.pdf>; for a journalistic account, see Hal Varian, "A Market Approach to Politics," *New York Times*, 8 May 2003, p. C2.
7. Kenneth Cmiel, "The Recent History of Human Rights," *American Historical Review*, 69 (2004), pp. 117–135; see also Carol C. Gould, *Globalizing Democracy and Human Rights* (New York: Cambridge University Press, 2004), for a more optimistic rendering that insists on the need for further change to accommodate innovative global criteria that will legitimate global diversity without jeopardizing all common standards. Studies of cosmopolitan democracy provide a related approach: David Held, *Democracy and the Global Order: From the Modern State to Cosmopolitan Governance* (Stanford: Stanford University Press, 1996); and Daniele Archibugi and David Held, eds., *Cosmopolitan Democracy: An Agenda for a New World Order* (Oxford: Blackwell, 1995).
8. For a significant recent comment on global diplomacy that overlaps considerably with the argument on behalf of world opinion and the need to promote its efficacy and recognition, see Amitai Etzioni, *From Empire to Community: A New Approach to International Relations* (London: Routledge, 2004).

FURTHER READING

Chapter 1

Boli, J. and G. Thomas, eds. *Constructing World Culture: International Non-governmental Organizations since 1875* (Stanford: Stanford University Press, 1999).

Meyer, J., J. Boli, G. Thomas, and F. Ramirez. "World Society and the Nation State," *American Journal of Sociology*, 103, 1977, pp. 144–181.

Public opinion

Bauer, W. *Die oeffentliche Meinung in der Weltgeschichte* (Potsdam: Akademiche Verlagsgesellschaft Athenaion, 1930).

Phillips Dawson, W. "The Public Opinion Process," *Public Opinion Quarterly*, 22, 1958, pp. 91–106.

Speier, H. *Historical Development of Public Opinion, in Social Order and the Risks of War* (New York: G. W. Stewart, 1952).

Starr, P. *The Creation of the Media: The Political Origins of Modern Communications* (New York: Basic Books, 2004).

Human rights

Cmiel, K. "The Recent History of Human Rights," *American Historical Review*, 169, 2004, pp. 117–135.

Lauren, P. G. *The Evolution of International Human Rights* (Philadelphia: University of Pennsylvania Press, 1998).

Wassertrom, J., L. Hubo, and M. Young, eds. *Human Rights and Revolution* (Lanham, MD: Rowman & Littlefield, 1996).

Chapter 2

Davis, D. B. "James Cropper and the British Anti-slavery Movement, 1823–1833," *Journal of Negro History*, 46, 1961, pp. 153–173

Drescher, S. *From Slavery to Freedom: Comparative Studies in the Rise and Fall of Atlantic Slavery* (New York, New York University Press, 1999).

Eltis, D. and J. Walvin, eds. *The Abolition of the Atlantic Slave Trade* (Madison: University of Wisconsin Press, 1981).

Haakongsen, K. *Natural and Moral Philosophy* (Cambridge, England: Cambridge University Press, 1996)

Haskell, T. "Capitalism and the Origins of the Humanitarian Sensibility," *American Historical Review*, 90, 1985, pp. 339–361, 547–566.

Hurwitz, E. *Politics and the Public Conscience: Slave Emancipation and the Abolitionist Movement in Britain* (London: Allen & Unwin, 1973).

Jennings, L. *French Reaction to British Slave Emancipation* (Baton Rouge: Louisiana State University, 1989).

Landon, F. "The Anti-Slavery Society of Canada," *Journal of Negro History*, 4, 1919, pp. 33–40.

Miers, S. *Britain and the Ending of the Slave Trade* (New York: Holmes & Meier, 1975).

Walvin, J. *English Slaves and Freedom 1776–1838* (Jackson: University Press of Mississippi, 1986).

Later antislavery and aftermath

Nadelmann, E. A. "Global Prohibition Regimes: The Evolution of Norms in International Society," *International Organization*, 44, 1990, pp. 479–526.

Chapter 3

Expanding moral obligation

Brown, J. M. *Eradicating This Evil: Women in the American Anti-lynching Movement* (New York: Garland, 2000).

Burton, A. *Burdens of History: British Feminists, Indian Women and Imperial Culture 1865–1915* (Chapel Hill: University of North Carolina Press, 1994).

Dray, P. *At the Hands of Persons Unknown: The Lynching of Black America* (New York: Random House, 2002).

Eny, D. "White Slavery, Public Health and the Socialist Position on Legalized Prostitution in Argentina," *Latin American Research Review*, 23, 1988, pp. 60–80.

Fan Hong, *Footbinding, Feminism and Freedom: The Liberation of Women's Bodies in Modern China* (London: Frank Cass, 1997).

Garon, S. *Molding Japanese Minds: The State in Everyday Life* (Princeton: Princeton University Press, 1997).

Guy, D. *Sex and Danger in Buenos Aires* (Lincoln, NE: University of Nebraska Press, 1991).

Hosking, G. *Russia and the Russians: A History* (Cambridge, MA: Harvard University Press, 2001).

Mackie, G. "Ending Footbinding and Infibulation: A Convention Account," *American Sociological Review*, 61, 1996, pp. 999–1017.

Owensby, B. *Intimate Ironies: Modernity and the Making of Middle-Class Lives in Brazil* (Stanford: Stanford University Press, 1999).

Plugfelder, G. *Cartographies of Desire: Male–Male Sexuality in Japanese Discourse* (Berkeley: University of California Press, 1999).

Potter, S. J. *News and the British World: The Emergence of an Imperial Press System* (Oxford: Oxford University Press, 2003).

Smyser, W. R. *The Humanitarian Conscience: Caring for Others in an Age of Terror* (New York: Palgrave Macmillan, 2003).

Walstedt, J. "Reform of Women's Roles and Family Structures in the Recent History of China," *Journal of Marriage and the Family*, 40, 1978, pp. 379–383.

Chapter 4

International feminism

Berkovitch, N. *From Motherhood to Citizenship: Women's Rights and International Organizations* (Baltimore: Johns Hopkins University Press, 1999).

McDougal, M. H. Lasswell, and Lung-chu Chen, "Human Rights for Women and World Public Order: The Outlawing of Sex-Based Discrimination," *American Journal of International Law*, 69, 1975, pp. 497–533.

Rupp, L. J. "Constructing Internationalism: The Case of Transnational Women's Organizations, 1888–1945," *American Historical Review*, 99, 1994, pp. 1571–1600.

Rupp, L. J. *Worlds of Women: The Making of an International Women's Movement* (Princeton: Princeton University Press, 1998).

Stienstra, D. *Women's Movements and International Organizations* (New York: St. Martin's Press, 1994).

Campaigns against international prostitution

Bristow, E. J. *Vice and Vigilance: Purity Movements in Britain since 1700* (Dublin: Gill & Macmillan, 1977).

Connelly, M. T. *The Response to Prostitution in the Progressive Era* (Chapel Hill: University of North Carolina Press, 1980), chapter 6.

Keire, M. "A Vice Trust: A Reinterpretation of the White Slavery Scare in the United States," *Journal of Social History*, 35, 2001, pp. 5–41.

Nadelmann, E. "Global Prohibition Regimes: The Evolution of Norms in International Society," *International Organization*, 44, 1990, pp. 479–526.

Rosen, R. C. *The Lost Sisterhood: Prostitution in America, 1900–1918* (Baltimore: Johns Hopkins University Press, 1983), chapter 7.

The International Labor Organization

Bartolomei de la Cruz, H., G. von Potobsky, and L. Sweptson. *The International Labor Organization: The International Standards System and Basic Human Rights* (Boulder, CO: Westview, 1999).

Endres, A. and G. Fleming. *International Organizations and the Analysis of Economic Policy, 1919–1950* (Cambridge, England: Cambridge University Press, 2002).

The Internationals

Joll, J. *The Second International, 1889–1914* (London: Routledge Kegan & Paul, 1955).

Katz, H. *The Emancipation of Labor: A History of the First International* (Westport, CT: Greenwood, 1992).

Chapter 5

The Ottoman Empire

Crakman, A. *From the "Terror of the World" to the "Sick Man of Europe": European Images of Ottoman Empire and Society from the Sixteenth Century to the Nineteenth* (New York: Peter Lang, 2002).

MacDermott, M. *A History of Bulgaria* (London: Allen & Unwin, 1962).

Saab, A. P. *Reluctant Icon: Gladstone, Bulgaria and the Working Classes, 1856–1878* (Cambridge, MA: Harvard University Press, 1991).

Shannon, R. *Gladstone and the Bulgarian Agitation, 1876* (London: Shoe String, 1975).

Tzanelli, R. "Haunted by the 'Enemy' within: Brigandage, Vlachian/Albanian Greekness, Turkish 'Contamination' and Narratives of Greek Nationhood in the Dilessi/Marathon Affair," *Journal of Modern Greek Studies*, 20, 2002, pp.47–74.

Wohl, A. "'Dizzy-Ben-Dizzi': Disraeli as Alien," *Journal of British Studies*, 34, 1995, pp. 375–411.

Armenia

Douglas, R. "Britain and the Armenian Questions, 1894–7," *Historical Journal*, 19, 1976, pp. 113–133.

Marsh, P. "Lord Salisbury and the Ottoman Massacres," *Journal of British Studies*, 11, 1972, pp. 63–83.

Melson, R. "A Theoretical Inquiry into the Armenian Massacres of 1894–1896," *Comparative Studies in Society and History*, 24, 1982, pp. 481–509.

Zeidner, R. "Britain and the Launching of the Armenian Question," *International Journal of Middle East Studies*, 7, 1976, pp. 465–483.

World War I

Zuckerman, L. *Rape of Belgium: The Untold Story of World War I* (New York: New York University Press, 2004).

Pacifism

Ceadel, M. "The First British Referendum: The Peace Ballot, 1934–5," *English Historical Review*, 95, 1980, pp. 810–839.

Chatfield, C. "Pacifists and Their Publics: The Politics of a Peace Movement," *Midwest Journal of Political Science*, 13, 1969, pp. 298–312.

Jacob, P. "Influences of World Events on U.S. 'Neutrality' Opinion," *Public Opinion Quarterly*, 4, 1940, pp. 48–65.

Nicolson, H. "British Public Opinion and Foreign Policy," *Public Opinion Quarterly*, 1, 1937, pp. 53–63.

Ethiopia

Baer, G. "Sanctions and Security: The League of Nations and the Italian–Ethiopian War," *International Organization*, 27, 1973, p. 79.

Diggins, J. P. *Mussolini and Fascism, The View from America* (Princeton: Princeton University Press, 1972).

Robertson, J. "The Origins of British Opposition to Mussolini over Ethiopia," *Journal of British Studies*, 9, 1969, pp. 122–142.

Spencer, J. "The Italian–Ethiopian Dispute and the League of Nations," *American Journal of International Law*, 31, 1937, pp. 614–641.

Spain

Hubbard, J. "British Public Opinion and the Spanish Civil War," Ph.D. dissertation, University of Texas, 1950.

Richardson, R. D. "Foreign Fighters in Spanish Militias," *Military Affairs*, 40, 1976, pp. 7–11.

Riegel, O. W. "Press, Radio and the Spanish Civil War," *Public Opinion Quarterly*, 1, 1937, pp. 131–136.

Valaik, D. "American Catholics and the Spanish Civil War," Ph.D. dissertation, University of Rochester.

Chapter 7

Context

Drinan, R. *The Mobilization of Shame: A World View of Human Rights* (New Haven: Yale University Press, 2001).

Forsythe, D. "The United Nations and Human Rights," *Political Science Quarterly*, 100, 1985, pp. 249–269.

Goodwin, G. "The Role of the United Nations in World Affairs," *International Affairs*, 34, 1958, pp. 25–37.

Kochavi, A. "Britain and the Establishment of the United Nations War Crimes Commission," *English Historical Review*, 107, 1992, pp. 323–349.

Luard, E. "Human Rights and Foreign Policy," *International Affairs*, 56, 1980, pp. 579–606.

Mullerson, R. A. *Human Rights Diplomacy* (London: Routledge, 1997).

Wilcox, F. "The Use of Atrocity Stories in War," *American Political Science Review*, 34, 1940, pp. 1167–1178.

Human rights NGOs

Amnesty International. <http://amnesty.org/web/web.nsf/printpages/AboutAI_facts>.

Clark, A. M. *Diplomacy of Conscience: Amnesty International and Changing Human Rights Norms* (Princeton: Princeton University Press, 2001).

Drinan, R. *The Mobilization of Shame: A World View of Human Rights* (New Haven: Yale University Press, 2001).

Foot, R. *Rights beyond Borders: The Global Community and the Struggle over Human Rights in China* (New York: Oxford University Press, 2000).

Human Rights Watch. <http://www.hrw.org/about/whocare/html.>

International Justice Mission. <http://www.ijm.org.>

Keck, M. E. and K. Sikkink. *Activists beyond Borders: Advocacy Networks in International Politics* (Ithaca, NY: Cornell University Press, 1998).

Korey, K. *NGOs and the Universal Declaration of Human Rights: A Curious Grapevine* (New York: St. Martin's Press, 1998).

Power, J. *Like Water on Stone: The Story of Amnesty International* (Boston: Northeastern University Press, 2001).

Rabben, L. *Fierce Legion of Friends: A History of Human Rights Campaigns and Campaigners* (Hyattsville, MD: Quixote, 2002).

Risse-Kappen, T. et al., eds. *The Power of Human Rights* (Oxford: Oxford University Press, 1999).

Sellars, K. *The Rise and Rise of Human Rights* (Thrupp, England: Sutton, 2002).

Thomas, D. C. *The Helsinki Effect: International Norms, Human Rights and the Demise of Communism* (Princeton: Princeton University Press, 2001).

Willetts, P., ed. *The Conscience of the World* (Washington: Brookings Institute, 1996).

The internet

Hick, S., E. F. Halpin, and E. Hoskins, eds. *Human Rights and the Internet* (London: Palgrave Macmillan, 2000).

Environmental world opinion and activism

Rubin, C. T. *The Green Crusade: Rethinking the Roots of Environmentalism* (New York: Free Press, 1994).

Taylor, B. R. ed. *Ecological Resistance Movements: The Global Emergence of Radical and Popular Environmentalism* (Albany: State University of New York Press, 1995).

Wall, D. *Earth First! and the Anti-roads Movement* (London: Routledge, 1999).

Wapner, P. K. *Environmental Activism and World Civic Politics* (Albany: State University of New York Press, 1996).

Chapter 8

Women's issues

Pietila, H. and J. Vickers. *Making Women Matter: The Role of the United Nations* (New York: Zed Books, 1990).

United Nations, *The United Nations and the Advancement of Women 1948–1996* (New York, 1996).

Winslow, A. ed. *Women, Politics and the United Nations* (Westport, CT: Greenwood, 1995).

Zinsser, J. "The United Nations Decade for Women: Quiet Revolution," *History Teacher*, November 1990, pp. 37–44.

Zoelle, D. *Globalizing Concerns for Women's Human Rights: The Failure of the American Model* (New York: Palgrave Macmillan, 2000).

Implementation

Bystydzienski, J. M., ed. *Women Transforming Politics, Worldwide Strategies for Empowerment* (Bloomington: Indiana University Press, 1992).

Charlton, E. E. *Women in Third World Development* (Boulder: Westview, 1984).

Coquery-Vidrovitch, C. and M. Sleden, eds. *African Women, A Modern History* (Boulder, CO: Westview, 1997).

Nelson, B. J. and N. Chowdhury. *Women and Politics Worldwide* (New Haven: Yale University Press, 1994).

Varma, S. *Women's Struggle for Political Space* (Jaipur: Rawat, 1997).

Labor

Bartolomei de la Cruz, H., G. von Potobsky, and L. Swepston. *The International Labor Organization* (Boulder, CO: Westview, 1999).

Jenks, C. W. "Universality and Ideology in the I.L.O.," *Annales d'Etudes Internationales*, 1, 1970, pp. 45–64.

Kaplansky, K. "Human Rights and the ILO," *Canadian Labour*, 12, 1967, pp. 7, 27.

Lawyer, J. et al., "The ILO at 50," *Monthly Labor Review*, 92, 1969, pp. 32–53.

Wills, Jane "Taking on the CosmoCorps? Experiments in Transnational Labor Organization," *Economic Geography*, 74, 1998, pp. 111–130.

Child labor

Arat, Z. "Analyzing Child Labor as a Human Rights Issue," *Human Rights Quarterly*, 24, 2002, pp. 304–325.

Basu, A. and N. Chau. "Targeting Child Labor in Debt Bondage: Evidence, Theory, and Policy Implications," *World Bank Economic Review*, 17, 2003, pp. 255–281.

Basu, K. "Child Labor: Cause, Consequence, and Cure, with Remarks on International Labor Standards," *Journal of Economic Literature*, 37, 1999, pp. 1083–1119.

Basu, K. and S. Tzannatos. "The Global Child Labor Problem: What Do We Know and What Can We Do?" *World Bank Economic Review*, 17, 2003, pp. 147–173.

Dennis, M. "Newly Adopted Protocols to the Convention on the Rights of the Child," *American Journal of International Law*, 94, 2000, pp. 789–796.

Dennis, M. "The ILO Convention on the Worst Forms of Child Labor," *American Journal of International Law*, 93, 1999, pp. 943–948.

Humphries, J. "Child Labor: Lessons from the Historical Experience of Today's Industrial Economies," *World Bank Economic Review*, 17, 2003, pp. 175–196.

Scoville, J. "Segmentation in the Market for Child Labor," *American Journal of Economics and Sociology*, 61, 2002, pp. 868–917.

Chapter 9

Nestlé and related issues

Dobbing, J., ed. *Infant Feeding: Anatomy of a Controversy 1972–1984* (Berlin: Springer Verlag, 1988).

Sethi, S. P. "A Conceptual Framework for Environmental Analysis of Social Issues and Evaluation of Business Response Patterns," *Academy of Management Review*, 4, 1979, pp. 63–74.

Sethi, S. P. *Multinational Corporations and the Impact of Public Advocacy on Corporate Strategy* (Boston: Beacon Press, 1994).

Sikkink, K. "Codes of Conduct for Transnational Corporations: The Case of the WHO/UNICEF Code," *International Organization*, 40, 1986, pp. 815–840.

Sweatshop campaigns

Bender, D. and R. Greenwald, eds. *Sweatshop USA: The American Sweatshop in Historical and Global Perspective* (London: Routledge, 2003).

Clean Clothes. <http://www.cleanclothes.org.>

Cooper, M. "No Sweat: Uniting Workers and Students. A New Movement Is Born," *Nation*, 7 June 1999, pp. 11–15.

Featherstone, F. *Students against Sweatshops: The Making of a Movement* (New York: Verso, 2002).

Greenhouse, S. "Anti-sweatshop Movement Is Achieving Gains Overseas," *Nation*, 26 January 2000, pp. 17–23.

Hanagan, M. "Labor and Globalization" special issue, *Social Science History*, 32, 2004.

International Labor Organization. <http://www.ilo.org/public/English/standards/norm/whatare/fundam/index.htm.>

Moberg, D. "Bringing Down Niketown: Consumers Can Help, but Only Unions and Labor Laws Will End Sweatshops," *Nation*, 7 June 1999, pp. 15–19

Ross, A., ed. *No Sweat: Fashion, Free Trade, and the Rights of Garment Workers* (New York: Verso, 1997).

Shaw, R. *Reclaiming America: Nike, Clean Air, and the New National Activism* (Berkeley: University of California Press, 1999).

Workers Rights Consortium. http://www.workersrights.org.

Environmentalism

Alfino, M., J. S. Caputo, R. Wynyard, and M. Alfino. *McDonaldization Revisited: Critical Essays on Consumer Culture* (Westport, CT: Greenwood, 1998).

Fortun, K. *Advocacy after Bhopal: Environmentalism, Disaster, New Global Orders* (Chicago: University of Chicago Press, 2001).

Hecht, S. B. and A. Cockburn. *The Fate of the Forest: Developers, Destroyers and Defenders of the Amazon* (New York: Harper Perennial, 1989).

Hoffman, A. J. *From Heresy to Dogma: An Institutional History of Corporate Environmentalism* (Stanford: Stanford University Press, 2001).

Kincheloe, J. L. *The Sign of the Burger: McDonald's and the Culture of Power* (Philadelphia: Temple University Press, 2002).

Love, J. F. *McDonald's: Behind the Arches*, rev. edn. (New York: Bantam Books, 1995).

Porter, G. and J. Welsh Brown. *Global Environmental Politics* (Boulder, CO: Westview, 1995).

Potter, D., ed. *NGOs and Environmental Policies: Asia and Africa* (London: Frank Cass, 1996).

Wapner, P. "Politics beyond the State: Environmental Activism and World Civic Politics," *World Politics*, 47, 1995, pp. 311–340.

Chapter 10

Context

Brysk, A., ed. *Globalization and Human Rights* (Berkeley: University of California Press, 2002).

Korey, K. *NGOs and the Universal Declaration of Human Rights* (New York: St. Martin's Press, 1998).

Disarmament and anti-nuclear movements

Evangelista, M. *Unarmed Forces: The Transnational Movement to End the Cold War* (Ithaca, NY: Cornell University Press, 1999).

Flam, H., ed. *States and Anti-nuclear Movements* (Edinburgh: Edinburgh University Press, 1994).

Solo, P. *From Protest to Policy: Beyond the Freeze to Common Security* (Cambridge, MA: Ballinger, 1988).

Wittner, L. S. *One World or None: A History of the World Nuclear Disarmament Movement through 1953* (Stanford: Stanford University Press, 1995)

Wittner, L. S. *Resisting the Bomb: A History of the World Nuclear Disarmament Movement 1954–1970* (Stanford: Stanford University Press, 1997).

Vietnam

Gardner, L. and T. Gittinger, eds. *International Perspectives on Vietnam* (College Station, TX: Texas A&M University Press, 2000).

Klinghoffer, J. A. *Vietnam, Jews and the Middle East: Unintended Consequences* (New York: Palgrave Macmillan, 1999).

Apartheid

Becker, C. M. "The Impact of Sanctions on South Africa and Its Periphery," *African Studies Review*, 31, 1988, pp. 61–88.

Culverson, D. "The Politics of the Anti-apartheid Movement in the United States, 1969–1986," *Political Science Quarterly*, 111, 1996, pp. 127–149.

Eades, L. M. *The End of Apartheid in South Africa* (Westport, CT: Greenwood, 1999).

El-Khawas, M. "The Third World Stance on Apartheid: The U.N. Record," *Journal of Modern African Studies*, 9, 1971, pp. 443–452.

Fierce, M. "Black and White American Opinion towards South Africa," *Journal of Modern African Studies*, 20, 1982, pp. 669–687.

Hill, K. A. "The Domestic Sources of Foreign Policymaking: Congressional Voting and American Mass Attitudes toward South Africa," *International Studies Quarterly*, 37, 1993, pp. 195–214.

Kaempfer, W. H., J. Lehman, and A. Lowenberg. "Divestment, Investment Sanctions, and Disinvestment: An Evaluation of Anti-apartheid Instruments," *International Organization*, 41, 1987, pp. 457–473.

Klotz, A. *Norms in International Relations: The Struggle against Apartheid* (Ithaca, NY: Cornell University, 1995).

Lowenberg, A. and W. Kaempfer. *The Origins and Demise of South African Apartheid; A Public Choice Analysis* (Ann Arbor: University of Michigan, 1998).

Metz, S. "The Anti-apartheid Movement and the Populist Instinct in American Politics," *Political Science Quarterly*, 101, 1986, pp. 379–395.

Rodman, K. "Public and Private Sanctions against South Africa," *Political Science Quarterly*, 109, 1994, pp. 313–334.

Singer, E. "South Africa's Press Restrictions: Effects on Press Coverage and Public Opinion toward South Africa," *Public Opinion Quarterly*, 51, 1987, pp. 315–334.

Central America and Cambodia

Burgerman, S. *Moral Victories: How Activists Provoke Multilateral Action* (Ithaca, NY: Cornell University Press, 2001).

Yugoslavia

Sobel, R. and E. Shapiro, eds. *International Public Opinion and the Bosnia Crisis* (Lanham, MD: Rowman & Littlefield, 2003).

Palestine

Suleiman, M. "Development of Public Opinion on the Palestine Question," *Journal of Palestine Studies*, 13, 1984, pp. 87–116.

East Timor

Hainsworth, P. and S. McCloskey, eds. *The East Timor Question* (London: I. B. Tavris, 2000).

Kingsbury, D. *Guns and Ballot Boxes: East Timor's Vote for Independence* (Victoria: Monash Asia Institute, 2000).

Tanter, R., M. Selden, and S. Shalom. *Bitter Flowers, Sweet Flowers: East Timor, Indonesia, and the World Community* (Lanham, MD: Roman & Littlefield, 2001).

Tiffen, R. *Diplomatic Deceits: Government, Media, and East Timor* (Sydney: University of New South Wales Press, 2001).

Death penalty campaigns

<http://www.deathpenaltyinfo.org/article.php?did=547&scid=37.>

Iraq

<http://www.codepink4peace.org/Get_Involved!_Ways_to_Help.shtml.>
<http://www.humanshields.org/about.htm.>
<http://www.stopwar.org.uk/links.asp.>

Chapter 11

Abdel-Kader Hatem, M. *Information and the Arab Cause* (London: Longman, 1974). Mandaville, P. *Transnational Muslim Politics: Reimagining the Umma* (London: Routeledge, 2001).

Boullata, I. J. *Trends and Issues in Contemporary Arab Thought* (Albany: State University of New York Press, 1990).

Feldman, N. *After Jihad: America and the Struggle for Islamic Democracy* (New York: Farrar Straus & Giroux, 2003).

Mandaville P. *Trasnational Muslim Politics: Reimagining the Umma* (London: Routledge, 2001).

Meuleman, J., ed. *Islam in the Era of Globalization* (London: RoutledgeCurzon, 2002).

Murden, S. W. *Islam, the Middle East, and the New Global Hegemony* (London: Lynne Rienner, 2002).

Pipes, D. *The Hidden Hand: Middle Eastern Fears of Conspiracy* (New York: St. Martin's Press, 1996).

Rejwan, N. ed. *The Many Faces of Islam* (Gainesville, FL: University Press of Florida, 2000).

INDEX

abuses, concealment of 39–40
Afghanistan 128, 202
Africa: pan-African community, mobilization of 83–84; property inheritance 128–29; racist resignation to tragedies in 192; women's groups in 124; world opinion, immunity to 197; *see also* apartheid; Rwanda
African Liberation Day marches (US) 161
African National Congress 80, 163
African Women's Task Force 124
al-Jazeera 187
Allbright, Madeleine 174
American Committee on Africa (ACOA) 161
Amin, Qassim 49–50
Amnesty International 6, 18, 94: abuses, scale of 193–94; activities of 107–8; anti-slavery movement 105; anti-violence campaign 127; death penalty campaigns 107–8, 173; 'disappeared' of Latin America 109; East Timor 172; geographic scope 108, 110–11; global standards 111; individual cases, and wider principles 109–10, 193; international relations 118–19; membership base 108; Middle East regimes 184; Nobel Peace Prize 107; organization of 109; prisoners of conscience 106–7; religious links 106; violence against women 124

animal rights 148–49
anti-globalization protests 101–2, 199
anti-lynching campaign, US 52–54
Anti-Slavery International 35–36, 135
anti-slavery movement: America, debate in 31; Amnesty International 105; boycotts 30; Christian values 27; empire, and world opinion 34–35, 36; Enlightenment 27–28, 33, 78; global responsibility 29; human rights causes 33, 35, 36, 73–74; humanitarian universalism 16, 26–28; international congresses 29; liberalism 33; moral justice 27–28, 35–36; organizations, proliferation of 28–29, 35–36; personal accounts 29–30; public opinion, impact of 26, 30–31, 35–36; real-world consequences, glossing over 34; single-minded focus 32; slavery, visibility of 31; success of 32–33; tactics of 28; technology 16; Western values 16–17, 31, 33–34; women's cause 59; *see also* white slavery movement
apartheid 84, 91, 97, 130, 212: Afrikaner triumph 160; British Commonwealth, expulsion of South Africa from 162–63; civil rights activism, US 161–63, 164; divestment policies, US 162, 163, 164–65; economic sanctions 163, 164–65; internal agitation 163; international outrage 160–61; public opinion,

239